THE POLITICS
OF SEXUALITY

THE POLITICS OF SEXUALITY

A Documentary and Reference Guide

Raymond A. Smith

AN IMPRINT OF ABC-CLIO, LLC
Santa Barbara, California • Denver, Colorado • Oxford, England

Library of Congress Cataloging-in-Publication Data

Smith, Raymond A., 1967–
  The politics of sexuality : a documentary and reference guide / Raymond A. Smith.
     p. cm.
  Includes bibliographical references and index.
     ISBN 978–0–313–34684–2 (hbk. : alk. paper) — ISBN 978–0–313–34685–9 (ebook)
1. Sex—Political aspects—United States. 2. Sex and law—United States. I. Title.
HQ23.S567   2010
342.7308´5—dc22   2010000625

ISBN: 978–0–313–34684–2
EISBN: 978–0–313–34685–9

14 13 12 11 10   1 2 3 4 5

This book is also available on the World Wide Web as an eBook.
Visit www.abc-clio.com for details.

Greenwood
An Imprint of ABC-CLIO, LLC

ABC-CLIO, LLC
130 Cremona Drive, P.O. Box 1911
Santa Barbara, California 93116-1911

This book is printed on acid-free paper ∞

Manufactured in the United States of America

CONTENTS

Contents

ACKNOWLEDGMENTS

The editor would like to thank several individuals who have made this project possible. Norly Jean-Charles, an undergraduate at Columbia University, served as an able editorial assistant, helping to collect and format many of the documents in this volume. Brandon L. H. Aultman provided critical help as an assistant editor of the manuscript as a whole, including drafting of the timeline and a number of sidebar articles (those authored by Aultman are so noted in the text). More broadly, the editor also wishes to thank his colleagues at Columbia University, including in the Department of Political Science and at the HIV Center for Clinical and Behavioral Studies.

Raymond A. Smith

INTRODUCTION: THE POLITICS OF SEXUALITY IN THE UNITED STATES SINCE 1965

Perhaps more than any other year, 1965 represents a turning point in the evolution of the United States toward greater acceptance of diversity and individual self-determination. It was in 1965 that the Voting Rights Act was passed to guarantee the electoral franchise to minorities. The year 1965 also marked the time that major immigration and naturalization reforms began the growth of the far more multicultural, multiethnic, and multiracial society that we know today. This same year saw the finalization of plans for launching of the National Organization for Women (NOW), the flagship of the feminist movement. It was in 1965 that the first major gay rights demonstrations were held, at Independence Hall in Philadelphia. And 1965 was also the year of the Supreme Court decision in the case of *Griswold v. Connecticut* that would shape the next 40 years of the politics of sexuality in the United States.

By 1965, the Supreme Court, under the leadership of Chief Justice Earl Warren, had already ordered wide-scale racial desegregation, strengthened freedom of speech and of the press, and enhanced the due-process protections of criminals and the accused. This "rights revolution" arrived in the bedroom through a ruling in the case of *Griswold v. Connecticut*. The specific controversy itself was not of great consequence: a challenge to a rarely enforced Connecticut law prohibiting married couples from practicing contraception. But the *reasoning* behind the *Griswold* ruling would prove to have enormous implications as the first definitive enunciation of a Constitutional right to "privacy" in relation to issues of sexuality and reproduction.

Before this, the government could still claim that it was within its legitimate constitutional authority, in the name of "public morality," to regulate nearly every aspect of the sexual lives of its citizens. Adultery, fornication, pornography, homosexuality, abortion, and contraception were still crimes punishable by the state. It was thus within the purview of government to specify, under threat of fines and imprisonment, exactly with whom its citizens could and could not be intimately involved and exactly which sexual activities they could or could not perform. Even though such "crimes," when consensual, were only erratically investigated and prosecuted, the criminal codes nonetheless forced a good deal of natural sexual activity into the shadows and imposed a code of silence in public discourse.

ABOUT THIS VOLUME

This volume of primary documents on the politics of sexuality takes as its starting point the 1965 *Griswold* decision, and lays out 62 key primary documents up until the year 2008.

Because the terms "politics" and "sexuality" both cover a vast array of issues, it was necessary to focus on documents that best illuminate the central political question of the past four decades: to what degree can government regulate aspects of sexuality among consenting adults? When choices need to be made about which topics to cover, the emphasis was placed on issues that have been major points of political contestation. Some themes related to sexuality have, of necessity, not been included. Two examples would be prostitution and age-of-consent laws. Both of these are controversial issues that raise potentially important issues, but neither area has experienced major changes in the law, new regulatory policies, important court cases, or other forms of political struggle.

Among the documents in this volume are excerpts from numerous rulings by the Supreme Court, the text of laws, testimony before Congress, transcripts of press conferences and speeches by political figures, and other official documents. All relate directly to the issue of the regulation of sexuality and, as government documents, all are taken from the public domain. The documents are of a few major types. Some represent landmarks in themselves, such as the U.S. Supreme Court ruling in *Roe v. Wade*, the Defense of Marriage Act, and the Articles of Impeachment against President Bill Clinton. Other documents are representative examples of a particular issue regarding the regulation of sexuality, such as the Virginia criminal code covering sexual offenses, or the California statute that created no-fault divorce. Others represent crucial public statements by major public officials, such as the Senate confirmation testimony of Chief Justice John Roberts and the resignation speech of New Jersey Governor Jim McGreevey.

Excerpting has been indicated by the use of ellipses (. . .). To improve readability, nonessential footnotes or citations have been eliminated, particularly in court rulings.

CHAPTER OUTLINE

Chapter 1 on reproductive rights begins with the *Griswold* decision and the closely related—if vastly more contentious—*Roe v. Wade* (1973), which guaranteed a woman's right to terminate a pregnancy. The chapter continues with documents regarding various attempts to limit and regulate access to abortion, which have narrowed the protections of *Roe* without actually overturning it.

Chapter 2 on women's equality continues with closely related questions of the extent to which the equal protection guarantees of the Fourteenth Amendment apply to women. It outlines attempts at constitutional amendments, the evolution of judicial interpretation, and efforts to ensure equality through public policy.

Chapter 3 considers controversies over the communication of information and ideas about sexuality, in terms of both so-called "adult speech" and also sex education for children and adolescents. The text provides key documents in the debates over "obscenity" and "indecency" and also whether sex education should take a comprehensive, scientific approach or should emphasize value-based priorities such as abstinence and fidelity.

Chapter 4 continues with a topic that has emerged as a political issue almost exclusively since 1965: the degree to which lesbian, gay, and bisexual individuals should be afforded the full social and political rights enjoyed by the heterosexual majority. The documents in this chapter revolve around the two critical ideas of personal privacy rights and equality protection of the law.

Chapter 5 focuses on changing norms and definitions of the institution of marriage and other forms of sexual and social partnership. As with other trends, greater freedom has been afforded since 1965 for individuals to make their own decisions about their choice of marriage partnerships. Topics covered include the right to marriage across racial lines and the now highly charged issue of providing marriage equality to same-sex partnerships, as well as the advent of innovations such as "no-fault divorce" and "covenant marriage."

Chapter 6 concludes with coverage of the various major sex scandals that have embroiled major political figures, both reflecting and influencing the linkages between politics and sexuality. From Justice Clarence Thomas to President Bill Clinton, Governor Eliot Spitzer to Senator Larry Craig, this chapter includes key documents that have risked, and in some cases ruined, the political careers of important government officials.

In addition to the documents in each chapter, this volume includes a number of special features, including:

- Commentary on the documents, providing context and analysis;
- "Historical View" sidebars discussing the politics of sexuality before 1965;
- "Comparative View" sidebars considering the politics of sexuality in other countries;
- "From the Left" and "From the Right" sidebars profiling major players in various political battles;
- Excerpts from the 2008 Republican and Democratic Party Platforms;
- More than 24 photos;
- Bibliographies for further reading on each topic.

TIMELINE OF
SIGNIFICANT EVENTS

.

This timeline provides a chronological guide to the documents in this volume, along with a number of important other contemporaneous major events in U.S. politics and government.

January 3, 1965	First session of the 89th Congress, both chambers of which were Democrat-led and would remain in Democrat control until 1995 (except for the Senate from 1981–1987).
June 7, 1965	The U.S. Supreme Court invalidates a Connecticut law banning the distribution of information concerning **contraception among married couples** in *Griswold v. Connecticut*. A landmark decision, the case heralded a new era of civil and political rights jurisprudence—the right to privacy.
August 6, 1965	Congress passes, and President Lyndon B. Johnson signs, the Voting Rights Act safeguarding the political rights of African Americans and other disenfranchised groups from encroachment from state governments.
June 12, 1967	In the landmark *Loving v. Virginia* case, the U.S. Supreme Court found Virginia's anti-miscegenation laws (banning **interracial marriage**) to be unconstitutional, holding that marriage is a "basic civil right of man."
October 13, 1967	President Lyndon B. Johnson issues Executive Order No. 11246, establishing **equal employment opportunities** for women in the federal government.
January 20, 1969	Richard Nixon, a Republican, is inaugurated as President of the United States.
June 23, 1969	The end of the tenure of Supreme Court Chief Justice Earl Warren—perhaps the most liberal chief justice and greatest proponent of civil liberties on the Court—and the beginning of the more conservative Chief Justice Warren Burger's tenure.
June 28, 1969	The Stonewall Riots, as they came to be called, began as gay patrons of the gay bar Stonewall Inn in New York City's Greenwich Village neighborhood began fighting police officers during an intrusive raid of the bar. The event launches the modern **gay and lesbian rights** movement.
January 1, 1970	California Governor Ronald Reagan signs into law "**No Fault Divorce**" legislation, the first of its kind in state law books. The laws allow for

	easier dissolution of marriages, removing substantial legal impediments that had historically protracted divorce hearings.
January 13, 1970	In an opinion that would give teeth to the Equal Pay Act, the Third Circuit delivered a decisive statement of **equal rights for female employees** in *Schultz v. Wheaton Glass Company*.
November 22, 1971	The U.S. Supreme Court strikes down an Idaho law **discriminating against women in inheritance law** as unconstitutional in *Reed v. Reed*.
March 22, 1972	Another landmark case for sexual politics, *Eisenstadt v. Baird* invalidated a Massachusetts law proscribing the use of **contraception among nonmarried couples**. The Court linked the right to the practice of contraception to all individuals as a Constitutional guarantee.
March 22, 1972	**Congress approves the Equal Rights Amendment** and sends it to the states for ratification. The ERA would safeguard equal protections across gender lines.
June 23, 1972	Congress amends the Civil Rights Act of 1964 with **Title IX, Education Amendments**, which entitled women equal access to athletic and other facilities in public school systems.
January 23, 1973	In one of the most controversial cases of its 200 year existence, the U.S. Supreme Court ruled in *Roe v. Wade* that **a women's right to obtain an abortion** is among many issues of privacy, shielded from governmental intrusion by the Constitution. The case's logic has been permuted over time, but its basic foundations remain intact law.
June 21, 1973	In *Miller v. California*, the U.S. Supreme Court struggled with the long elusive **concept of obscenity** by stating that in order to be found obscenity, material must offend community standards, be patently offensive, and lack serious political, artistic, or scientific value.
August 9, 1974	President Richard Nixon resigns from his office and is replaced by his vice president, Gerald Ford, a Republican.
December 20, 1976	Building from the framework of *Reed*, the U.S. Supreme Court creates the **"intermediate scrutiny" standard** for any legal classification of gender in *Craig v. Boren*.
January 20, 1977	Jimmy Carter, a Democrat, is sworn in as President of the United States.
July 3, 1978	The U.S. Supreme Court held, in *FCC v. Pacifica*, that indecent language could be regulated on the airwaves and is not a protected class of free speech. This case is commonly referred to as the **"Seven Dirty Words" case**, based on George Carlin's act upon which the FCC filed suit.
January 3, 1981	First session of the 97th Congress: the House remains a Democrat-controlled House, but the Republicans control the Senate for the first time since 1954.
January 20, 1981	Ronald Reagan, a Republican, is sworn in as President of the United States.
January 13, 1984	President Ronald Reagan delivers his "National Sanctity of Human Life" proclamation to the U.S. people that, in addition to establishing January 22 as **national day to recognize human life**, unequivocally denounces the tenets of *Roe*, holding that all humans were "given the gift of life," asserting certain legal rights to the unborn.
June 30, 1986	In the case of *Bowers v. Hardwick*, the Supreme Court dealt a major setback to the gay and lesbian movement by **upholding the anti-sodomy laws** of Georgia, reasoning that there is no inherent constitutional protection for same-sex couples engaging in sexual practices.

September 26, 1986	The end of Chief Justice Burger's tenure and the beginning of the conservative Chief Justice William Rehnquist's tenure as head of the Supreme Court.
January 3, 1987	First session of the 100th Congress: Democrats once again reclaimed majority lead of both chambers, until 1995.
January 20, 1989	George H. W. Bush, a Republican, is sworn in as President of the United States.
November 6, 1990	San Francisco voters pass Proposition K, creating the institution of **domestic partnership** for same-sex couples.
October 10, 1991	Ohio adopts a legislative end to **"common law" marriage**, one of many such forthcoming state acts that ended this traditional practice.
October 11, 1991	Anita Hill delivers her testimony before the Senate Judiciary Committee accusing Clarence Thomas—then nominee for the Supreme Court and her former employer at the Justice Department—of **sexual harassment**. Thomas indignantly denies the accusations and goes on to win confirmation from the Senate.
June 29, 1992	Hoped by pro-life advocates to be the case to finally dismantle *Roe*, *Planned Parenthood v. Casey* worked to underscore the basic right of women to terminate pregnancy; however, the **states' power to regulate abortion** is expanded as long as statutes do not place "undue burdens" upon the woman seeking an abortion.
January 20, 1993	William Jefferson Clinton, a Democrat, is sworn in as President of the United States.
May 5, 1993	The Supreme Court in the state of Hawaii finds that the **denial of marriage licenses to same-sex couples** violates the Equal Protection clause of the state constitution and is therefore invalid. The decision ignited a U.S. controversy regarding whether other states would have to recognize a same-sex marriage validated in another state, and it is soon overturned by a state constitutional amendment.
September 16, 1993	The **"Don't Ask, Don't Tell" policy statement for gay and lesbian people** is enacted, barring military officials from prying into the sexual orientation of their personnel. However, servicemen/women can still be discharged if found to be homosexual, and several thousands gradually will continue to be.
September 13, 1994	Congress passes and President Bill Clinton signs into law the **Violence Against Women Act** to curb **domestic violence against women** nationwide.
January 3, 1995	First session of the 104th Congress: Republicans win control of both houses of Congress, by substantial margins, for the first time in four decades.
January 3, 1996	The U.S. Congress passes, and President Bill Clinton signs into law, the Defense of Marriage Act, allowing states to **not recognize same-sex marriage licenses** procured in other states as well as providing a "one man, one woman" federal definition of marriage.
August 22, 1996	The U.S. Congress amends portions of the Social Security Act to appropriate funds to organizations that promote **abstinence-only sex education.**
May 20, 1996	The Supreme Court held in *Romer v. Evans* that Colorado's attempt at wholly **denying constitutional protections to gay and lesbian people** through "Amendment 2" was, of itself, unconstitutional. This holding established the gay and lesbian community as a "class of persons" for the first time in U.S. jurisprudence.

June 26, 1997	In *Reno v. ACLU*, the U.S. government attempted to extend its boundaries of **regulatory power over indecency on the Internet.** The U.S. Supreme Court struck down portions of the Communications Decency Act, preventing Congress from blocking Constitutionally protected expressions in cyberspace.
May 21, 1998	In reaction to the loosening standards of marriage laws in the United States, Arizona is one of several states to pass "**covenant marriage**" policies seeking to instill a firmer, more substantial union between married couples by narrowing the range of allowable reasons for divorce.
August 18, 1998	At the height of his latest controversy as president, Bill Clinton is **accused of adultery with a White House intern**, Monica Lewinsky. He offers a live televised admission to the nation, hoping to head off impeachment.
September 3, 1998	Senator Joseph Lieberman argues that although Clinton's actions were morally reprehensible, impeachment was not a necessary course of action, rebuffing it as political maneuvering.
September 9, 1998	Kenneth Starr, chief counsel investigating the Clinton-Lewinsky sexual scandal, issues his infamous "**Starr Report**" listing eight potential violations by President Clinton during the scandal.
December 15, 1998	For only the second time in U.S. history, the House passes **articles of impeachment against the president** because of the Lewinsky scandal and sends them to the Senate. The Senate, however, acquits President Clinton, who finishes his term in office.
January 20, 2001	George W. Bush, a Republican and son of former President George H. W. Bush, is sworn in as President of the United States following a controversial and contested election against Vice President Al Gore.
January 7, 2003	After three decades of *Roe*, with its central holdings still intact, the Congress adopts the **Partial Birth Abortion Act of 2003**, banning a rarely performed practice of "dilation and extraction." Although limited, the law narrows the protections of *Roe*.
June 26, 2003	In a reversal of the infamous *Bowers* case of 1986, the Supreme Court holds in *Lawrence v. Texas* that state **anti-sodomy statutes violate privacy rights.** So long as sexual acts are noncommercial and consensual among private adults, the government's regulatory boundary ends at the bedroom door.
August 2, 2003	Oregon is among one of a number of states to pass a **nondiscrimination law on the basis of sexual orientation.** The law differs from that in most states by including "gender identity" as a protected category.
November 18, 2003	The Supreme Court of Massachusetts holds in *Goodridge v. Department of Health* that all benefits of marriage, including the term **"marriage" must include same-sex couples**—thus invalidating its "one man, one woman" marriage statute.
August 12, 2004	**New Jersey Governor Jim McGreevey** makes a shocking announcement to the public that he was a closeted gay man who, although married, had carried on an affair with another man, and he resigns as governor.
December 2004	Democrats in Congress issue a report that critiques the narrowness of federal abstinence-only sexual education, endorsing a promotion of **comprehensive sex-education programs** instead.
March 2005	The U.S. Department of State issues a policy statement adopting the "ABC" approach to global sexual education to stem the HIV epidemic: "**A**bstinence, **B**e faithful, correct **C**ondom use."

September 5, 2005	Chief Justice William Rehnquist dies in office; later that month, new Chief Justice John Roberts, Jr., is sworn in as his replacement.
October 1, 2005	Connecticut passes **civil union legislation** conferring basic marriage rights—all but in name—upon same-sex couples. Connecticut thus becomes the first state to do so without prior court order.
January 31, 2006	With the retirement of U.S. Supreme Court Associate Justice Sandra Day O'Connor, a long-standing balance is ended; the court shifts sharply to the political right with the confirmation of Associate Justice Samuel Alito.
July 1, 2006	The Equal Opportunity Employment Commission revises its regulatory code to enforce Title VII of the Civil Rights Act to penalize **sexual harassment in the workplace**.
January 3, 2007	First session of the 110th Congress: Democrats achieve majorities in both chambers.
April 18, 2007	In the case of *Gonzales v. Carhart*, the U.S. Supreme Court **upholds the federal Partial Birth Abortion Ban of 2003**, indicating the furthering political trend of eroding *Roe*'s long-standing principles.
April 24, 2007	The Employment Non-Discrimination Act, first proposed in 1996, finally passes the U.S. House of Representatives, despite a veto threat from President George W. Bush. It is the first such law to pass even a single chamber of Congress to include **sexual orientation as a protected category** in federal discrimination policy.
June 11, 2007	Senator Larry Craig is arrested for **lewd conduct in a men's public bathroom**, allegedly soliciting an undercover officer for sex. Larry Craig denounced the accusations, asserting that "I am not gay and have never been gay."
March 5, 2008	Governor Eliot Spitzer is accused, via an FBI affidavit showing his **involvement in a prostitution ring**, of paying for the services of a high-end prostitute named "Kristen." He consequently resigns from his office.
May 15, 2008	The California Supreme Court, in the *In Re: Marriage Cases*, holds that the state **must open the institution of marriage** to same-sex couples and that its failure to do so violates the equal protection clause of the California constitution. The ruling is overturned that November by the controversial Proposition 8, a referendum that amended the California State Constitution.

Timeline by Brandon L. H. Aultman

READER'S GUIDE TO THE DOCUMENTS AND SIDEBARS

Reader's Guide to the Documents and Sidebars

Reader's Guide to the Documents and Sidebars

Reader's Guide to the Documents and Sidebars

Women's Rights Movement

1

REPRODUCTIVE RIGHTS: CONTRACEPTION AND ABORTION

"[A] zone of privacy [is] created by several fundamental constitutional guarantees."

THE POLITICS OF PRIVACY

1.1 Married Couples and Contraception: U.S. Supreme Court opinion in *Griswold v. Connecticut* (1965)

1.2 Single People and Contraception: U.S. Supreme Court opinion in *Eisenstadt v. Baird* (1972)

1.3 A Woman's Right to an Abortion: U.S. Supreme Court opinion in *Roe v. Wade* (1973)

1.4 Evolving Notions of Privacy Rights: Confirmation hearing remarks by Chief Justice John Roberts (2005)

"The essential holding of Roe v. Wade *should be retained and once again reaffirmed . . ."*

THE BATTLE TO REGULATE ABORTION

1.5 Ronald Reagan on Abortion: Presidential Proclamation of National Right to Life Day (1984)

1.6 The "Global Gag Rule" on Abortion: The Mexico City Policy on Global Abortion Funding (1984)

1.7 Expanding States' Regulatory Power over Abortion: U.S. Supreme Court opinion in *Casey v. Planned Parenthood* (1992)

1.8 Regulating Late Term Abortions: The Partial Birth Abortion Ban of 2003

1.9 Narrowing *Roe*: U.S. Supreme Court opinion in *Gonzales v. Carhart* (2007)

1.10 A Direct Challenge to *Roe*: The South Dakota law banning abortion (2006)

Introduction

Among all the polarizing issues of the "culture wars" of the 1960s to today, none has been more hotly contested than the politics of abortion. The so-called trio of "God, guns, and gays"—referring to such issues as prayer in school, gun control laws, and gay rights—have all been controversial, yet none have had quite the incendiary effect of the debate over abortion.

At the conservative extreme are those committed to the "right to life" who believe that a new human being exists from the moment that an ovum is fertilized by a spermatozoa. They claim that every abortion is thus the murder of an innocent life and that abortions over the past 35 years have constituted an "American holocaust." At the other end are those who argue that the issue is solely about women's constitutional right to autonomy and self-determination as equal citizens, rather than as "slaves" to the biology of reproduction. Anti-abortion statutes, from this view, are a vehicle for the continued subordination of women, who in times of desperation will still seek to end unwanted pregnancies but will be driven to unsafe, even life-threatening "back alley abortions." The most strident advocates of abortion right would argue that a fetus has no moral or legal standing that can in any way override the rights of the woman who is carrying it.

Yet it does not take long for the seeming clarity of this situation to quickly become far more obscure. On the question of the value of human life, for instance, those who are "pro-choice" are more likely also to oppose the death penalty and violent warfare, suggesting a deep-seated respect for human life. Similarly, those who are "pro-life" may also be more prone to oppose education about sexuality and access to contraception, which could drastically reduce demand for abortion. Further, polls have repeatedly indicated that most people take a more nuanced position that is mostly absent from the rhetoric of the two extremes: they may favor legalization in certain situations (such as rape, incest, or protection of the life of the mother) but may also prefer greater regulation under other circumstances (such as in the case of minors, married women, or late-term pregnancies).

The practice of abortion, using chemicals or surgical intervention, has been known for millennia; indeed, the original Hippocratic Oath from Ancient Greece barred physicians from practicing certain forms of abortion. In the British common law tradition inherited by the United States, abortion was permitted until the moment of "quickening" or the stirring of a fetus that signaled the progress of its development. Throughout the nineteenth century, increasingly restrictive laws on abortion were passed by the individual states in the United States, with liberalization by state legislatures beginning only in the late 1960s. In 1973, the U.S. Supreme Court ruled, rather suddenly in the view of many, that all state laws banning abortion were unconstitutional. The effect of their epochal ruling in *Roe v. Wade* (Document 1.3) was to essentially provide access to "abortion on demand" throughout the country. By placing the right to abortion beyond the control of state legislatures and of Congress, they also opened the floodgates of political controversy that continues to the current day.

Roe was the third, and in some ways the culmination, of a series of major rulings regarding individual autonomy in the context of sexuality and reproduction. The first of these was *Griswold v. Connecticut* in 1965 (Document 1.1), in which the U.S. Supreme Court found that married individuals had a constitutional "zone of privacy" that guaranteed their right to use contraceptive devices. As discussed below, *Griswold* initiated the modern conception of privacy rights, which were expanded and strengthened to include unmarried people in the 1972 U.S. Supreme Court case of *Eisenstadt v. Baird* (Document 1.2). The basic concept of a zone of privacy, although it does not appear as such in the text of the Constitution, is largely accepted even by conservatives as reflected in comments from the confirmation hearing of Chief Justice of the United States John Roberts (Document 1.4). *Roe* itself, however, remains highly charged, although the contemporary debate revolves much less around the concept of a woman's right to privacy than on the countervailing value of the government's interest in fetal life.

Eschewing the two extreme views of the pro-life and pro-choice camps, and perhaps reflecting the view of most Americans, the U.S. Supreme Court has repeatedly declined to overturn *Roe* but has narrowed it considerably. In the most important post-*Roe* case, the Court ruled in *Casey* (Document 1.6) that states may regulate abortion, but only to the extent that they do not create an "undue burden" on the rights of women. In another front of the battle, in 2003 Congress banned a late-term abortion practice via the Partial Birth Abortion Act (Document 1.7), which was later upheld by the Supreme Court in the case of *Carhart* (Document 1.8). Emboldened by this development, state legislatures with anti-abortion majorities continue to find new ways to restrict abortion, up to and including attempts at complete bans (for example, in South Dakota in Document 1.9). Court battles—and political rancor—seem likely to continue well into the foreseeable future.

"[A] zone of privacy [is] created by several fundamental constitutional guarantees."

The Politics of Privacy

INTRODUCTION

Forty years after its end, the Warren Court remains as controversial as ever in American politics. Following the convention of naming a "court" for the tenure of each chief justice, the term "Warren Court" refers to the 16-year period during which Chief Justice Earl Warren presided over the Supreme Court, from 1953–1969 (although its influence extended a few years longer, perhaps as late as 1975, after which the Supreme Court began a long-term rightward tilt).

The impact of the Warren Court on American culture and society was enormous and enormously polarizing. Many of their landmark decisions are beyond the scope of this volume, such as *Brown v. Board of Education* (1954), which prohibited racial segregation, *Engle v. Vitale* (1962), which ended mandatory prayer in public schools, and *New York Times Co. v. Sullivan* (1964), which expanded protections for the press. Some other landmarks are covered elsewhere in this volume, including *Loving v. Virginia* (1968) (Document 5.1), which struck down bans on interracial marriage, and *Griwsold v. Connecticut*, which is discussed below.

Conservatives tend to revile the Warren Court as the epitome of "judicial activism" in which judges impose their own views rather than limit themselves to interpreting the law. Many conservatives prefer instead to apply the concept of "original intent," in which the meaning of the Constitution is essentially static, linked to whatever the framers "intended" in 1787 (however unclear or inadequately documented that may be). By contrast, liberals tend to revere the Warren Court, seeing it as the protector of disfavored and disempowered groups against discrimination by electoral majorities. They tend to endorse the idea of a "Living Constitution," which offers flexibility for interpretation in light of changing circumstances. Once a jurist moves beyond literal text and original intent, however, there is a danger of excessive subjectivity in the interpretation of the law. This is particularly problematic in a democracy given that federal judges in the United States are appointed rather than elected.

One of the most important examples of the "Living Constitution" approach is to be found in the concept of privacy articulated in the Supreme Court's ruling in *Griswold v. Connecticut* (Document 1.1). Although the word "privacy" does not appear in the text of the Constitution, prior court rulings had articulated privacy as one value among many to be protected. *Griswold* went even further, arguing that: "[S]pecific guarantees in the Bill of Rights have penumbras, formed by emanations from those guarantees that help give them life and substance. Various guarantees create zones of privacy." Conservatives decried the vague language of "penumbras," "emanations," and "zones." The fact that *Griswold* involved the always-sensitive subject of human sexuality only exacerbated the controversies.

Originally, *Griswold*, which guaranteed married couples the right to access contraception, seemed to be as much about the nature of the marital relationship as about the reproductive rights. But just a few years later, in the case of *Eisenstadt v. Baird* (Document 1.2), the Supreme Court clarified that the right to use contraception—and thus by extension to control one's own reproductive life—also extended to single adults, clarifying that the right to privacy pertains to the individual rather than the marital relationship. Today, contraception is widely available and largely uncontroversial (except in the context of sex education, which is discussed in Chapter 2). And these precedents have even been accepted by as conservative a jurist as Chief Justice John Roberts (see Document 1.8).

Far more contested, however, is the 1973 ruling in the case of *Roe v. Wade*, which struck down anti-abortion laws in every state of the Union. Although *Roe* was handed down after the end of the Warren Court, it was still very much in its spirit. The Court affirmed that women have a privacy right to end an unintended or unwanted pregnancy, although its rationale is built more on the Constitution's "due process" guarantees than on the much-criticized "penumbras and emanations" of *Griswold*.

Although it is sometimes mischaracterized as such, the ruling is not "absolutist" in its language or reasoning. Notably, it acknowledges a governmental interest in the developing fetus, particularly as it reaches the point of viability. Since the Fourteenth Amendment specifically applies to persons "born or naturalized" in the United States, however, the Supreme Court determined that constitutional due process guarantees (relating to "life, liberty, and property") do not apply to those not yet born.

In an approach that conservatives have criticized as "legislating from the bench," the *Roe* opinion establishes a trimester approach. During the first trimester (i.e., the first three months), clearly before viability, a woman had essentially an unlimited right to procure an abortion. During the second trimester, a state may regulate abortion but only in ways "reasonably related to maternal health." In the third trimester, when fetal viability is most likely, states may regulate abortion "except where it is necessary, in appropriate medical judgment, for the preservation of the life or health of the mother." In practice, the "life or health" exception has been construed broadly, such as to include mental health, making even third trimester regulation quite difficult.

The *Roe* ruling had the effect of taking the issue of abortion out of the usual arena of politics and onto a Constitutional level. Several unsuccessful attempts have been made to pass a "human life amendment" that would alter the Constitution either to prohibit abortion outright or to indicate that abortion rights are not guaranteed by the Constitution. Another approach—which has led to a great politicization in the choice of Supreme Court justices as well as other federal judges—has been to seek to have the Supreme Court overturn its own precedent. The shifting fortunes of attempts to alter *Roe* are discussed in the second part of this chapter.

Document 1.1: Married Couples and Contraception

- **Document:** Excerpts from the Supreme Court ruling in *Griswold v. Connecticut*, including portions of the syllabus (summary), the majority opinion, and a dissenting opinion
- **Date:** June 7, 1965
- **Where:** U.S. Supreme Court, Washington, DC
- **Significance:** This decision had the immediate effect of guaranteeing that married people could practice contraception without government interference. The more far-reaching impact was to initiate and articulate the modern concept of "privacy rights," particularly with regard to issues of reproduction and sexuality.

SUPREME COURT OF THE UNITED STATES

381 U.S. 479

Griswold v. Connecticut

APPEAL FROM THE SUPREME COURT OF ERRORS OF CONNECTICUT

No. 496

Argued: March 29–30, 1965—Decided: June 7, 1965

"Would we allow the police to search the sacred precincts of marital bedrooms for telltale signs of the use of contraceptives? The very idea is repulsive to the notions of privacy surrounding the marriage relationship."

Syllabus

Appellants, the Executive Director of the Planned Parenthood League of Connecticut, and its medical director, a licensed physician, were convicted as accessories for giving married persons information and medical advice on how to prevent conception and, following examination, prescribing a contraceptive device or material for the wife's use. A Connecticut statute makes it a crime for any person to use any drug or article to prevent conception. Appellants claimed that the accessory statute, as applied, violated the Fourteenth Amendment. An intermediate appellate court and the State's highest court affirmed the judgment.

Held:

1. Appellants have standing to assert the constitutional rights of the married people.

2. The Connecticut statute forbidding use of contraceptives violates the right of marital privacy which is within the penumbra of specific guarantees of the Bill of Rights.

MR. JUSTICE DOUGLAS delivered the opinion of the Court.

Appellant Griswold is Executive Director of the Planned Parenthood League of Connecticut. Appellant Buxton is a licensed physician and a professor at the Yale Medical School who served as Medical Director for the League at its Center in New Haven—a center open and operating from November 1 to November 10, 1961, when appellants were arrested.

They gave information, instruction, and medical advice to *married persons* as to the means of preventing conception. They examined the wife and prescribed the best contraceptive device or material for her use. Fees were usually charged, although some couples were serviced free.

The statutes whose constitutionality is involved in this appeal are §§ 53-32 and 54-196 of the General Statutes of Connecticut (1958 rev.). The former provides:

Any person who uses any drug, medicinal article or instrument for the purpose of preventing conception shall be fined not less than fifty dollars or imprisoned not less than sixty days nor more than one year or be both fined and imprisoned.

Section 54-196 provides:

Any person who assists, abets, counsels, causes, hires or commands another to commit any offense may be prosecuted and punished as if he were the principal offender.

The appellants were found guilty as accessories and fined $100 each, against the claim that the accessory statute, as so applied, violated the Fourteenth Amendment. The Appellate Division of the Circuit Court affirmed. The Supreme Court of Errors affirmed that judgment . . .

Coming to the merits, we are met with a wide range of questions that implicate the Due Process Clause of the Fourteenth Amendment . . . We do not sit as a super-legislature to determine the wisdom, need, and propriety of laws that touch economic problems, business affairs, or social conditions. This law, however, operates directly on an intimate relation of husband and wife and their physician's role in one aspect of that relation.

The association of people is not mentioned in the Constitution nor in the Bill of Rights. The right to educate a child in a school of the parents' choice—whether public or private or parochial—is also not mentioned. Nor is the right to study any particular subject or any foreign language. Yet the First Amendment has been construed to include certain of those rights . . .

In other words, the First Amendment has a penumbra where privacy is protected from governmental intrusion. In like context, we have protected forms of "association" that are not political in the customary sense, but pertain to the social, legal, and economic benefit of the members . . .

The foregoing cases suggest that specific guarantees in the Bill of Rights have penumbras, formed by emanations from those guarantees that help give them life and substance. Various guarantees create zones of privacy. The right of association contained in the penumbra of the First Amendment is one, as we have seen. The Third Amendment, in its prohibition against the quartering of soldiers "in any house" in time of peace without the consent of the owner, is another facet of that privacy. The Fourth Amendment explicitly affirms the "right of the people to be secure in their persons, houses, papers, and effects, against unreasonable searches and seizures." The Fifth Amendment, in its Self-Incrimination Clause, enables the citizen to create a zone of privacy which government may not force him to surrender to his detriment. The Ninth Amendment provides: "The enumeration in the Constitution, of certain rights, shall not be construed to deny or disparage others retained by the people." . . .

The present case, then, concerns a relationship lying within the zone of privacy created by several fundamental constitutional guarantees. And it concerns a law which, in forbidding the use of contraceptives, rather than regulating their manufacture or sale, seeks to achieve its goals by means having a maximum destructive impact upon that relationship. Such a law cannot stand in light of the familiar principle, so often applied by this Court, that a governmental purpose to control or prevent activities constitutionally subject to state regulation may not be achieved by means which sweep unnecessarily broadly and thereby invade the area of protected freedoms.

Would we allow the police to search the sacred precincts of marital bedrooms for telltale signs of the use of contraceptives? The very idea is repulsive to the notions of privacy surrounding the marriage relationship.

We deal with a right of privacy older than the Bill of Rights—older than our political parties, older than our school system. Marriage is a coming together for better or for worse, hopefully enduring, and intimate to the degree of being sacred. It is an association that promotes a way of life, not causes; a harmony in living, not political faiths; a bilateral loyalty, not commercial or social projects. Yet it is an association for as noble a purpose as any involved in our prior decisions.

MR. JUSTICE GOLDBERG, whom THE CHIEF JUSTICE and MR. JUSTICE BRENNAN join, concurring.

I agree with the Court that Connecticut's birth control law unconstitutionally intrudes upon the right of marital privacy, and I join in its opinion and judgment . . .

I agree fully with the Court that, applying these tests, the right of privacy is a fundamental personal right, emanating "from the totality of the constitutional scheme under which we live." ...The protection guaranteed by the [Fourth and Fifth] Amendments is much broader in scope. The makers of our Constitution undertook to secure conditions favorable to the pursuit of happiness. They recognized the significance of man's spiritual nature of his feelings and of his intellect. They knew that only a part of the pain, pleasure and satisfactions of life are to be found in material things. They sought to protect Americans in their beliefs, their thoughts, their emotions and their sensations. They conferred, as against the Government, the right to be let alone—the most comprehensive of rights and the right most valued by civilized men.

The Connecticut statutes here involved deal with a particularly important and sensitive area of privacy—that of the marital relation and the marital home. ... Although the Constitution does not speak in so many words of the right of privacy in marriage, I cannot believe that it offers these fundamental rights no protection. The fact that no particular provision of the Constitution explicitly forbids the State from disrupting the traditional relation of the family—a relation as old and as fundamental as our entire civilization—surely does not show that the Government was meant to have the power to do so. Rather, as the Ninth Amendment expressly recognizes, there are fundamental personal rights such as this one, which are protected from abridgment by the Government, though not specifically mentioned in the Constitution ...

In a long series of cases, this Court has held that, where fundamental personal liberties are involved, they may not be abridged by the States simply on a showing that a regulatory statute has some rational relationship to the effectuation of a proper state purpose.

Where there is a significant encroachment upon personal liberty, the State may prevail only upon showing a subordinating interest which is compelling ...

Although the Connecticut birth control law obviously encroaches upon a fundamental personal liberty, the State does not show that the law serves any "subordinating [state] interest which is compelling," or that it is "necessary ... to the accomplishment of a permissible state policy." The State, at most, argues that there is some rational relation between this statute and what is admittedly a legitimate subject of state concern—the discouraging of extramarital relations. It says that preventing the use of birth control devices by married persons helps prevent the indulgence by some in such extramarital relations. The rationality of this justification is dubious, particularly in light of the admitted widespread availability to all persons in the State of Connecticut. unmarried as well as married, of birth control devices for the prevention of disease, as distinguished from the prevention of conception, ... Finally, it should be said of the Court's holding today that it in no way interferes with a State's proper regulation of sexual promiscuity or misconduct ...

Adultery, homosexuality and the like are sexual intimacies which the State forbids, but the intimacy of husband and wife is necessarily an essential and accepted feature of the institution of marriage, an institution which the State not only must allow, but which, always and in every age, it has fostered and protected. It is one thing when the State exerts its power either to forbid extramarital sexuality or to say who may marry, but it is quite another when, having acknowledged a marriage and the intimacies inherent in it, it undertakes to regulate by means of the criminal law the details of that intimacy. ...

Historical View: Margaret Sanger and the Birth Control Movement

Decades before the landmark U.S. Supreme Court decision in *Griswold v. Connecticut*—which struck down a law criminalizing the distribution of even *information* about contraception—Margaret Sanger was *the* family planning pioneer. But her role in the slow progress toward sociopolitical acceptance of contraception was checkered with controversy. A nurse by training and socialist by political affiliation, Sanger grew increasingly disconcerted with what she saw as unacceptable lay medical practices among the poor women she treated in the Lower East Side of New York City. Poor women would often induce abortions without medical supervision, and numerous unwanted pregnancies increased maternal and infant death rates. She became convinced that "birth control," a term she has been credited with coining, was intrinsically linked to the health and well-being of women.

During the period before women's suffrage, "Comstock" laws in the United States criminalized published details about contraception and abortion. In 1913, after having circulated her *Family Limitations* pamphlet on the practices of safer sex and contraceptive devices, Sanger left for Europe to escape these strictures. While away, her unflagging drive to seek out better contraceptive tools led to a number of such devices making their way back to the United States. The diaphragm, for instance, had been transported from France via "bonbon" crates—she would later sell these devices in a small "illegal" clinic in New York. A number of other pregnancy prevention devices made transatlantic voyages to the United States during that time, and Sanger founded the first family planning clinic in the United States upon her return in 1916.

In her *Case for Birth Control*, first published in 1920, Sanger presented a basic treatise to U.S. women and the health care profession as a whole. The document is essentially a mission statement for family planning policies. Her short-lived American Birth Control League had been established in 1921. Undergoing numerous name changes, the organization would eventually become the Planned Parenthood Federation of America. By 1923, Sanger founded the Birth Control Clinical Research Bureau in Manhattan, distributing contraception and gathering ongoing statistics about birth control.

Sanger openly held that discussion concerning abortion and contraception should be based on rational, not religious, tenets. This flew in the face of a number of American laws based on Christian precepts. Her secular views on family planning were eventually shared by a number of physicians and social scientists, aiding in the creation of a strong popular base during the mid-twentieth century. She and this group of intellectuals would later take on the Comstock Laws of several states, ending in a number of nullifications. Sanger believed her controversial means—

Margaret Sanger (1879–1966), shown here in an undated photograph, worked as a nurse on New York City's Lower East Side. Her experiences with poor women there led her to launch the American birth-control movement. (Library of Congress Prints & Photographs Division/George Grantham Bain Collection/LC-DIG-ggbain-23669)

illegally distributing of contraceptive devices and establishing birth control clinics in a politically hostile atmosphere—were certainly justified by what she understood as an inherent right: health.—*Brandon L. H. Aultman*

MR. JUSTICE STEWART, whom MR. JUSTICE BLACK joins, dissenting.

Since 1879, Connecticut has had on its books a law which forbids the use of contraceptives by anyone. I think this is an uncommonly silly law. As a practical matter, the law is obviously unenforceable, except in the oblique context of the present case. As a philosophical matter, I believe the use of contraceptives in the relationship of marriage should be left to personal and private choice, based upon each individual's moral, ethical, and religious beliefs. As a matter of social policy, I think professional counsel about methods of birth control should be available to all, so that each individual's choice can be meaningfully made. But we are not asked in this case to say whether we think this law is unwise, or even asinine. We are asked to hold that it violates the United States Constitution. And that I cannot do.

In the course of its opinion, the Court refers to no less than six Amendments to the Constitution: the First, the Third, the Fourth, the Fifth, the Ninth, and the Fourteenth. But the Court does not say which of these Amendments, if any, it thinks is infringed by this Connecticut law.

We are told that the Due Process Clause of the Fourteenth Amendment is not, as such, the "guide" in this case. With that much, I agree. There is no claim that this law, duly enacted by the Connecticut Legislature, is unconstitutionally vague. There is no claim that the appellants were denied any of the elements of procedural due process at their trial, so as to make their convictions constitutionally invalid. And, as the Court says, the day has long passed since the Due Process Clause was regarded as a proper instrument for determining "the wisdom, need, and propriety" of state laws.

As to the First, Third, Fourth, and Fifth Amendments, I can find nothing in any of them to invalidate this Connecticut law, even assuming that all those Amendments are fully applicable against the States. It has not even been argued that this is a law "respecting an establishment of religion, or prohibiting the free exercise thereof." And surely, unless the solemn process of constitutional adjudication is to descend to the level of a play on words, there is not involved here any abridgment of the freedom of speech, or of the press; or the right of the people peaceably to assemble, and to petition the Government for a redress of grievances. No soldier has been quartered in any house. There has been no search, and no seizure. Nobody has been compelled to be a witness against himself.

The Court also quotes the Ninth Amendment, and my Brother GOLDBERG's concurring opinion relies heavily upon it. But to say that the Ninth Amendment has anything to do with this case is to turn somersaults with history . . .

What provision of the Constitution, then, does make this state law invalid? The Court says it is the right of privacy "created by several fundamental constitutional guarantees." With all deference, I can find no such general right of privacy in the Bill of Rights, in any other part of the Constitution, or in any case ever before decided by this Court . . .

Document 1.2: Single People and Contraception

- **Document:** Excerpts from the majority opinion in the Supreme Court case of *Eisenstadt v. Baird*
- **Date:** March 22, 1972
- **Where:** The U.S. Supreme Court, Washington, DC
- **Significance:** This ruling clearly established that the right to practice contraception is linked to individual liberty rather than to the marital relationship, broadening individual rights to self-determination with regard to issues of reproduction and sexuality.

SUPREME COURT OF THE UNITED STATES

405 U.S. 438
EISENSTADT, SHERIFF v. BAIRD
APPEAL FROM THE UNITED STATES COURT OF APPEALS FOR THE FIRST
CIRCUIT
No. 70-17.
Argued November 17–18, 1971
Decided March 22, 1972

MR. JUSTICE BRENNAN delivered the opinion of the Court.

Appellee William Baird was convicted at a bench trial in the Massachusetts Superior Court under Massachusetts General Laws Ann., first, for exhibiting contraceptive articles in the course of delivering a lecture on contraception to a group of students at Boston University and, second, for giving a young woman a package of Emko vaginal foam at the close of his address. . . .

"If the right of privacy means anything, it is the right of the individual, married or single, to be free from unwarranted governmental intrusion into matters so fundamentally affecting a person as the decision whether to bear or beget a child."

The legislative purposes that the statute is meant to serve are not altogether clear. In Commonwealth v. Baird, supra, the Supreme Judicial Court noted only the State's interest in protecting the health of its citizens: "[T]he prohibition in 21," the court declared, "is directly related to" the State's goal of "preventing the distribution of articles designed to prevent conception which may have undesirable, if not dangerous, physical consequences." In a subsequent decision, the court, however, found "a second and more compelling ground for upholding the statute"—namely, to protect morals through "regulating the private sexual lives of single persons." The Court of Appeals, for reasons that will appear, did not consider the promotion of health or the protection of morals through the deterrence of fornication to be the legislative aim. Instead, the court concluded that the statutory goal was to limit contraception in and of itself—a purpose that the court held conflicted "with fundamental human rights" under Griswold v. Connecticut, where this Court struck down Connecticut's prohibition against the use of contraceptives as an unconstitutional infringement of the right of marital privacy.

We agree that the goals of deterring premarital sex and regulating the distribution of potentially harmful articles cannot reasonably be regarded as legislative aims of 21 and 21A. And we hold that the statute, viewed as a prohibition on contraception per se, violates the rights of single persons under the Equal Protection Clause of the Fourteenth Amendment . . .

[W]e hold that the statute, viewed as a prohibition on contraception per se, violates the rights of single persons under the Equal Protection Clause of the Fourteenth Amendment. . . . If under Griswold the distribution of contraceptives to married persons cannot be prohibited, a ban on distribution to unmarried persons would be equally impermissible. It is true that in Griswold the right of privacy in question inhered in the marital relationship. Yet the marital couple is not an independent entity with a mind and heart of its own, but an association of two individuals each with a separate intellectual and emotional makeup. If the right of privacy means anything, it is the right of the individual, married or single, to be free from unwarranted governmental intrusion into matters so fundamentally affecting a person as the decision whether to bear or beget a child.

Document 1.3: A Woman's Right to an Abortion

- **Document:** Excerpts from the Supreme Court ruling in *Roe v. Wade*, including portions of the majority opinion and the dissenting opinion
- **Date:** January 23, 1973
- **Where:** The U.S. Supreme Court, Washington, DC
- **Significance:** In one of the most controversial rulings in its history, the U.S. Supreme Court effectively struck down all state laws against abortion with this ruling. Polarizing since the outset, *Roe* has been a cornerstone of the "culture wars" in American politics for the past 35 years. To a considerable extent, the "pro-life" view is presented in the dissent by Justice William Rehnquist.

SUPREME COURT OF THE UNITED STATES

410 U.S. 113

Roe v. Wade

APPEAL FROM THE UNITED STATES DISTRICT COURT FOR THE NORTHERN DISTRICT OF TEXAS

No. 70-18

Argued: December 13, 1971—Decided: January 22, 1973

"We, therefore, conclude that the right of personal privacy includes the abortion decision, but that this right is not unqualified, and must be considered against important state interests in regulation."

MR. JUSTICE BLACKMUN delivered the opinion of the Court.

This Texas federal appeal and its Georgia companion, *Doe v. Bolton*, present constitutional challenges to state criminal abortion legislation. The Texas statutes under attack here are typical of those that have been in effect in many States for approximately a century. The Georgia statutes, in contrast, have a modern cast, and are a legislative product that, to an extent at least, obviously reflects the influences of recent attitudinal change, of advancing medical knowledge and techniques, and of new thinking about an old issue.

We forthwith acknowledge our awareness of the sensitive and emotional nature of the abortion controversy, of the vigorous opposing views, even among physicians, and of the deep and seemingly absolute convictions that the subject inspires. One's philosophy, one's experiences, one's exposure to the raw edges of human existence, one's religious training, one's attitudes toward life and family and their values, and the moral standards one establishes and seeks to observe, are all likely to influence and to color one's thinking and conclusions about abortion.

In addition, population growth, pollution, poverty, and racial overtones tend to complicate and not to simplify the problem.

Our task, of course, is to resolve the issue by constitutional measurement, free of emotion and of predilection. We seek earnestly to do this, and, because we do, we have inquired into, and in this opinion place some emphasis upon, medical and medical-legal history and what that history reveals about man's attitudes toward the abortion procedure over the centuries . . .

I

The Texas statutes that concern us here are Arts. 1191-1194 and 1196 of the State's Penal Code. These make it a crime to "procure an abortion," as therein defined, or to attempt one, except with respect to "an abortion procured or attempted by medical advice for the purpose of saving the life of the mother." Similar statutes are in existence in a majority of the States. . . .

Jane Roe, a single woman who was residing in Dallas County, Texas, instituted this federal action in March 1970 against the District Attorney of the county. She sought a declaratory judgment that the Texas criminal abortion statutes were unconstitutional on their face, and an injunction restraining the defendant from enforcing the statutes. Roe alleged that she was unmarried and pregnant; that she wished to terminate her pregnancy by an abortion "performed by a competent, licensed physician, under safe, clinical conditions"; that she was unable to get a "legal" abortion in Texas because her life did not appear to be threatened by the continuation of her pregnancy; and that she could not afford to travel to another jurisdiction in order to secure a legal abortion under safe conditions. She claimed that the Texas statutes were unconstitutionally vague and that they abridged her right of personal privacy, protected by the First, Fourth, Fifth, Ninth, and Fourteenth Amendments. By an amendment to her complaint, Roe purported to sue "on behalf of herself and all other women" similarly situated.

James Hubert Hallford, a licensed physician, sought and was granted leave to intervene in Roe's action. In his complaint, he alleged that he had been arrested previously for violations of the Texas abortion statutes, and that two such prosecutions were pending against him. He described conditions of patients who came to him seeking abortions, and he claimed that for many cases he, as a physician, was unable to determine whether they fell within or outside the exception recognized by Article 1196. He alleged that, as a consequence, the statutes were vague and uncertain, in violation of the Fourteenth Amendment, and that they violated his own and his patients' rights to privacy in the doctor-patient relationship and his own right to practice medicine, rights he claimed were guaranteed by the First, Fourth, Fifth, Ninth, and Fourteenth Amendments....

The principal thrust of appellant's attack on the Texas statutes is that they improperly invade a right, said to be possessed by the pregnant woman, to choose to terminate her pregnancy. Appellant would discover this right in the concept of personal "liberty" embodied in the Fourteenth Amendment's Due Process Clause; or in personal, marital, familial, and sexual privacy said to be protected by the Bill of Rights or its penumbras, *see Griswold v. Connecticut*, (1965); *Eisenstadt v. Baird*, (1972); or among those rights reserved to the people by the Ninth Amendment, *Griswold v. Connecticut* . . .

VIII

The Constitution does not explicitly mention any right of privacy. In a line of decisions, however, going back perhaps as far as *Union Pacific R. Co. v. Botsford* (1891), the Court has recognized that a right of personal privacy, or a guarantee of certain areas or zones of privacy, does exist under the Constitution.... This right of privacy, whether it be founded in the Fourteenth Amendment's concept of personal liberty and restrictions upon state action, as we feel it is, or, as the District Court determined, in the Ninth Amendment's reservation of rights to the people, is broad enough to encompass a woman's decision whether or not to terminate her pregnancy. The detriment that the State would impose upon the pregnant woman by denying this choice altogether is apparent. Specific and direct harm medically diagnosable even in early pregnancy may be involved. Maternity, or additional offspring, may force upon the woman a distressful life and future. Psychological harm may be imminent. Mental and physical health may be taxed by child care. There is also the distress, for all concerned, associated with the unwanted child, and there is the problem of bringing a child into a family already unable, psychologically and otherwise, to care for it. In other cases, as in this one, the additional difficulties and continuing stigma of unwed motherhood may be involved. All these are factors the woman and her responsible physician necessarily will consider in consultation.

On the basis of elements such as these, appellant and some *amici* argue that the woman's right is absolute and that she is entitled to terminate her pregnancy at whatever time, in whatever way, and for whatever reason she alone chooses. With this we do not agree. Appellant's arguments that Texas either has no valid interest at all in regulating the abortion decision, or no interest strong enough to support any limitation upon the woman's sole determination, are unpersuasive. The Court's decisions recognizing a right of privacy also acknowledge that some state regulation in areas protected by that right is appropriate. As noted above, a State may properly assert important interests in safeguarding health, in maintaining medical standards, and in protecting potential life. At some point in pregnancy, these respective interests become sufficiently compelling to sustain regulation of the factors that govern the abortion decision. The privacy right involved, therefore, cannot be said to be absolute. In fact, it is not clear to us that the claim asserted by some *amici* that one has an unlimited right to do with one's body as one pleases bears a close relationship to the right of privacy previously articulated in the Court's decisions. The Court has refused to recognize an unlimited right of this kind in the past....

We, therefore, conclude that the right of personal privacy includes the abortion decision, but that this right is not unqualified, and must be considered against important state interests in regulation....

Although the results are divided, most of these courts have agreed that the right of privacy, however based, is broad enough to cover the abortion decision; that the right, nonetheless, is not absolute, and is subject to some limitations; and that, at some point, the state interests as to protection of health, medical standards, and prenatal life, become dominant. We agree with this approach.

Where certain "fundamental rights" are involved, the Court has held that regulation limiting these rights may be justified only by a "compelling state interest and that legislative enactments must be narrowly drawn to express only the legitimate state interests at stake. In the recent abortion cases cited above, courts have recognized these principles. Those striking down state laws have generally scrutinized the State's interests in protecting health and potential life, and have concluded that neither interest justified broad limitations on the reasons for which a physician and his pregnant patient might decide that she should have an abortion in the early stages of pregnancy. Courts sustaining state laws have held that the State's determinations to protect health or prenatal life are dominant and constitutionally justifiable . . .

X

[W]e do not agree that, by adopting one theory of life, Texas may override the rights of the pregnant woman that are at stake. We repeat, however, that the State does have an important and legitimate interest in preserving and protecting the health of the pregnant woman, whether she be a resident of the State or a nonresident who seeks medical consultation and treatment there, and that it has still *another* important and legitimate interest in protecting the potentiality of human life. These interests are separate and distinct. Each grows in substantiality as the woman approaches term and, at a point during pregnancy, each becomes "compelling."

With respect to the State's important and legitimate interest in the health of the mother, the "compelling" point, in the light of present medical knowledge, is at approximately the end of the first trimester. This is so because of the now-established medical fact that, until the end of the first trimester mortality in abortion may be less than mortality in normal childbirth. It follows that, from and after this point, a State may regulate the abortion procedure to the extent that the regulation reasonably relates to the preservation and protection of maternal health. Examples of permissible state regulation in this area are requirements as to the qualifications of the person who is to perform the abortion; as to the licensure of that person; as to the facility in which the procedure is to be performed, that is, whether it must be a hospital or may be a clinic or some other place of less-than-hospital status; as to the licensing of the facility; and the like.

This means, on the other hand, that, for the period of pregnancy prior to this "compelling" point, the attending physician, in consultation with his patient, is free to determine, without regulation by the State, that, in his medical judgment, the patient's pregnancy should be terminated. If that decision is reached, the judgment may be effectuated by an abortion free of interference by the State.

With respect to the State's important and legitimate interest in potential life, the "compelling" point is at viability. This is so because the fetus then presumably has the capability of meaningful life outside the mother's womb. State regulation protective of fetal life after viability thus has both logical and biological justifications. If the State is interested in protecting fetal life after viability, it may go so far as to proscribe abortion during that period, except when it is necessary to preserve the life or health of the mother.

Measured against these standards, Art. 1196 of the Texas Penal Code, in restricting legal abortions to those "procured or attempted by medical advice for the purpose of saving the life of the mother," sweeps too broadly. The statute makes no distinction between abortions performed early in pregnancy and those performed later, and it limits to a single reason, "saving" the mother's life, the legal justification for the procedure. The statute, therefore, cannot survive the constitutional attack made upon it here.

This conclusion makes it unnecessary for us to consider the additional challenge to the Texas statute asserted on grounds of vagueness. *See United States v. Vuitch*, 402 U.S. at 67-72.

XI To summarize and to repeat:

1. A state criminal abortion statute of the current Texas type, that excepts from criminality only a lifesaving procedure on behalf of the mother, without regard to pregnancy stage and without recognition of the other interests involved, is violative of the Due Process Clause of the Fourteenth Amendment.

(a) For the stage prior to approximately the end of the first trimester, the abortion decision and its effectuation must be left to the medical judgment of the pregnant woman's attending physician.

(b) For the stage subsequent to approximately the end of the first trimester, the State, in promoting its interest in the health of the mother, may, if it chooses, regulate the abortion procedure in ways that are reasonably related to maternal health.

(c) For the stage subsequent to viability, the State in promoting its interest in the potentiality of human life may, if it chooses, regulate, and even proscribe, abortion except where it is necessary, in appropriate medical judgment, for the preservation of the life or health of the mother...

This holding, we feel, is consistent with the relative weights of the respective interests involved, with the lessons and examples of medical and legal history, with the lenity of the common law, and with the demands of the profound problems of the present day. The decision leaves the State free to place increasing restrictions on abortion as the period of pregnancy lengthens, so long as those restrictions are tailored to the recognized state interests. The decision vindicates the right of the physician to administer medical treatment according to his professional judgment up to the points where important state interests provide compelling justifications for intervention. Up to those points, the abortion decision in all its aspects is inherently, and primarily, a medical decision, and basic responsibility for it must rest with the physician. If an individual practitioner abuses the privilege of exercising proper medical judgment, the usual remedies, judicial and intra-professional, are available.

XII Our conclusion that Art. 1196 is unconstitutional means, of course, that the Texas abortion statutes, as a unit, must fall. The exception of Art. 1196 cannot be struck down separately, for then the State would be left with a statute proscribing all abortion procedures no matter how medically urgent the case....

MR. JUSTICE REHNQUIST, dissenting.

The Court's opinion brings to the decision of this troubling question both extensive historical fact and a wealth of legal scholarship. While the opinion thus commands my respect, I find myself nonetheless in fundamental disagreement with those parts of it that invalidate the Texas statute in question, and therefore dissent...

Comparative View: Abortion Policies in Argentina

While the battle over abortion has been hard fought in the United States, the pro-choice side has fared much better than in Latin America. A case in point is Argentina, one of the more progressive nations in many ways, yet one that also lags considerably with regard to reproductive rights.

An anti-abortion protest at a Buenos Aires theater disrupted a December 2004 conference on contraception led by the founder of a Dutch abortion rights organization. (AP Photo/Natacha Pisarenko)

Of the roughly 40 million people who live in the Argentine Republic, 92 percent at least nominally identify themselves as Roman Catholic. Laws concerning abortion reflect this sectarian majority: according to Human Rights Watch (HRW), abortion is strictly prohibited. Only when the pregnancy places the mother's life in immediate jeopardy or when a mentally disabled woman is raped may she seek to legally terminate her pregnancy.

Reports worldwide clearly demonstrate that criminalizing abortion merely drives it underground, leading women to a number of unsafe and potentially lethal methods of abortion. For example, an estimated 500,000 abortions take place each in year in Argentina in reportedly unhygienic conditions. Moreover, the extent of maternal mortality as a result of these illegal abortions is high: 1 out of every 250 abortions results in the mother's death.

The women's rights movement in Argentina has seen relatively slow progress, making overt gains only in the 1980s and 1990s. The movement played a particularly prominent role in 1994 when the Argentine government undertook a campaign to codify anti-abortion policy in the national constitution. The efforts of the movement paid off: the constitutional reform did not make specific reference to anti-abortion policies. However, the new provisions had implicit pro-life sentiments, and by presidential decree, March 25 is "Day of the Unborn Child" in Argentina.

Still, small gains in pro-choice policies have been made. The central government adopted provisions in 2005 to ensure adequate post-abortion care. Considering the high numbers of illegal abortions each year, the decision also took into account the high level of maternal deaths associated with the act. It was the government's hope that such care would lessen the deleterious effects of illegal abortions. However, abortion as an active option for unintended pregnancy remains unavailable in Argentina and elsewhere in most of Latin America.—*by Brandon L. H. Aultman*

I have difficulty in concluding, as the Court does, that the right of "privacy" is involved in this case. Texas, by the statute here challenged, bars the performance of a medical abortion by a licensed physician on a plaintiff such as Roe. A transaction resulting in an operation such as this is not "private" in the ordinary usage of that word. Nor is the "privacy" that the Court finds here even a distant relative of the freedom from searches and seizures protected by the Fourth Amendment to the Constitution, which the Court has referred to as embodying a right to privacy.

If the Court means by the term "privacy" no more than that the claim of a person to be free from unwanted state regulation of consensual transactions may be a form of "liberty" protected by the Fourteenth Amendment, there is no doubt that similar claims have been upheld in our earlier decisions on the basis of that liberty. I agree with the statement of MR. JUSTICE STEWART in his concurring opinion that the "liberty," against deprivation of which without due process the Fourteenth Amendment protects, embraces more than the rights found in the Bill of Rights. But that liberty is not guaranteed absolutely against deprivation, only against deprivation without due process of law. The test traditionally applied in the area of social and economic legislation is whether or not a law such as that challenged has a rational relation to a valid state objective. The Due Process Clause of the Fourteenth Amendment undoubtedly does place a limit, albeit a broad one, on legislative power to enact laws such as this. If the Texas statute were to prohibit an abortion even where the mother's life is in jeopardy, I have little doubt that such a statute would lack a rational relation to a valid state objective under the test stated in *Williamson, supra*. But the Court's sweeping invalidation of any restrictions on abortion during the first trimester is impossible to justify under that standard, and the conscious weighing of competing factors that the Court's opinion apparently substitutes for the established test is far more appropriate to a legislative judgment than to a judicial one.... [T]he adoption of the compelling state interest standard will inevitably require this Court to examine the legislative policies and pass on the wisdom of these policies in the very process of deciding whether a particular state interest put forward may or may not be "compelling." The decision here to break pregnancy into three distinct terms and to outline the permissible restrictions the State may impose in each one, for example, partakes more of judicial legislation than it does of a determination of the intent of the drafters of the Fourteenth Amendment.

The fact that a majority of the States reflecting, after all, the majority sentiment in those States, have had restrictions on abortions for at least a century is a strong indication, it seems to me, that the asserted right to an abortion is not "so rooted in the traditions and conscience of our people as to be ranked as fundamental," *Snyder v. Massachusetts* (1934). Even today, when society's views on abortion are changing, the very existence of the debate is evidence that the "right" to an abortion is not so universally accepted as the appellant would have us believe ...

For all of the foregoing reasons, I respectfully dissent.

Document 1.4: Evolving Notions of Privacy Rights

- *Document:* Excerpts from John Roberts's replies to questions by Senators during his confirmation hearings for the position of Chief Justice
- *Date:* September 12, 2005
- *Where:* U.S. Senate Judiciary Committee, Washington, DC
- *Significance:* In these excerpts, one of the nation's most respected, and now powerful, jurists sheds light on current conservative thinking about privacy rights. Given his position as Chief Justice, these remarks may suggest the future direction of the U.S. Supreme Court on issues of constitutional protections relating to reproduction and sexuality.

JOHN ROBERTS CONFIRMATION HEARING

Topic: A Woman's Right To Choose & Roe vs. Wade

Senator: [Arlen] Specter

SPECTER: It is 9:30. The confirmation hearing of Judge Roberts will now proceed.

Welcome, again, Judge Roberts.

ROBERTS: Thank you, Mr. Chairman.

SPECTER: We begin the first round of questioning in order of seniority, with 30 minutes allotted to each senator . . .

SPECTER: I move now to Casey v. Planned Parenthood . . . In Casey, the key test on following precedents moved to the extent of reliance by the people on the precedent.

And Casey had this to say in a rather earthy way: "People have ordered their thinking and living around Roe. To eliminate the issue of reliance, one would need to limit cognizable reliance to specific instances of sexual activity. For two decades of economic and social developments, people have organized intimate relationships in reliance on the availability of abortion in the event contraception should fail."

That's the joint opinion; rather earthy in its context. Would you agree with that?

ROBERTS: Well, Senator, the importance of settled expectations in the application of stare decisis is a very important consideration. That was emphasized in the Casey opinion, but also in other opinions outside that area of the law.

The principles of stare decisis look at a number of factors. Settled expectations is one of them, as you mentioned . . .

SPECTER: When you and I met on our first so-called courtesy call, I discussed with you the concept of a "super" stare decisis, and this was a phrase used by a circuit Judge Luttig in Richmond Medical Center v. Governor Gilmore in the year 2000, when he refers to Casey being a "super" stare decisis decision with respect to the fundamental right to choose.

And a number of the academics—Professor Farber has talked about the "super" stare decisis, and Professor Eskridge has, as it applies to statutory lines.

Do you think that the cases which have followed Roe fall into the category of a "super" stare decisis designation?

ROBERTS: Well, it's a term that hasn't found its way into the Supreme Court opinions yet.

SPECTER: Well, there's an opportunity for that.

(LAUGHTER)

ROBERTS: I think one way to look at it is that the Casey decision itself, which applies the principles of stare decisis to Roe v. Wade, is itself a precedent of the court entitled to respect under principles of stare decisis. And that would be the body of law that any judge confronting an issue in this area would begin with; not simply the decision in Roe v. Wade, but it's reaffirmation in the Casey decision.

That is itself a precedent. It's a precedent on whether or not to revisit the Roe v. Wade precedent. And, under principles of stare decisis, that would be where any judge considering an issue in this area would begin . . .

SPECTER: Judge Roberts, in your confirmation hearing for the circuit court, your testimony read to this effect, and it's been widely quoted: "Roe is the settled law of the land."

Do you mean settled for you, settled only for your capacity as a circuit judge, or settled beyond that?

ROBERTS: Well, beyond that, it's settled as a precedent of the court, entitled to respect under principles of stare decisis. And those principles, applied in the Casey case, explain when cases should be revisited and when they should not.
And it is settled as a precedent of the court, yes.

SPECTER: You went on then to say, quote, "It's a little more than settled. It was reaffirmed in the face of a challenge that it should be overruled in the Casey decision."

So it has that added precedential value.

ROBERTS:

I think the initial question for the judge confronting an issue in this area, you don't go straight to the Roe decision; you begin with Casey, which modified the Roe framework and reaffirmed its central holding.

SPECTER: And you went on to say, accordingly: "It is the settled law of the land," using the term "settled" again.

Then your final statement as to this quotation: "There is nothing in my personal views that would prevent me from fully and faithfully applying the precedent, as well as Casey." . . .

SPECTER: Judge Roberts, the change in positions have been frequently noted. Early on, in one of your memoranda, you had made a comment on the "so-called right to privacy."

SPECTER: This was a 1981 memo to Attorney General Smith, December 11th, 1981. You were referring to a lecture which Solicitor General Griswold had given six years earlier and you wrote, quote, that, "Solicitor General Griswold devotes a section to the so-called right to privacy; acquiring, as we have—that such an amorphous arguing, as we have, that such an amorphous right was not to be found in the Constitution."

Do you believe today that the right to privacy does exist in the Constitution?

ROBERTS: Senator, I do. The right to privacy is protected under the Constitution in various ways.

It's protected by the Fourth Amendment which provides that the right of people to be secure in their persons, houses, effects and papers is protected.

It's protected under the First Amendment dealing with prohibition on establishment of a religion and guarantee of free exercise.

It protects privacy in matters of conscience.

It was protected by the framers in areas that were of particular concern to them. It may not seem so significant today: the Third Amendment, protecting their homes against the quartering of troops.

And in addition, the court has—it was a series of decisions going back 80 years—has recognized that personal privacy is a component of the liberty protected by the due process clause.

The court has explained that the liberty protected is not limited to freedom from physical restraint and that it's protected not simply procedurally, but as a substantive matter as well.

And those decisions have sketched out, over a period of 80 years, certain aspects of privacy that are protected as part of the liberty in the due process clause under the Constitution.

SPECTER: So that the views that you expressed back in 1981, raising an issue about "amorphous" and "so-called," would not be the views you'd express today?

ROBERTS: Those views reflected the dean's speech. If you read his speech, he's quite skeptical of that right. I knew the attorney general was. And I was transmitting the dean's speech to the attorney general, but my views today are as I've just stated them.

SPECTER: OK.

So they weren't necessarily your views then, but they certainly aren't your views now?

ROBERTS: I think that's fair, yes . . .

Topic: Right to Privacy

Senator: Schumer
Date: SEPTEMBER 13, 2005

SCHUMER: OK. I'd like to go over some other things here.

I have to say I've been pleasantly surprised by some of your answers today.

As you know from our private meetings and my opening statement yesterday, my principal concern is ensuring that we don't have people on our court who will dismantle the structural protections that have guaranteed our most fundamental constitutional rights.

And what troubles me and why I think many people are bothered by this right now, is that the president has openly stated that nominees will be chosen in the mold of justices who have stated, repeatedly, their desire to roll back the clock on some of these basic protections.

In my view, over the past 60 or 70 years, maybe longer, three legs have sustained our constitutional rights: the Fourteenth Amendment's guarantees of equal protection and substantive due process; the right to privacy; and a broad delegation of authority to Congress to pass legislation—usually under the commerce clause—necessary to protect our nation's security, the environment, Americans' health and workers' civil rights.

On the first two, you have given answers that I think show that you want to protect those rights. And I just want to repeat them and just make sure that you're on the record for them.

To Senator Biden—he asked: Do you agree there's a right to privacy to be found in the liberty clause of the Fourteenth Amendment? And you responded, "I do, Senator. Liberty is not limited to freedom from physical restraint. It does cover areas, as you said, such as privacy, and it's not protected only in procedural terms but it's protected substantively as well."

That accurately states your view?

ROBERTS: Yes.

SCHUMER: And on the Griswold case and the right to privacy there, you said, in reference to Senator Kohl's question, quote, "I agree with the Griswold's court's conclusion that marital

> "The court, since Griswold, has grounded the privacy right discussed in that case in the liberty interests protected under the due process clause."

privacy extends to contraception and availability of that.

"The court, since Griswold, has grounded the privacy right discussed in that case in the liberty interests protected under the due process clause."

That is your accurate view?

ROBERTS: Yes, sir . . .

"The essential holding of Roe v. Wade *should be retained and once again reaffirmed . . ."*

The Battle to Regulate Abortion

Despite its polarizing nature, the Supreme Court's 1973 decision in *Roe v. Wade*, which guarantees abortion rights nationwide, has remained the law of the land. What makes this particularly remarkable is that the period since 1980 has coincided with a sharp rightward shift in American politics, including the 20 years of the presidencies of Ronald Reagan and both George H. W. and George W. Bush, plus 12 years of Republican control of Congress. The basic sentiments of the pro-life movement are clear, as reflected in a presidential proclamation by Ronald Reagan in 1984 (Document 1.4). And by 2008, only two justices had been appointed to the Supreme Court by a Democratic president since 1968. Yet to the frustration of a generation of conservatives, their control of all three branches of the national government has not been enough to overcome the powerful precedent of *Roe*.

Pro-life demonstrators and pro-choice counterdemonstrators clash at the January 2004 March for Life rally in Washington, DC. (AP Photo/Gerald Herbert)

Still, if it has not reached its "Holy Grail" of a complete banning of abortion, the pro-life movement has nonetheless achieved many of its goals through targeted protests, demonstrations, and other forms of political pressure. Abortion is far more stigmatized in the United States than in other developed countries, and it has all but vanished from discussion in movies or on television. Fewer and fewer medical students elect to learn how to perform abortions, the number of abortion providers has been dwindling, and public funding for abortions has been curtailed. In large swathes of the country, women must travel long distances to obtain an abortion, since many local providers have closed down rather than contend with the harassment and, at times, violence directed at clinics and doctors that provide abortion.

There have also been numerous test cases in which states have enacted laws designed to challenge *Roe*, several of which have proven successful in narrowing the scope of abortion rights. The single most important was the ruling in the 1992 case of *Casey v. Planned Parenthood of Southeastern Pennsylvania* (Document 1.5), regarding attempts by Pennsylvania to regulate abortion. In this case, a Supreme Court with eight justices appointed by Republican presidents had a major opportunity to overturn *Roe* but instead narrowly upheld its central holding. "We conclude that the basic decision in *Roe* was based on a constitutional analysis which we cannot now repudiate. The woman's liberty is not so unlimited, however, that, from the outset, the State cannot show its concern for the life of the unborn," wrote the majority in *Casey*.

Setting aside the trimester scheme from *Roe*, the Court in *Casey* established a new standard, which persists as of 2008. States may regulate abortion but not establish an "undue burden" on women, defined as "the purpose or effect of placing a substantial obstacle in the path of a woman seeking an abortion of a nonviable fetus." In the Pennsylvania case, the Court struck down a spousal notification requirement for married women as an undue burden, but upheld such provisions as a 24-waiting period, counseling, and parental notification for minors.

Frustrated that *Roe* had not been overturned outright, the anti-abortion camp began focusing in a different direction—toward finding a consensus on banning the most "extreme" manifestations of abortion. To this end, they identified the procedure of "intact dilation and evacuation" in which the skull of a fully formed fetus is crushed *in utero* after the rest of the body has passed through the birth canal. Termed "partial-birth abortion," such procedures accounted for only a small percentage of all abortions performed, but its details were exceedingly gruesome and seemed to some observers to approximate infanticide.

Heeding medical arguments that abortions may sometimes need to be performed even very late in pregnancy—as well as reacting to political pressure from the left—President Bill Clinton vetoed legislation sent to him by Congress to ban such "partial-birth" abortions. Then in 2000, the Supreme Court overturned a similar Nebraska state law in the case of *Stenberg*, stating that it did not provide an exception for abortions that were "medically necessary" for the health of the mother. In 2003, however, Congress passed the Partial Birth Abortion Ban (Document 1.5) without an exception for the health of the mother, and Republican President George W. Bush signed the bill into law. The ban found a way around the *Stenberg* ruling by making the dubious assertion that, in fact, "partial birth" abortion was never medically necessary and thus no exception for the health of the mother.

Nonetheless, the ban did provide an exception for the life of the mother. This apparent contradiction was added in order to improve the bill's chances of surviving scrutiny by the Supreme Court—which it did indeed do in the case *Gonzales v, Carhart* (Document 1.6). Along with *Casey*, *Carhart* is widely considered to have significantly undermined the sweeping protections afforded by *Roe*. Equally striking in *Carhart* is language in the ruling that seemed to return to a more paternalistic era, suggesting that women may not fully understand their decision to have an abortion, and as such need to be protected by the state.

In part emboldened by the passage of the Partial Birth Abortion Ban and the result in *Carhart*, still others in the pro-life movement continued to seek avenues to challenge *Roe* itself. In 2006 the South Dakota legislature passed a statewide law banning all abortions under all circumstances, one that knowingly conflicted with *Roe* in order to set up a legal "showdown." Although the voters of South Dakota, through a referendum later that year, prevented the absolute ban from taking effect, it seems all but certain that abortion will remain a central struggle in American political life.

Ironically, the overturning of *Roe* would not be the end of the politics of abortion in the United States. Rather, should the day come that *Roe* is fully overturned, then the battle would simply move from one arena to 50, with each of the states once again reaching its own conclusions about the appropriate balance between the rights of women and those of fetuses. Short of the unlikely eventuality of a Constitutional amendment either outright banning or outright guaranteeing abortion, the struggle over abortion seems likely to remain a perennial preoccupation of American politics.

Document 1.5: Ronald Reagan on Abortion

- *Document:* Proclamation by President Ronald Reagan of National Sanctity of Human Life Day
- *Date:* January 13, 1984
- *Where:* The White House, Washington, DC
- *Significance:* This proclamation articulates the pro-life view that abortion violates a fundamental "right to life" of the unborn, encapsulating the conservative position in the abortion debates.

By the President of the United States of America

A Proclamation

The values and freedoms we cherish as Americans rest on our fundamental commitment to the sanctity of human life. The first of the "unalienable rights" affirmed by our Declaration of Independence is the right to life itself, a right the Declaration states has been endowed by our Creator on all human beings—whether young or old, weak or strong, healthy or handicapped.

Since 1973, however, more than 15 million unborn children have died in legalized abortions—a tragedy of stunning dimensions that stands in sad contrast to our belief that each life is sacred. These children, over tenfold the number of Americans lost in all our Nation's wars, will never laugh, never sing, never experience the joy of human love; nor will they strive to heal the sick, or feed the poor, or make peace among nations. Abortion has denied them the first and most basic of human rights, and we are infinitely poorer for their loss.

We are poorer not simply for lives not led and for contributions not made, but also for the erosion of our sense of the worth and dignity of every individual. To diminish the value of one category of human life is to diminish us all. Slavery, which treated Blacks as something less than human, to be bought and sold if convenient, cheapened human life and mocked our dedication to the freedom and equality of all men and women. Can we say that abortion—which treats the unborn as something less than human, to be destroyed if convenient—will be less corrosive to the values we hold dear?

"I call upon the citizens of this blessed land to gather on that day in homes and places of worship to give thanks for the gift of life, and to reaffirm our commitment to the dignity of every human being and the sanctity of each human life."

We have been given the precious gift of human life, made more precious still by our births in or pilgrimages to a land of freedom. It is fitting, then, on the anniversary of the Supreme Court decision in Roe v. Wade that struck down State anti-abortion laws, that we reflect anew on these blessings, and on our corresponding responsibility to guard with care the lives and freedoms of even the weakest of our fellow human beings.

Now, Therefore, I, Ronald Reagan, President of the United States of America, do hereby proclaim Sunday, January 22, 1984, as National Sanctity of Human Life Day. I call upon the citizens of this blessed land to gather on that day in homes and places of worship to give thanks for the gift of life, and to reaffirm our commitment to the dignity of every human being and the sanctity of each human life.

In Witness Whereof, I have hereunto set my hand this 13th day of January, in the year of our Lord nineteen hundred and eighty-four, and of the Independence of the United States of America the two hundred and eighth.

Ronald Reagan

Document 1.6: The "Global Gag Rule" on Abortion

- *Document:* Excerpts from the "Mexico City Policy" prohibiting U.S. funding for organizations abroad that "promote" abortion
- *Date:* August 8, 1984
- *Where:* International Conference on Population, Mexico City, Mexico
- *Significance:* With this policy, delivered by UN Ambassador James Buckley on behalf of the Reagan administration, the United States effectively ended funding for any international organizations that even discussed abortion services. Opponents have dubbed this the "global gag rule" and claim that its effect has been to undermine women's rights and reproductive freedom in developing nations.

POLICY STATEMENT OF THE UNITED STATES OF AMERICA

AT THE UNITED NATIONS INTERNATIONAL CONFERENCE ON POPULATION (SECOND SESSION)

MEXICO, D.F., AUGUST 16–13, 1984

The world's rapid population growth is a recent phenomenon. Only several decades ago, the population of developing countries was relatively stable, the result of a balance between high fertility and high mortality. There are now 4.5 billion people in the world, and six billion are projected by the year 2000. Such rapid growth places tremendous pressures on governments without concomitant economic growth.

The International Conference on Population offers the U.S. an opportunity to strengthen the international consensus on the interrelationships between economic development and population, which has emerged since the last such conference in Bucharest in 1974. Our primary objective will be to encourage developing countries to adopt sound economic policies and, where appropriate, population policies consistent with respect for human dignity and family values. As President Reagan stated in his message to the Mexico City Conference:

We believe population programs can and must be truly voluntary, cognizant of the rights and responsibilities of individuals and families, and respectful of religious and cultural values. When they are, such programs can make an important contribution to economic and social development, to the health of mothers and children, and to the stability of the family and of society.

U.S. support for family planning programs is based on respect for human life, enhancement of human dignity, and strengthening of the family. Attempts to use abortion, involuntary sterilization, or other coercive measures in family planning must be shunned, whether exercised against families within a society or against nations within the family of man.

The United Nations Declaration of the Rights of the Child (1959) calls for legal protection for children before birth as well as after birth. In keeping with this obligation, the United States does not consider abortion an acceptable element of family planning programs and will no longer contribute to those of which it is a part. Accordingly, when dealing with nations which support abortion with funds not provided by the United States Government, the United States will contribute to such nations through segregated accounts which cannot be used for abortion. Moreover, the United States will no longer contribute to separate nongovernmental organizations which perform or actively promote abortion as a method of family planning in other nations.

With regard to the United Nations Fund for Population Activities (UNFPA), the U.S. will insist that no part of its contribution be used for abortion. The U.S. will also call for concrete assurances that the UNFPA is not engaged in, or does not provide funding for, abortion or coercive family planning programs; if such assurances are not forthcoming, the U.S. will redirect the amount of its contribution to other, non-UNFPA, family planning programs.

In addition, when efforts to lower population growth are deemed advisable, U.S. policy considers it imperative that such efforts respect the religious beliefs and culture of each society, and the right of couples to determine the size of heir own families. Accordingly, the U.S. will not provide family planning funds to any nation which engages in forcible coercion to achieve population growth objectives.

U.S. Government authorities will immediately begin negotiations to implement the above policies with the appropriate governments and organizations. It is time to put additional emphasis upon those root problems which frequently exacerbate population pressures, but which have too often been given scant attention. By focusing upon real remedies for underdeveloped economies, the International Conference on Population can reduce demographic issues to their proper place. It is an important place, but not the controlling one. It requires our continuing attention within the broader context of economic growth and of the economic freedom that is its prerequisite.

Document 1.7: Expanding States' Regulatory Power over Abortion

- **Document:** Excerpts from the Supreme Court ruling in *Planned Parenthood of Southeastern Pa. v. Casey*, including portions of the syllabus, majority opinion, and dissenting opinion
- **Date:** June 29, 1992
- **Where:** The U.S. Supreme Court, Washington, DC
- **Significance:** In the most important decision on abortion since *Roe v. Wade*, the Supreme Court upheld the basic right to abortion while allowing states wider discretion to regulate abortion while not imposing an "undue burden."

SUPREME COURT OF THE UNITED STATES

PLANNED PARENTHOOD OF SOUTHEASTERN PENNSYLVANIA et al. *v.* CASEY, GOVERNOR OF PENNSYLVANIA, et al.

No. 91-744.

Argued April 22, 1992—Decided June 29, 1992

Syllabus

At issue are five provisions of the Pennsylvania Abortion Control Act of 1982: § 3205, which requires that a woman seeking an abortion give her informed consent prior to the procedure, and specifies that she be provided with certain information at least 24 hours before the abortion is performed; § 3206, which mandates the informed consent of one parent for a minor to obtain an abortion, but provides a judicial bypass procedure; § 3209, which commands that, unless certain exceptions apply, a married woman seeking an abortion must sign a statement indicating that she has notified her husband; § 3203, which defines a "medical emergency" that will excuse compliance with the foregoing requirements; and §§ 3207(b), 3214(a), and 3214(f), which impose certain reporting requirements on facilities providing abortion services. Before any of the provisions took effect, the petitioners, five abortion clinics and a physician representing himself and a class of doctors who provide abortion services, brought this suit seeking a declaratory judgment that each of the provisions was unconstitutional on its face, as well as injunctive relief. The District Court held all the provisions unconstitutional and permanently enjoined their enforcement. The Court of Appeals affirmed in part and reversed in part, striking down the husband notification provision but upholding the others . . .

O'CONNOR, KENNEDY, SOUTER, JJ., Opinion of the Court

After considering the fundamental constitutional questions resolved by *Roe*, principles of institutional integrity, and the rule of *stare decisis*, we are led to conclude this: the essential holding of *Roe v. Wade* should be retained and once again reaffirmed.

It must be stated at the outset and with clarity that *Roe's* essential holding, the holding we reaffirm, has three parts. First is a recognition of the right of the woman to choose to have an abortion before viability and to obtain it without undue interference from the State. Before viability, the State's interests are not strong enough to support a prohibition of abortion or the imposition of a substantial obstacle to the woman's effective right to elect the procedure. Second is a confirmation of the State's power to restrict abortions after fetal viability if the law contains exceptions for pregnancies which endanger a woman's life or health. And third is the principle that the State has legitimate interests from the outset of the pregnancy in protecting the health of the woman and the life of the fetus that may become a child. These principles do not contradict one another; and we adhere to each . . .

Our law affords constitutional protection to personal decisions relating to marriage, procreation, contraception, family relationships, child rearing, and education. Carey v. Population Services International, 431 U.S., at 685. Our cases recognize the right of the individual, married or single, to be free from unwarranted governmental intrusion into matters so fundamentally affecting a person as the decision whether to bear or beget a child. Eisenstadt v. Baird, supra, 405 U.S., at 453 (emphasis in original). Our precedents "have respected the private realm of family life which the state cannot enter." Prince v. Massachusetts, 321 U.S. 158, 166 (1944). These matters, involving the most intimate and personal choices a person may make in a lifetime, choices central to personal dignity and autonomy, are central to the liberty protected by the Fourteenth Amendment. At the heart of liberty is the right to define one's own concept of existence, of meaning, of the universe, and of the mystery of human life. Beliefs about these matters could not define the attributes of personhood were they formed under compulsion of the State . . .

IV

From what we have said so far, it follows that it is a constitutional liberty of the woman to have some freedom to terminate her pregnancy. We conclude that the basic decision in *Roe* was based on a constitutional analysis which we cannot now repudiate. The woman's liberty is not so unlimited, however, that, from the outset, the State cannot show its concern for the life of the unborn and, at a later point in fetal development, the State's interest in life has sufficient force so that the right of the woman to terminate the pregnancy can be restricted.

That brings us, of course, to the point where much criticism has been directed at *Roe*, a criticism that always inheres when the Court draws a specific rule from what in the Constitution is but a general standard. We conclude, however, that the urgent claims of the woman to retain the ultimate control over her destiny and her body, claims implicit in the meaning of liberty, require us to perform that function. Liberty must not be extinguished for want of a line that is clear. And it falls to us to give some real substance to the woman's liberty to determine whether to carry her pregnancy to full term.

We conclude the line should be drawn at viability, so that, before that time, the woman has a right to choose to terminate her pregnancy . . .

_____

We have seen how time has overtaken some of *Roe's* factual assumptions: advances in maternal health care allow for abortions safe to the mother later in pregnancy than was true in 1973, and advances in neonatal care have advanced viability to a point somewhat earlier. But these facts go only to the scheme of time limits on the realization of competing interests, and the divergences from the factual premises of 1973 have no bearing on the validity of *Roe's* central holding, that viability marks the earliest point at which the State's interest in fetal life is constitutionally adequate to justify a legislative ban on nontherapeutic abortions. The soundness or unsoundness of that constitutional judgment in no sense turns on whether viability occurs at approximately 28 weeks, as was usual at the time of *Roe*, at 23 to 24 weeks, as it sometimes does today, or at some moment even slightly earlier in pregnancy, as it may if fetal respiratory capacity can somehow be enhanced in the future. Whenever it may occur, the attainment of viability may continue to serve as the critical fact, just as it has done since *Roe* was decided; which is to say that no change in *Roe's* factual underpinning has left its central holding obsolete, and none supports an argument for overruling it.

_____

The abortion right is similar. Numerous forms of state regulation might have the incidental effect of increasing the cost or decreasing the availability of medical care, whether for abortion or any other medical procedure. The fact that a law which serves a valid purpose, one not designed to strike at the right itself, has the incidental effect of making it more difficult or more expensive to procure an abortion cannot be enough to invalidate it. Only where state regulation imposes an undue burden on a woman's ability to make this decision does the power of the State reach into the heart of the liberty protected by the Due Process Clause . . .

_____

Section 3209 of Pennsylvania's abortion law provides, except in cases of medical emergency, that no physician shall perform an abortion on a married woman without receiving a signed statement from the woman that she has notified her spouse that she is about to undergo an abortion. . . .

By selecting as the controlling class women who wish to obtain abortions, rather than all women or all pregnant women, respondents, in effect, concede that § 3209 must be judged by reference to those for whom it is an actual, rather than irrelevant, restriction. Of course, as we have said, § 3209's real target is narrower even than the class of women seeking abortions identified by the State: it is married women seeking abortions who do not wish to notify their husbands of their intentions and who do not qualify for one of the statutory exceptions to the notice requirement. The unfortunate yet persisting conditions we document above will mean that, in a large fraction of the cases in which § 3209 is relevant, it will operate as a substantial obstacle to a woman's choice to undergo an abortion. It is an undue burden, and therefore invalid.

This conclusion is in no way inconsistent with our decisions upholding parental notification or consent requirements. Those enactments, and our judgment that they are constitutional, are based on the quite reasonable assumption that minors will benefit from consultation with their parents and that children will often not realize that their parents have their best interests at heart. We cannot adopt a parallel assumption about adult women....

CHIEF JUSTICE REHNQUIST, with whom JUSTICE WHITE, JUSTICE SCALIA, and JUSTICE THOMAS join, concurring in the judgment in part and dissenting in part ...

We believe that *Roe* was wrongly decided, and that it can and should be overruled consistently with our traditional approach to *stare decisis* in constitutional cases. We would adopt the approach of the plurality in 410 U.S. 113 (1973), but beats a wholesale retreat from the substance of that case. We believe that *Roe* was wrongly decided, and that it can and should be overruled consistently with our traditional approach to *stare decisis* in constitutional cases. We would adopt the approach of the plurality in *Webster v. Reproductive Health Services*, 492 U.S. 490 (1989), and uphold the challenged provisions of the Pennsylvania statute in their entirety ...

[T]he state of our post-*Roe* decisional law dealing with the regulation of abortion is confusing and uncertain, indicating that a reexamination of that line of cases is in order. Unfortunately for those who must apply this Court's decisions, the reexamination undertaken today leaves the Court no less divided than beforehand. Although they reject the trimester framework that formed the underpinning of *Roe*, JUSTICES O'CONNOR, KENNEDY, and SOUTER adopt a revised undue burden standard to analyze the challenged regulations. We conclude, however, that such an outcome is an unjustified constitutional compromise, one which leaves the Court in a position to closely scrutinize all types of abortion regulations despite the fact that it lacks the power to do so under the Constitution.

In *Roe*, the Court opined that the State does have an important and legitimate interest in preserving and protecting the health of the pregnant woman, ... and that it has still another important and legitimate interest in protecting the potentiality of human life.

Furthermore, while striking down the spousal *notice* regulation, the joint opinion would uphold a parental *consent* restriction that certainly places very substantial obstacles in the path of a minor's abortion choice. The joint opinion is forthright in admitting that it draws this distinction based on a policy judgment that parents will have the best interests of their children at heart, while the same is not necessarily true of husbands as to their wives. Ante at 895. This may or may not be a correct judgment, but it is quintessentially a legislative one. The "undue burden" inquiry does not in any way supply the distinction between parental consent and spousal consent which the joint opinion adopts. Despite the efforts of the joint opinion, the undue burden standard presents nothing more workable than the trimester framework which it discards today. Under the guise of the Constitution, this Court will still impart its own preferences on the States in the form of a complex abortion code.

The sum of the joint opinion's labors in the name of *stare decisis* and "legitimacy" is this: *Roe v. Wade* stands as a sort of judicial Potemkin Village, which may be pointed out to passers by as a monument to the importance of adhering to precedent. But behind the facade, an entirely new method of analysis, without any roots in constitutional law, is imported to decide the constitutionality of state laws regulating abortion. Neither *stare decisis* nor "legitimacy" are truly served by such an effort . . .

JUSTICE SCALIA, with whom THE CHIEF JUSTICE, JUSTICE WHITE, and JUSTICE THOMAS join, concurring in the judgment in part and dissenting in part . . .

The States may, if they wish, permit abortion on demand, but the Constitution does not *require* them to do so. The permissibility of abortion, and the limitations upon it, are to be resolved like most important questions in our democracy: by citizens trying to persuade one another and then voting. As the Court acknowledges, "where reasonable people disagree, the government can adopt one position or the other." The Court is correct in adding the qualification that this "assumes a state of affairs in which the choice does not intrude upon a protected liberty," but the crucial part of that qualification is the penultimate word. A State's choice between two positions on which reasonable people can disagree is constitutional even when (as is often the case) it intrudes upon a "liberty" in the absolute sense. Laws against bigamy, for example—which entire societies of reasonable people disagree with—intrude upon men and women's liberty to marry and live with one another. But bigamy happens not to be a liberty specially "protected" by the Constitution.

That is, quite simply, the issue in this case: not whether the power of a woman to abort her unborn child is a "liberty" in the absolute sense; or even whether it is a liberty of great importance to many women. Of course it is both. The issue is whether it is a liberty protected by the Constitution of the United States. I am sure it is not. I reach that conclusion not because of anything so exalted as my views concerning the "concept of existence, of meaning, of the universe, and of the mystery of human life." Rather, I reach it for the same reason I reach the conclusion that bigamy is not constitutionally protected—because of two simple facts: (1) the Constitution says absolutely nothing about it, and (2) the longstanding traditions of American society have permitted it to be legally . . .

I am certainly not in a good position to dispute that the Court *has saved* the "central holding" of *Roe*, since, to do that effectively, I would have to know what the Court has saved, which in turn would require me to understand (as I do not) what the "undue burden" test means. I must confess, however, that I have always thought, and I think a lot of other people have always thought, that the arbitrary trimester framework, which the Court today discards, was quite as central to *Roe* as the arbitrary viability test, which the Court today retains. It seems particularly ungrateful to carve the trimester framework out of the core of *Roe* . . .

The Court's description of the place of *Roe* in the social history of the United States is unrecognizable. Not only did *Roe* not, as the Court suggests, *resolve* the deeply divisive issue of abortion; it did more than anything else to nourish it, by elevating it to the national level, where it is infinitely more difficult to resolve. National politics were not plagued by abortion protests, national abortion lobbying, or abortion marches on Congress, before *Roe v. Wade* was decided. Profound disagreement existed among our citizens over the issue—as it does over other issues,

such as the death penalty—but that disagreement was being worked out at the state level.
As with many other issues, the division of
sentiment within each State was not as closely
balanced as it was among the population of the
Nation as a whole, meaning not only that more

> "At the heart of liberty is the right to define one's own concept of exist-
> ence, of meaning, of the universe, and of the mystery of human life."

people would be satisfied with the results of state-by-state resolution, but also that those results
would be more stable. Pre-*Roe*, moreover, political compromise was possible.

Roe's mandate for abortion on demand destroyed the compromises of the past, rendered compromise impossible for the future, and required the entire issue to be resolved uniformly, at
the national level. At the same time, *Roe* created a vast new class of abortion consumers and
abortion proponents by eliminating the moral opprobrium that had attached to the act.
("If the Constitution *guarantees* abortion, how can it be bad?"—not an accurate line of thought,
but a natural one.) Many favor all of those developments, and it is not for me to say that they
are wrong. But to portray *Roe* as the statesmanlike "settlement" of a divisive issue, a jurispru-
dential Peace of Westphalia that is worth preserving, is nothing less than Orwellian.
Roe fanned into life an issue that has inflamed our national politics in general, and has obscured
with its smoke the selection of Justices to this Court, in particular, ever since. And by keeping
us in the abortion-umpiring business, it is the perpetuation of that disruption, rather than of any
pax Roeana that the Court's new majority decrees . . .

Document 1.8: Regulating Late Term Abortions

- *Document:* The Partial Birth Abortion Act of 2003, a federal law banning late-term "intact dilation and evacuation" or "partial-birth" abortion
- *Date:* January 7, 2003
- **Where:** *The U.S. Congress, Washington, DC*
- *Significance:* This law does not seek to overturn abortion rights themselves, but rather to ban a particular form of abortion. However, analysts on both sides viewed the law as the beginning of a process of undermining the protections afforded by *Roe.*

An Act to prohibit the procedure commonly known as partial-birth abortion.

Be it enacted by the Senate and House of Representatives of the United States of America in Congress assembled,

SECTION 1. SHORT TITLE.

This Act may be cited as the "Partial-Birth Abortion Ban Act of 2003."

SEC. 2. FINDINGS.

The Congress finds and declares the following:

(1) A moral, medical, and ethical consensus exists that the practice of performing a partial-birth abortion—an abortion in which a physician deliberately and intentionally vaginally delivers a living, unborn child's body until either the entire baby's head is outside the body of the mother, or any part of the baby's trunk past the navel is outside the body of the mother and only the head remains inside the womb, for the purpose of performing an overt act (usually

the puncturing of the back of the child's skull and removing the baby's brains) that the person knows will kill the partially delivered infant, performs this act, and then completes delivery of the dead infant—is a gruesome and inhumane procedure that is never medically necessary and should be prohibited.

"Implicitly approving such a brutal and inhumane procedure by choosing not to prohibit it will further coarsen society to the humanity of not only newborns, but all vulnerable and innocent human life, making it increasingly difficult to protect such life."

(2) Rather than being an abortion procedure that is embraced by the medical community, particularly among physicians who routinely perform other abortion procedures, partial-birth abortion remains a disfavored procedure that is not only unnecessary to preserve the health of the mother, but in fact poses serious risks to the long-term health of women and in some circumstances, their lives. As a result, at least 27 States banned the procedure as did the United States Congress which voted to ban the procedure during the 104th, 105th, and 106th Congresses . . .

(14) Pursuant to the testimony received during extensive legislative hearings during the 104th, 105th, 107th, and 108th Congresses, Congress finds and declares that:

(A) Partial-birth abortion poses serious risks to the health of a woman undergoing the procedure . . .

(B) There is no credible medical evidence that partial-birth abortions are safe or are safer than other abortion procedures. No controlled studies of partial-birth abortions have been conducted nor have any comparative studies been conducted to demonstrate its safety and efficacy compared to other abortion methods . . .

(G) Congress and the States have a compelling interest in prohibiting partial-birth abortions. In addition to promoting maternal health, such a prohibition will draw a bright line that clearly distinguishes abortion and infanticide, that preserves the integrity of the medical profession, and promotes respect for human life.

(H) Based upon Roe v. Wade, 410 U.S. 113 (1973) and Planned Parenthood v. Casey, 505 U.S. 833 (1992), a governmental interest in protecting the life of a child during the delivery process arises by virtue of the fact that during a partial-birth abortion, labor is induced and the birth process has begun. This distinction was recognized in Roe when the Court noted, without comment, that the Texas parturition statute, which prohibited one from killing a child "in a state of being born and before actual birth," was not under attack. This interest becomes compelling as the child emerges from the maternal body. A child that is completely born is a full, legal person entitled to constitutional protections afforded a "person" under the United States Constitution. Partial-birth abortions involve the killing of a child that is in the process, in fact mere inches away from, becoming a "person." Thus, the government has a heightened interest in protecting the life of the partially-born child . . .

(K) Thus, by aborting a child in the manner that purposefully seeks to kill the child after he or she has begun the process of birth, partial-birth abortion undermines the public's perception of the appropriate role of a physician during the delivery process, and perverts a process during which life is brought into the world, in order to destroy a partially-born child.

(L) The gruesome and inhumane nature of the partial-birth abortion procedure and its disturbing similarity to the killing of a newborn infant promotes a complete disregard for infant human life that can only be countered by a prohibition of the procedure.

The Republican Party Platform, 2008: Abortion

Faithful to the first guarantee of the Declaration of Independence, we assert the inherent dignity and sanctity of all human life and affirm that the unborn child has a fundamental individual right to life which cannot be infringed. We support a human life amendment to the Constitution, and we endorse legislation to make clear that the Fourteenth Amendment's protections apply to unborn children.

We oppose using public revenues to promote or perform abortion and will not fund organizations which advocate it. We support the appointment of judges who respect traditional family values and the sanctity and dignity of innocent human life.

We have made progress. The Supreme Court has upheld prohibitions against the barbaric practice of partial-birth abortion. States are now permitted to extend health-care coverage to children before birth. And the Born Alive Infants Protection Act has become law; this law ensures that infants who are born alive during an abortion receive all treatment and care that is provided to all newborn infants and are not neglected and left to die.

We must protect girls from exploitation and statutory rape through a parental notification requirement. We all have a moral obligation to assist, not to penalize, women struggling with the challenges of an unplanned pregnancy.

At its core, abortion is a fundamental assault on the sanctity of innocent human life. Women deserve better than abortion. Every effort should be made to work with women considering abortion to enable and empower them to choose life. We salute those who provide them alternatives, including pregnancy care centers, and we take pride in the tremendous increase in adoptions that has followed Republican legislative initiatives."

(M) The vast majority of babies killed during partial-birth abortions are alive until the end of the procedure. It is a medical fact, however, that unborn infants at this stage can feel pain when subjected to painful stimuli and that their perception of this pain is even more intense than that of newborn infants and older children when subjected to the same stimuli. Thus, during a partial-birth abortion procedure, the child will fully experience the pain associated with piercing his or her skull and sucking out his or her brain.

(N) Implicitly approving such a brutal and inhumane procedure by choosing not to prohibit it will further coarsen society to the humanity of not only newborns, but all vulnerable and innocent human life, making it increasingly difficult to protect such life. Thus, Congress has a compelling interest in acting—indeed it must act—to prohibit this inhumane procedure.

(O) For these reasons, Congress finds that partial-birth abortion is never medically indicated to preserve the health of the mother; is in fact unrecognized as a valid abortion procedure by the mainstream medical community; poses additional health risks to the mother; blurs the line between abortion and infanticide in the killing of a partially-born child just inches from birth; and confuses the role of the physician in childbirth and should, therefore, be banned.

SEC. 3. PROHIBITION ON PARTIAL-BIRTH ABORTIONS . . .

Sec. 1531. Partial-birth abortions prohibited

(a) Any physician who, in or affecting interstate or foreign commerce, knowingly performs a partial-birth abortion and thereby kills a human fetus shall be fined under this title or imprisoned not more than 2 years, or both. This subsection does not apply to a partial-birth abortion that is necessary to save the life of a mother whose life is endangered by a physical disorder, physical illness, or physical injury, including a life-endangering physical condition caused by or arising from the pregnancy itself. This subsection takes effect 1 day after the enactment . . .

(e) A woman upon whom a partial-birth abortion is performed may not be prosecuted under this section, for a conspiracy to violate this section, or for an offense under section 2, 3, or 4 of this title based on a violation of this section.'

Speaker of the House of Representatives.

Vice President of the United States and President of the Senate.

Document 1.9: Narrowing *Roe*

- *Document:* Excerpts from the Supreme Court ruling in *Gonzales v. Carhart*, including portions of the majority opinion and the dissenting opinion
- *Date:* April 18, 2007
- *Where:* The U.S. Supreme Court, Washington, DC
- *Significance:* In the first-of-its-kind case since *Roe*, the U.S. Supreme Court upheld a national law banning the practice of certain types of late-term abortions termed "partial birth abortions" even without an exception for the health of the mother. The ruling further erodes the protections of *Roe*, and was criticized for implying that the law may prevent some women from regretting having an abortion.

SUPREME COURT OF THE UNITED STATES

550 U. S. ___(2007)

ALBERTO R. GONZALES, ATTORNEY GENERAL, PETITIONER

v.

LEROY CARHART et al.

on writ of certiorari to the United States Court of Appeals for the Eighth Circuit

No. 05–380.

Argued November 8, 2006—Decided April 18, 2007*

In July 2005 reproductive rights advocates demonstrated in Boston against erosion of the protections contained in the U.S. Supreme Court's *Roe v. Wade* decision of 1973. (AP Photo/Lisa Poole)

Justice Kennedy delivered the opinion of the Court . . .

We begin with a determination of the Act's operation and effect. A straightforward reading of the Act's text demonstrates its purpose and the scope of its provisions: It regulates and proscribes, with exceptions or qualifications to be discussed, performing the intact D&E procedure.

Respondents agree the Act encompasses intact D&E, but they contend its additional reach is both unclear and excessive. Respondents assert that, at the least, the Act is void for vagueness because its scope is indefinite. In the alternative, respondents argue the Act's text proscribes all D&Es. Because D&E is the most common second-trimester abortion method, respondents suggest the Act imposes an undue burden. In this litigation the Attorney General does not dispute that the Act would impose an undue burden if it covered standard D&E.

We conclude that the Act is not void for vagueness, does not impose an undue burden from any overbreadth, and is not invalid on its face . . .

> "[A] mother who comes to regret her choice to abort must struggle with grief more anguished and sorrow more profound when she learns ... that she allowed a doctor to pierce the skull and vacuum the fast-developing brain of her unborn child."

Under the principles accepted as controlling here, the Act, as we have interpreted it, would be unconstitutional "if its purpose or effect is to place a substantial obstacle in the path of a woman seeking an abortion before the fetus attains viability." Casey, 505 U.S., at 878 (plurality opinion). The abortions affected by the Act's regulations take place both previability and postviability; so the quoted language and the undue burden analysis it relies upon are applicable. The question is whether the Act, measured by its text in this facial attack, imposes a substantial obstacle to late-term, but pre-viability, abortions. The Act does not on its face impose a substantial obstacle, and we reject this further facial challenge to its validity ...

The Act's ban on abortions that involve partial delivery of a living fetus furthers the Government's objectives. No one would dispute that, for many, D&E is a procedure itself laden with the power to devalue human life. Congress could nonetheless conclude that the type of abortion proscribed by the Act requires specific regulation because it implicates additional ethical and moral concerns that justify a special prohibition. Congress determined that the abortion methods it proscribed had a "disturbing similarity to the killing of a newborn infant," and thus it was concerned with "draw[ing] a bright line that clearly distinguishes abortion and infanticide." Congressional Findings (14)(G), ibid. The Court has in the past confirmed the validity of drawing boundaries to prevent certain practices that extinguish life and are close to actions that are condemned. Glucksberg found reasonable the State's "fear that permitting assisted suicide will start it down the path to voluntary and perhaps even involuntary euthanasia."

Respect for human life finds an ultimate expression in the bond of love the mother has for her child. The Act recognizes this reality as well. Whether to have an abortion requires a difficult and painful moral decision. While we find no reliable data to measure the phenomenon, it seems unexceptionable to conclude some women come to regret their choice to abort the infant life they once created and sustained. Severe depression and loss of esteem can follow.

In a decision so fraught with emotional consequence some doctors may prefer not to disclose precise details of the means that will be used, confining themselves to the required statement of risks the procedure entails. From one standpoint this ought not to be surprising. Any number of patients facing imminent surgical procedures would prefer not to hear all details, lest the usual anxiety preceding invasive medical procedures become the more intense. This is likely the case with the abortion procedures here in issue ...

It is, however, precisely this lack of information concerning the way in which the fetus will be killed that is of legitimate concern to the State. Casey, supra, at 873 (plurality opinion) ("States are free to enact laws to provide a reasonable framework for a woman to make a decision that has such profound and lasting meaning"). The State has an interest in ensuring so grave a choice is well informed. It is self-evident that a mother who comes to regret her choice to abort must struggle with grief more anguished and sorrow more profound when she learns, only after the event, what she once did not know: that she allowed a doctor to pierce the skull and vacuum the fast-developing brain of her unborn child, a child assuming the human form.

It is a reasonable inference that a necessary effect of the regulation and the knowledge it conveys will be to encourage some women to carry the infant to full term, thus reducing the absolute number of late-term abortions. The medical profession, furthermore, may find different and less shocking methods to abort the fetus in the second trimester, thereby accommodating

---

The Democratic Party Platform, 2008: Reproductive Rights and Abortion

We oppose the current Administration's consistent attempts to undermine a woman's ability to make her own life choices and obtain reproductive health care, including birth control. We will end health insurance discrimination against contraception and provide compassionate care to rape victims. We will never put ideology above women's health . . .

The Democratic Party strongly and unequivocally supports *Roe v. Wade* and a woman's right to choose a safe and legal abortion, regardless of ability to pay, and we oppose any and all efforts to weaken or undermine that right.

The Democratic Party also strongly supports access to comprehensive affordable family planning services and age-appropriate sex education which empower people to make informed choices and live healthy lives. We also recognize that such health care and education help reduce the number of unintended pregnancies and thereby also reduce the need for abortions.

The Democratic Party also strongly supports a woman's decision to have a child by ensuring access to and availability of programs for pre- and post-natal health care, parenting skills, 51 income support, and caring adoption programs.

---

legislative demand. The State's interest in respect for life is advanced by the dialogue that better informs the political and legal systems, the medical profession, expectant mothers, and society as a whole of the consequences that follow from a decision to elect a late-term abortion.

Justice Ginsburg, with whom Justice Stevens, Justice Souter, and Justice Breyer join, dissenting.

In Planned Parenthood of Southeastern Pa. v. Casey, (1992), the Court declared that "[l]iberty finds no refuge in a jurisprudence of doubt." There was, the Court said, an "imperative" need to dispel doubt as to "the meaning and reach" of the Court's 7-to-2 judgment, rendered nearly two decades earlier in Roe v. Wade. Responsive to that need, the Court endeavored to provide secure guidance to "[s]tate and federal courts as well as legislatures throughout the Union," by defining "the rights of the woman and the legitimate authority of the State respecting the termination of pregnancies by abortion procedures."

Taking care to speak plainly, the Casey Court restated and reaffirmed Roe's essential holding. First, the Court addressed the type of abortion regulation permissible prior to fetal viability. It recognized "the right of the woman to choose to have an abortion before viability and to obtain it without undue interference from the State." Second, the Court acknowledged "the State's power to restrict abortions after fetal viability, if the law contains exceptions for pregnancies which endanger the woman's life or health." Third, the Court confirmed that "the State has legitimate interests from the outset of the pregnancy in protecting the health of the woman and the life of the fetus that may become a child."

In reaffirming Roe, the Casey Court described the centrality of "the decision whether to bear . . . a child," Eisenstadt v. Baird, (1972), to a woman's "dignity and autonomy," her "personhood" and "destiny," her "conception of . . . her place in society." Of signal importance here, the Casey Court stated with unmistakable clarity that state regulation of access to abortion procedures, even after viability, must protect "the health of the woman."

Seven years ago, in Stenberg v. Carhart, (2000) , the Court invalidated a Nebraska statute criminalizing the performance of a medical procedure that, in the political arena, has been dubbed "partial-birth abortion." With fidelity to the Roe-Casey line of precedent, the Court held the Nebraska statute unconstitutional in part because it lacked the requisite protection for the preservation of a woman's health.

Today's decision is alarming. It refuses to take Casey and Stenberg seriously. It tolerates, indeed applauds, federal intervention to ban nationwide a procedure found necessary and proper in certain cases by the American College of Obstetricians and Gynecologists (ACOG). It blurs the line, firmly drawn in Casey, between previability and postviability abortions. And, for the first time since Roe, the Court blesses a prohibition with no exception safeguarding a woman's health.

I dissent from the Court's disposition. Retreating from prior rulings that abortion restrictions cannot be imposed absent an exception safeguarding a woman's health, the Court upholds an Act that surely would not survive under the close scrutiny that previously attended state-decreed limitations on a woman's reproductive choices.

Document 1.10: A Direct Challenge to *Roe*

- *Document:* South Dakota state law banning abortion under all circumstances
- *Date:* February 17, 2006
- *Where:* State of South Dakota, Legislative Assembly
- *Significance:* In a direct challenge to *Roe*, and an attempt to have it overturned, the legislature of South Dakota passed an absolute ban on abortion except to protect the life of the mother. The struck-out portions reflect repealed sections of the prior law. Although the law was overturned by the voters of South Dakota in a subsequent referendum later in 2006, this model seems likely to be repeated in states with anti-abortion majorities.

State of South Dakota

EIGHTY-FIRST SESSION
LEGISLATIVE ASSEMBLY, 2006

FOR AN ACT ENTITLED, An Act to establish certain legislative findings, to reinstate the prohibition against certain acts causing the termination of an unborn human life, to prescribe a penalty therefor, and to provide for the implementation of such provisions under certain circumstances.

BE IT ENACTED BY THE LEGISLATURE OF THE STATE OF SOUTH DAKOTA:

Section 1. The Legislature accepts and concurs with the conclusion of the South Dakota Task Force to Study Abortion, based upon written materials, scientific studies, and testimony of witnesses presented to the task force, that life begins at the time of conception, a conclusion confirmed by scientific advances since the 1973 decision of Roe v. Wade, including the fact that each human being is totally unique immediately at fertilization. Moreover, the Legislature finds, based upon the conclusions of the South Dakota Task Force to Study Abortion, and in recognition of the technological advances and medical experience and body of knowledge about abortions produced and made available since the 1973 decision of Roe v. Wade, that to fully protect the rights, interests, and health of the pregnant mother, the rights, interest, and life of her unborn child, and the mother's fundamental natural intrinsic right to a relationship with her child, abortions in South Dakota should be prohibited. Moreover, the Legislature finds that the guarantee of due process of law under the Constitution of South Dakota applies equally to born and unborn human beings, and that under the Constitution of South Dakota, a pregnant mother and her unborn child, each possess a natural and inalienable right to life.

Section 2. That chapter 22-17 be amended by adding thereto a NEW SECTION to read as follows:

No person may knowingly administer to, prescribe for, or procure for, or sell to any pregnant woman any medicine, drug, or other substance with the specific intent of causing or abetting the termination of the life of an unborn human being. No person may knowingly use or employ any instrument or procedure upon a pregnant woman with the specific intent of causing or abetting the termination of the life of an unborn human being.

Any violation of this section is a Class 5 felony.

Section 3. That chapter 22-17 be amended by adding thereto a NEW SECTION to read as follows:

Nothing in section 2 of this Act may be construed to prohibit the sale, use, prescription, or administration of a contraceptive measure, drug or chemical, if it is administered prior to the time when a pregnancy could be determined through conventional medical testing and if the contraceptive measure is sold, used, prescribed, or administered in accordance with manufacturer instructions.

Section 4. That chapter 22-17 be amended by adding thereto a NEW SECTION to read as follows:

NARAL Pro-Choice America

Founded as The National Association for the Repeal of Abortion Laws (NARAL) in 1969, NARAL Pro-Choice America argues that "while it's critical to promote policies that help prevent unintended pregnancies and make abortion less necessary, NARAL Pro-Choice America also fights to protect the right to safe, legal abortion."

According to the organization's Web site (www.prochoiceamerica.org), "in 1973, the Supreme Court guaranteed American women the right to choose abortion in its landmark decision *Roe v. Wade*. In *Roe*, the Court issued a compromise between the state's ability to restrict abortion and a woman's right to choose. Since that time, the anti-choice movement has worked furiously to dismantle it—with the ultimate goal of overturning the decision altogether. Anti-choice activists are working hard in state legislatures, the courts, and Congress to take away our rights."

NARAL Pro-Choice America argues that "making abortion access more difficult and dangerous is a key tactic of the anti-choice movement. Even with *Roe v. Wade*'s protections still in place, 87 percent of U.S. counties have no abortion provider . . . The anti-choice movement's ultimate goal is to outlaw abortion in all circumstances." The group works against efforts to overturn *Roe v. Wade*, as well as to enact other limitations on access to abortion via traditional surgical techniques as well as newer chemical means such as the drug RU 486.

The National Right to Life Committee

Immediately after the Supreme Court legalized abortion in all 50 states in its opinion in the case of *Roe v. Wade* in 1973, The National Right to Life Committee was founded to "restore legal protection to innocent human life." According to its Web site (www.nrlc.org), "the primary interest of the National Right to Life Committee and its members has been the abortion controversy; however, it is also concerned with related matters of medical ethics which relate to the right to life issues of euthanasia and infanticide."

On the 35th anniversary of *Roe v. Wade* in 2008, the National Right to Life committee argued that the ruling had "resulted in nearly 50 million deaths. . . . "These are not just statistics: each of those abortions stopped the heartbeat of a living, unborn baby . . ."

Noting that abortion rates had decreased in recent years, the Web site noted that: "Much of the decrease can be attributed to efforts by National Right to Life and its network of state affiliates and local chapters to educate the public about abortion and the biological development of the unborn child, as well as legislative measures designed to help women at a time when they are most in need."

No licensed physician who performs a medical procedure designed or intended to prevent the death of a pregnant mother is guilty of violating section 2 of this Act. However, the physician shall make reasonable medical efforts under the circumstances to preserve both the life of the mother and the life of her unborn child in a manner consistent with conventional medical practice.

Medical treatment provided to the mother by a licensed physician which results in the accidental or unintentional injury or death to the unborn child is not a violation of this statute.

Nothing in this Act may be construed to subject the pregnant mother upon whom any abortion is performed or attempted to any criminal conviction and penalty.

Section 5. That chapter 22-17 be amended by adding thereto a NEW SECTION to read as follows:

Terms used in this Act mean:

(1) "Pregnant," the human female reproductive condition, of having a living unborn human being within her body throughout the entire embryonic and fetal ages of the unborn child from fertilization to full gestation and child birth;

(2) "Unborn human being," an individual living member of the species, homo sapiens, throughout the entire embryonic and fetal ages of the unborn child from fertilization to full gestation and childbirth;

(3) "Fertilization," that point in time when a male human sperm penetrates the zona pellucida of a female human ovum.

Section 6. That § 34-23A-2 be repealed.
~~34-23A-2. An abortion may be performed in this state only if it is performed in compliance with § 34-23A-3, 34-23A-4, or 34-23A-5.~~
Section 7. That § 34-23A-3 be repealed.

~~34-23A-3. An abortion may be performed by a physician during the first twelve weeks of pregnancy. The abortion decision and its effectuation must be left to the medical judgment of the pregnant woman's attending physician during the first twelve weeks of pregnancy.~~

Section 8. That § 34-23A-4 be repealed.

~~34-23A-4. An abortion may be performed following the twelfth week of pregnancy and through the twenty-fourth week of pregnancy by a physician only in a hospital licensed under the provisions of chapter 34-12 or in a hospital operated by the United States, this state, or any department, agency, or political subdivision of either or in the case of hospital facilities not being available, in the licensed physician's medical clinic or office of practice subject to the requirements of § 34-23A-6.~~

Section 9. That § 34-23A-5 be repealed.

~~34-23A-5. An abortion may be performed following the twenty-fourth week of pregnancy by a physician only in a hospital authorized under § 34-23A-4 and only if there is appropriate and reasonable medical judgment that performance of an abortion is necessary to preserve the life or health of the mother.~~ . . .

Section 12. This Act shall be known, and may be cited, as the Women's Health and Human Life Protection Act.

BIBLIOGRAPHY

Evans, John H. "Polarization in Abortion Attitudes in U.S. Religious Traditions, 1972–1998." *Sociological Forum* 17.3 (September 2002): 397–422.

Garrow, David J. *Liberty and Sexuality: The Right to Privacy and the Making of Roe v. Wade.* New York: Macmillan, 1994.

Gitchens, M. *Abortion Politics: Public Policy in Cross-Cultural Perspective.* New York: Routledge, 1996.

Hull, N. E. H., and Peter Charles Hoffer. *Roe v. Wade: The Abortion Rights Controversy in American History.* Lawrence: University of Kansas Press, 2001.

Johnson, John W. *Griswold v. Connecticut: Birth Control and the Constitutional Right of Privacy.* Lawrence: University of Kansas Press, 2005.

Luker, Kristin. *Abortion and the Politics of Motherhood.* Berkeley: University of California Press, 1984.

McDonnell, Kathleen. *Not an Easy Choice: A Feminist Re-Examines Abortion.* Boston: South End Press, 1984.

Rosenblatt, Roger. *Life Itself: Abortion in the American Mind.* New York: Random House, 1992.

Solinger, Rickie. *Abortion Wars: A Half-Century of Struggle, 1950–2000.* Berkeley: University of California Press, 1998.

Whitman, Chris. "Looking Back on Planned Parenthood v. Casey." *Michigan Law Review* 100.7 (June 2002): 1980–1996.

2

WOMEN'S EQUALITY

*No person shall be denied "liberty, or property,
without due process of law; nor . . . the equal
protection of the laws."*

RECOGNIZING EQUAL RIGHTS FOR WOMEN

2.1 Enforcing the Equal Pay Act: U.S. Supreme Court ruling in *Schultz v. Wheaton Glass Company* (1970)

2.2 Strengthening Equal Protection: U.S. Supreme Court ruling in *Reed v. Reed* (1971)

2.3 Debating Equal Rights: Excerpts from a House Hearing on an Equal Rights Amendment (1971)

2.4 Guaranteeing Constitutional Equality: Federal and State Equal Rights Amendments (1973)

2.5 Establishing "Intermediate Scrutiny" for Women's Issues: Supreme Court ruling in *Craig v. Boren* (1976)

*"It is the policy of the United States
Government to provide equal opportunity."*

MAKING WOMEN'S EQUALITY A REALITY

2.6 Equal Employment Opportunities for Women: President Lyndon Johnson's Executive Order 11375 (1967)

2.7 Curbing Gender-Based Violence: The Violence against Women Act (1994)

2.8 Advancing Educational Opportunity: Title IX of the Education Amendments of 1972 to the Civil Rights Act of 1964

2.9 Preventing Sexual Harassment: Policy of the Equal Opportunity Employment Commission (2006)

Introduction

Perhaps the most universal of all forms of discrimination is sexism. While minorities on the basis of religious, cultural, linguistic, or other characteristics have often been subject to persecution of various kinds, such groups could often be segregated off by the majority or they could find ways to separate themselves from their oppressors. But women are, inevitably, omnipresent in all societies, present in every region, every class, and every family.

As a result, oppression by men has often had to take on other forms of subjugation, such as depriving women of economic independence, subjecting them to violence, subordinating them in family decision making, and legally relegating them to "second-class citizenship." Yet women have always found ways to resist and assert themselves, even if only through their connections with the men in their lives. As early as 411 BC, the Greek playwright Aristophanes wrote the satirical work *Lysistrata* in which women tried to bring about an end to the Peloponnesian War by the only means at their disposal—withholding sex from their husbands.

Early in the American Republic, (white) women were counted as citizens and enjoyed such constitutional rights as freedom of speech and religion. Still, women's rights as such were not enshrined in any of the nation's founding documents, despite Abigail Adam's famous plea to her husband John to "remember the ladies, and be more generous and favorable to them than your ancestors. Do not put such unlimited power into the hands of the Husbands." John replied: "as to your extraordinary code of laws, I cannot but laugh . . ." For more than the first century of U.S. independence, women's rights were to be maintained instead through representation via fathers, brothers, husbands, and sons, with women holding only limited legal rights.

Half a century later, at the Seneca Falls Convention of 1848, leading women's rights advocates such as Elizabeth Cady Stanton and Lucretia Mott helped to pen a "Declaration of Sentiments" (which is the subject of the "Historical View" sidebar in this chapter.) The document, which self-consciously paralleled the Declaration of Independence, was considered by many men to be a shocking, even scandalous, debasement of one of the nation's greatest founding documents, and it brought about little immediate change. But the Seneca Falls Convention is often regarded as the historic founding moment of the "first wave" feminist movement.

Although some western states gradually began to extend the electoral franchise to women, it would be yet another 70 years before women would finally gain the right to vote throughout the country. Linked to the Progressive Movement of the late nineteenth and early twentieth centuries, so-called "suffragettes" fought for equal access to the ballot, a goal at least realized with the passage of the Nineteenth Amendment in 1920. However, because of traditionalist political socialization, lower levels of education, and other influences, women did not vote in numbers completely commensurate with their numbers until the 1970s. (Today, they constitute a little more than half the American electorate, largely because women live somewhat longer and are much less likely to be incarcerated than men.)

Another key interlude for women's rights was the World War II era. With so many of the nation's young men conscripted for the military effort, women were swept up as part of "total war mobilization." Once deemed unfit for many types of heavy labor, women ably took over roles in heavy industry and manufacture, most iconically represented by posters of "Rosie the Riveter" who flexed her bicep and declared "We Can Do It." Upon the end of the war, thousands of men returned to the United States and to the workforce, displacing women and sending them back to their roles as "housewives."

Yet these women were the mothers of girls who would come of age in the 1960s and 1970s and launch the "second wave" feminist movement, the variety best known in the United States through association with leaders such as Betty Friedan and Gloria Steinem and political crusades such as support for the gender wage parity, educational opportunities, access to safe and legal contraception and abortion, and a range of other rights. One of the most influential vehicles of second-wave feminism was the National Organization for Women (NOW), which is profiled in the "From the Left" sidebar in this chapter. Other women have asserted their right to be politically active without specifically adopting the term "feminist," including Concerned Women for America (CWA), which is profiled in the "From the Right" sidebar in this chapter. Still others have attempted to fuse the two, such as the anti-abortion group "Feminists for Life."

Questions relating to women's rights pervade this entire volume, including issues of reproductive rights (Chapter 1), the rights of lesbian, bisexual, and transgender women (Chapter 4), and rights within the context of marriage (Chapter 5). This chapter focuses more specifically on attempts over the past half-century to completely secure the promise of full equality for women. The cornerstone of this crusade was the attempt to pass an Equal Rights Amendment to the U.S. Constitution, as well as to various state constitutions (Document 2.4). Building on the Fourteenth Amendment to the U.S. constitution, the ERA would explicitly outlaw all forms of discrimination on the basis of sex. As recounted in excerpt from Congressional debate (Document 2.3), this was not as uncontroversial an idea as it may seem today. In fact, the ERA ultimately was not enacted at the federal level but was implemented in a number of states. However, judicial rulings have done through constitutional interpretation what the ERA sought through textual change. A series of rulings have been limited in their immediate scope to such areas as equal pay (Document 2.1), inheritance rights (Document 2.2), and the age at which one can purchase alcohol (Document 2.5). But collectively, their implications have gone much further, recognizing women as a distinctive category of citizens who have been, and remain, subject to widespread discrimination.

Of course, a simple recognition of the inherent equality of women is not sufficient to eradicate sexism in practice, whether interpersonal sexism in the culture at large or the legacy of institutional sexism in both the public and private sectors. To that end, a number of additional steps have been taken to make women's equality a reality. These include an Executive Order by Lyndon Johnson extending affirmative action programs to women (Document 2.6), and laws ensuring equal access to educational facilities (Document 2.7), curbing gender-based violence (Document 2.8), and detering sexual harassment (Document 2.9). While the work of establishing full equality for women remains unfinished, the period since 1965 has yielded considerable, and continuing, gains.

No person shall be denied "liberty, or property, without due process of law; nor . . . the equal protection of the laws."

Recognizing Equal Rights for Women

The Fourteenth Amendment was enacted in the immediate aftermath of the Civil War, and its original intentions were clearly to provide citizenship and equal protection of the law to the millions of former slaves of African descent who were emancipated by means of the Thirteenth Amendment. Yet the meaning and scope of the Fourteenth Amendment, and its fundamental promise of equality, have continued to be lively areas of discussion and controversy, not only in the case of race and ethnicity but also with regard to other characteristics, including sex or gender.

With the extension of voting rights to women through the Nineteenth Amendment of 1920, women achieved a near-equal say in the political process, at least at the ballot box. But the electoral franchise alone could not eradicate centuries of patriarchal precedents that subordinated women in almost every realm of social, political, and economic life. Such deep-seated sexism, its opponents argued, demanded the full weight of a textual addition to the Constitution, with the broad national dialogue and consensus that such an amendment would require. Thus was born the idea for the Equal Rights Amendment (ERA, Document 2.4).

The battle for and against ratification of the ERA was one of the signature domestic political events of the 1970s. As required of all Constitutional amendments, the ERA first had to receive support from a two-thirds majority of both houses of Congress. It did so by large margins in the House in October 1971 and the Senate in March 1972, from which it moved to the states. Before the seven-year deadline specified by Congress, three-quarters of the state legislatures—a total of 38—would also have to provide ratification in order for the amendment to take effect. (The final outcomes are outlined in Document 2.4).

Opponents argued that the ERA would erase all distinctions between the genders, and thus might require women to be drafted into combat, demand single-sex locker rooms, or require same-sex marriages. Although most people, and most states, approved the ERA, only 35 states had ratified (and five had rescinded their earlier ratifications) by the time of the amendment's deadline in 1979, and thus the ERA lapsed into history. In every Congress since then, supporters have reintroduced the ERA but in many ways the ratification process—and resultant raising of national consciousness—was a form of victory in itself.

One important by-product of the campaign was that a number of states incorporated versions of the ERA into their own constitutions, guaranteeing equal protection at least within their states (Document 2.3). The citizens of these states already enjoy, at the statewide level, the full protection afforded by guarantees of equal rights.

Perhaps even more importantly, a string of judicial decisions at the federal level have achieved some of the same goals through a more expansive interpretation of the Fourteenth Amendment. In 1970, a federal circuit court provided a robust interpretation of the Equal Pay Act of 1963, indicating that it would not allow the intent of the law to be circumvented on technicalities (Document 2.1). Shortly thereafter, the Supreme Court took a further step in determining that women were a so-called "suspect class," and that any government action affecting them adversely must have a "rational basis" (Document 2.2). The major breakthrough occurred in the case of *Craig v. Boren* (Document 2.5), in which the Court articulated a new level of "intermediate scrutiny," which would apply to government action involving women. This new standard requires that government action must be "substantially related" to a legitimate government aim, not simply "rationally related." However, the protection did not rise to the most rigorous standard of "strict scrutiny" established by the courts. Although the ERA would, by its nature, have imposed the higher level of strict scrutiny, intermediate scrutiny has proved to be an enduring and powerful form of anti-discrimination protection for women. Subsequent court rulings, such as 1996's *U.S. v. Virginia*, requiring the admission of women to the Virginia Military Institute, have further enhanced intermediate scrutiny, demanding "exceedingly persuasive justification" for government action that treats women unequally.

Document 2.1: Enforcing the Equal Pay Act

- **Document:** Excerpt from U.S. 3rd Circuit Court of Appeals Case *Schultz v. Wheaton Glass Company*
- **Date:** January 13, 1970
- **Where:** Third Circuit Court of Appeals, Philadelphia, Pennsylvania
- **Significance:** In their unanimous opinion, the 3rd Circuit Court of Appeals held that wage disparity between men and women who occupied the same job role violated the Equal Pay Act's protection against discriminatory wage differences based on sex.

George P. Shultz, Secretary of Labor, United States Department of Labor, Appellant v. Wheaton Glass Company, Appellee

No. 17517

UNITED STATES COURT OF APPEALS FOR THE THIRD CIRCUIT

421 F.2d 259 (1970)

Decided: January 13, 1970

JUDGES: Freedman, Seitz and Aldisert, Circuit Judges.

FREEDMAN, C. J., delivered the opinion of the Court:

This appeal presents important problems in the construction of the Equal Pay Act of 1963, which was added as an amendment to the Fair Labor Standards Act of 1938.

The Equal Pay Act prohibits an employer from discriminating "between employees on the basis of sex by paying wages to employees . . . at a rate less than the rate at which he pays wages to employees of the opposite sex . . . for equal work on jobs the performance of which requires equal skill, effort, and responsibility, and which are performed under similar working conditions, except where such payment is made pursuant to . . . (iv) a differential based on any other factor other than sex . . ."

Invoking the enforcement provisions of the Fair Labor Standards Act the Secretary of Labor brought this action against Wheaton Glass Co., claiming that it discriminated against its "female selector-packers" on the basis of sex by paying them at an hourly rate of $2.14, which is 10% less than the $2.355 rate it pays to its "male selector-packers." The Secretary sought an injunction against future violations and the recovery of back pay for past violations. The company denied that the female selector-packers perform equal work within the terms of the Act and claimed that in any event the 10% pay differential is within exception (iv) of the Act because it is based on a "factor other than sex" . . .

Selector-packers are employed in the Bottle Inspection Department. They work at long tables and visually inspect the bottles for defects as they emerge on a conveyor from the oven, or "lehr." The defective products are discarded into waste containers. Those which meet the specifications are packed in cardboard cartons on a stand within arm's reach of the selector-packers and then lifted onto an adjacent conveyor or rollers and sent off to the Quality Control Department for further examination and processing. In the Bottle Inspection Department is another category of employees known as "snap-up boys," who crate and move bottles and generally function as handymen, sweeping and cleaning and performing other unskilled miscellaneous tasks. They are paid at the hourly rate of $2.16.

Prior to 1956, the company employed only male selector-packers. In that year, however, the shortage of available men in the Millville area forced the company to employ for the first time female selector-packers. On the insistence of the Glass Bottle Blowers Association of the United States and Canada, AFL-CIO, Local 219, with which the company had a collective bargaining agreement, there was, in the language of the district court, "carved out of the total job of selector-packer . . . a new role of female selector-packer." This new classification was written into the collective bargaining agreement, and pursuant to it female selector-packers were not to lift bulky cartons or cartons weighing more than 35 pounds. At the union's insistence a provision was added to the collective bargaining agreement that no male selector-packer was to be replaced by a female selector-packer except to fill a vacancy resulting from retirement, resignation, or dismissal for just cause.

On its face the record presents the incongruity that because male selector-packers spend a relatively small portion of their time doing the work of snap-up boys whose hourly rate of pay is $2.16, they are paid $2.355 per hour for their own work, while female selector-packers receive only $2.14. This immediately casts doubt on any contention that the difference in the work done by male and female selector-packers, which amounts substantially to what the snap-up boys do, is of itself enough to explain the difference in the rate of pay for male and female selector-packers on grounds other than sex.

The district court explored this difference in some detail. The court found that while male and female selector-packers perform substantially identical work at the ovens, the work of the male selector-packers is substantially different because they perform sixteen additional tasks . . .

The district court pointed to evidence submitted by the company that the male selector-packers spent an average of approximately 18 percent of their total time on this work, which was forbidden to women. It made no finding, however, that this was a fact, nor did it make any finding as to what percentage of time was spent by male selector-packers either on the average or individually in performing this different work. Indeed, it made no finding that all male selector-packers performed this extra work, but only that the extra work when not performed by snap-up boys was done by male selector-packers. There is, therefore, no basis for an assumption that all male selector-packers performed any or all of these 16 additional tasks.

Even if there had been a finding that all the male selector-packers performed all of the 16 additional tasks and that these consumed a substantial amount of their time, there would still be lacking an adequate basis for the differential in wages paid to male and female selector-packers. For there would be no rational explanation why men who at times perform work paying two cents per hour more than their female counterparts should for that reason receive 21 1/2 cents per hour more than females for the work they do in common.

The district court, therefore, placed its conclusion on a factor of "flexibility." . . . The district court found that this availability of male selector-packers to perform the work of snap-up boys during shutdowns was an element of flexibility and deemed it to be of economic value to the company in the operation of its unique, customized plant. It is on this element of flexibility that the judgment of the district court ultimately rests . . .

Whatever difference may exist in the total work of male and female selector-packers because men also perform work of snap-up boys does not justify a class wage differential in the absence of any finding regarding the number of male selector-packers who perform or are available for the work of snap-up boys. While all male selector-packers receive the higher rate of pay, there is no finding that all of them are either available for or actually perform snap-up boys' work.

An even more serious imperfection in the claim of flexibility is the absence, as we have already indicated, of any finding or explanation why availability of men to perform work which pays two cents per hour more than women receive should result in overall payment to men of 21 1/2 cents more than women for their common work. A 10% wage differential is not automatically justified by showing that some advantage exists to the employer because of a flexibility whose extent and economic value is neither measured nor determined and which is attained by the performance of work carrying a much lower rate of pay. In short, there is no finding of the economic value of the element of flexibility on which the district court justified the 10% discrimination in pay rate between male and female selector-packers . . .

These disparities in rates of pay under which snap-up boys performing physical labor receive a higher rate than female selector-packers while male selector-packers receive a much higher rate because they are available also to do some of the work of snap-up boys, take on an even more discriminatory aspect when viewed in the light of their history. For as the district court indicated, the classification of female selector-packers at the lowest rate of pay of these three categories was made at a time of labor shortage when the company was forced to hire women and the union insisted on conditions which would minimize their future competition against the men with whom they would now be working. The motive, therefore, clearly appears to have been to keep women in a subordinate role rather than to confer flexibility on the company and to emphasize this subordination by both the 10% differential between male and female selector-packers and the two cents difference between snap-up boys and female selector-packers.

The effect of such a motive and the evaluation of the distinction in the work done by male and female selector-packers requires us to turn to the construction of the Equal Pay Act of 1963. The Act was the culmination of many years of striving to eliminate discrimination in pay because of sex. Similar bills were before Congress for many years before the Act ultimately was adopted, and in its final form it bears evidence of the competing tendencies which surrounded its birth. There are problems of construction which leap up from the reading of its language. It has not been authoritatively construed by the Supreme Court and a study of its legislative history and the bills which preceded it yields little guidance in the construction of its provisions in concrete circumstances.

In adopting the Act, Congress chose to specify equal pay for "equal" work. In doing so, Congress was well aware of the experience of the National War Labor Board during World War II and its regulations requiring equal pay for "comparable" work. The National War Labor Board made job evaluations to determine whether inequities existed within a plant even between dissimilar occupations. Since Congress was aware of the Board's policy and chose to require equal pay for "equal" rather than "comparable" work, it is clear that the references in the legislative history to the Board's regulations were only to show the feasibility of administering a federal equal pay policy and do not warrant use of the Board's decisions as guiding principles for the construction of the Equal Pay Act.

On the other hand, Congress in prescribing equal work did not require that the jobs be identical, but only that they must be substantially equal. Any other interpretation would destroy the remedial purposes of the Act.

The Act was intended as a broad charter of women's rights in the economic field. It sought to overcome the age-old belief in women's inferiority and to eliminate the depressing effects on living standards of reduced wages for female workers and the economic and social consequences which flow from it.

Differences in job classifications were in general expected to be beyond the coverage of the Equal Pay Act. . . . Congress never intended, however, that an artificially created job classification which did not substantially differ from the genuine one could provide an escape for an employer from the operation of the Equal Pay Act. This would be too wide a door through which the content of the Act would disappear.

This view is strengthened by the subsequent adoption of Title VII of the Civil Rights Act of 1964 which prohibits discrimination because of sex in the classification of employees as well as in their employment and compensation. Although the Civil Rights Act is much broader than the Equal Pay Act, its provisions regarding discrimination based on sex are in pari materia with the Equal Pay Act. This is recognized in the provision of § 703(h) of the Civil Rights Act that an employer's differentiation upon the basis of sex in determining wages or compensation shall not be an unlawful employment practice under the Civil Rights Act if the differentiation is authorized by the Equal Pay Act. Since both statutes serve the same fundamental purpose against discrimination based on sex, the Equal Pay Act may not be construed in a manner which by virtue of § 703(h) would undermine the Civil Rights Act . . .

Under the statute, the burden of proof there-upon fell on the company to prove its claim that it came within exception (iv). This burden the district court held the company had successfully met . . .

"Congress in prescribing equal work did not require that the jobs be identical, but only that they must be substantially equal. Any other interpretation would destroy the remedial purposes of the Equal Pay Act."

The district court held that the company met its burden of proving that it came within the exception because "the acceptable proof demonstrates that the defendant's disparity in wages is based upon factors other than sex . . ." It also stated that "substantial differences exist, in fact, in the full job cycles between the sexes, thereby justifying the disparity in their wages." These, however, are statements of ultimate conclusions for which there is no adequate support either in findings of fact or in the record.

We are, of course, bound by findings of fact unless they are clearly erroneous . . . Since the Secretary established his prima facie case and the company failed to prove that the discrimination in wages paid to female selector-packers was based on any factor other than sex, the claim of the Secretary was established and an appropriate judgment should have been entered in his favor.

The judgment of the district court, therefore, will be reversed with direction to enter an appropriate judgment in favor of plaintiff.

Document 2.2: Strengthening Equal Protection

- *Document:* Excerpt from the U.S. Supreme Court case *Reed v. Reed*
- *Date:* November 22, 1971
- *Where:* U.S. Supreme Court, Washington, DC
- *Significance:* Unanimously, the Supreme Court struck down an Idaho statute that automatically advantaged males under inheritance law. The ruling strengthened the idea that women were protected by the Equal Protection Clause of the Fourteenth Amendment.

U.S. Supreme Court

Reed v. Reed, 404 U.S. 71 (1971)

No. 70-4

Argued October 19, 1971

Decided November 22, 1971

MR. CHIEF JUSTICE BURGER delivered the unanimous opinion of the Court.

Richard Lynn Reed, a minor, died intestate in Ada County, Idaho, on March 29, 1967. His adoptive parents, who had separated sometime prior to his death, are the parties to this appeal. Approximately seven months after Richard's death, his mother, appellant Sally Reed, filed a petition in the Probate Court of Ada County, seeking appointment as administratrix of her son's estate. Prior to the date set for a hearing on the mother's petition, appellee Cecil Reed, the father of the decedent, filed a competing petition seeking to have himself appointed administrator of the son's estate. The probate court held a joint hearing on the two petitions and thereafter ordered that letters of administration be issued to appellee Cecil Reed upon his taking the oath and filing the bond required by law. The court treated §§ 15-312 and 15-314 of the Idaho Code as the controlling statutes, and read those sections as compelling a preference for Cecil Reed because he was a male.

Section 15-312 designates the persons who are entitled to administer the estate of one who dies intestate. In making these designations, that section lists 11 classes of persons who are so entitled, and provides, in substance, that the order in which those classes are listed in the section shall be determinative of the relative rights of competing applicants for letters of administration. One of the 11 classes so enumerated is "[t]he father or mother" of the person dying intestate. Under this section, then, appellant and appellee, being members of the same entitlement class, would seem to have been equally entitled to administer their son's estate. Section 1314 provides, however, that "[o]f several persons claiming and equally entitled [under § 1312] to administer, males must be preferred to females, and relatives of the whole to those of the half blood."

In issuing its order, the probate court implicitly recognized the equality of entitlement of the two applicants under § 15-312, and noted that neither of the applicants was under any legal disability; the court ruled, however, that appellee, being a male, was to be preferred to the female appellant "by reason of Section 15-314 of the Idaho Code." In stating this conclusion, the probate judge gave no indication that he had attempted to determine the relative capabilities of the competing applicants to perform the functions incident to the administration of an estate. It seems clear the probate judge considered himself bound by statute to give preference to the male candidate over the female, each being otherwise "equally entitled."

Sally Reed appealed from the probate court order, and her appeal was treated by the District Court of the Fourth Judicial District of Idaho as a constitutional attack on § 15-314. In dealing with the attack, that court held that the challenged section violated the Equal Protection Clause of the Fourteenth Amendment, and was, therefore, void; the matter was ordered "returned to the Probate Court for its determination of which of the two parties" was better qualified to administer the estate.

This order was never carried out, however, for Cecil Reed took a further appeal to the Idaho Supreme Court, which reversed the District Court and reinstated the original order naming the father administrator of the estate. In reaching this result, the Idaho Supreme Court first dealt with the governing statutory law and held that, under § 15-312 "a father and mother are equally entitled to letters of administration," but the preference given to males by § 15-314 is "mandatory" and leaves no room for the exercise of a probate court's discretion in the appointment of administrators. Having thus definitively and authoritatively interpreted the statutory provisions involved, the Idaho Supreme Court then proceeded to examine, and reject, Sally Reed's contention that § 15-314 violates the Equal Protection Clause by giving a mandatory preference to males over females, without regard to their individual qualifications as potential estate administrators.

Sally Reed thereupon appealed for review by this Court pursuant and we noted probable jurisdiction. Having examined the record and considered the briefs and oral arguments of the parties, we have concluded that the arbitrary preference established in favor of males by § 15-314 of the Idaho Code cannot stand in the face of the Fourteenth Amendment's command that no State deny the equal protection of the laws to any person within its jurisdiction.

Idaho does not, of course, deny letters of administration to women altogether. Indeed, under § 15-312, a woman whose spouse dies intestate has a preference over a son, father, brother, or any other male relative of the decedent. Moreover, we can judicially notice that, in this country, presumably due to the greater longevity of women, a large proportion of estates, both intestate and under wills of decedents, are administered by surviving widows.

"To give a mandatory preference to members of either sex over members of the other, merely to accomplish the elimination of hearings on the merits, is to make the very kind of arbitrary legislative choice forbidden by the Equal Protection Clause of the Fourteenth Amendment...."

Section 15-314 is restricted in its operation to those situations where competing applications for letters of administration have been filed by both male and female members of the same entitlement class established by § 15-312. In such situations, § 15-314 provides that different treatment be accorded to the applicants on the basis of their sex; it thus establishes a classification subject to scrutiny under the Equal Protection Clause.

In applying that clause, this Court has consistently recognized that the Fourteenth Amendment does not deny to States the power to treat different classes of persons in different ways. The Equal Protection Clause of that amendment does, however, deny to States the power to legislate that different treatment be accorded to persons placed by a statute into different classes on the basis of criteria wholly unrelated to the objective of that statute. A classification "must be reasonable, not arbitrary, and must rest upon some ground of difference having a fair and substantial relation to the object of the legislation, so that all persons similarly circumstanced shall be treated alike." The question presented by this case, then, is whether a difference in the sex of competing applicants for letters of administration bears a rational relationship to a state objective that is sought to be advanced by the operation of §§ 15-312 and 15-314.

In upholding the latter section, the Idaho Supreme Court concluded that its objective was to eliminate one area of controversy when two or more persons, equally entitled under § 15-312, seek letters of administration, and thereby present the probate court "with the issue of which one should be named." The court also concluded that, where such persons are not of the same sex, the elimination of females from consideration "is neither an illogical nor arbitrary method devised by the legislature to resolve an issue that would otherwise require a hearing as to the relative merits . . . of the two or more petitioning relatives . . . "

Clearly the objective of reducing the workload on probate courts by eliminating one class of contests is not without some legitimacy. The crucial question, however, is whether § 15-314 advances that objective in a manner consistent with the command of the Equal Protection Clause. We hold that it does not. To give a mandatory preference to members of either sex over members of the other, merely to accomplish the elimination of hearings on the merits, is to make the very kind of arbitrary legislative choice forbidden by the Equal Protection Clause of the Fourteenth Amendment; and whatever may be said as to the positive values of avoiding intrafamily controversy, the choice in this context may not lawfully be mandated solely on the basis of sex.

We note finally that, if § 15-314 is viewed merely as a modifying appendage to § 15-312 and as aimed at the same objective, its constitutionality is not thereby saved. The objective of § 15-312 clearly is to establish degrees of entitlement of various classes of persons in accordance with their varying degrees and kinds of relationship to the intestate. Regardless of their sex, persons within any one of the enumerated classes of that section are similarly situated with respect to that objective. By providing dissimilar treatment for men and women who are thus similarly situated, the challenged section violates the Equal Protection Clause.

The judgment of the Idaho Supreme Court is reversed, and the case remanded for further proceedings not inconsistent with this opinion.

Reversed and remanded.

Document 2.3: Debating Equal Rights

- *Document:* Hearings before Subcommittee No. 4 of the Committee on the Judiciary, House of Representatives, 92nd Congress, First Session
- *Date:* March 24, 1972
- *Significance:* During the initial hearings on an Equal Rights Amendment to the U.S. Constitution, Senator Ervin delivers his legal argument that an amendment is not necessary for equal rights and that a slow path of incremental change would suffice. Representatives Edwards and Conyers rebut. Lucille Shriver, of a women's professional organization, delivers an incisive statement regarding why the passage is necessary for equality between the sexes

---

People Quoted: Senator Sam J. Ervin, Jr., North Carolina; Representative John Conyers, Michigan; Representative Don Edwards, California; Shriver, Lucille H., Federation Director of the National Federation of Business and Professional Women's Clubs.

Sen. Sam J. Ervin, Jr: . . . It is the better part of wisdom to recognize that discriminations not created by law cannot be abolished by law. They must be abolished by changed attitudes in the society which imposes them.

From the many conversations I have had with advocates of the equal rights amendment since coming to the Senate, I am convinced that many of their just grievances are founded upon discriminations not created by law, and that for this reason the equal rights amendment will have no effect whatsoever in respect to them . . .

Congress has also decreed by the equal employment provisions in title VII of the Civil Rights Act of 1964 that there can be no discrimination whatever against women in employment in industries employing 25 or more persons, whose business affects interstate commerce, except in those instances where sex is a bona fide occupational qualification reasonably necessary to the normal operation of the enterprise. Furthermore, it is to be noted that the President and virtually all of the departments and agencies of the Federal

Government have issued orders prohibiting discrimination against women in Federal employment.

Moreover, State legislatures have adopted many enlightened statutes in recent years prohibiting discrimination against women in employment.

If women are not enjoying the full benefit of this Federal and State legislation and these executive orders of the Federal Government, it is due to a defect in enforcement rather than a want of fair laws and regulations . . .

Mr. Edwards: . . . You believe apparently that whatever qualification may exist in equality, be it in education or employment, will be taken care of by law.

Senator Ervin: By statutes. . . . I think we can accept now the Supreme Court will hold that any statute of any State which makes a legal distinction between the rights of responsibilities of men and women is unconstitutional under the equal protection clause unless it is based upon rational grounds which justify the distinction.

Mr. Edwards: Senator Ervin, if I may go one step further, you are asking the proponents of this legislation to be patient. You are asking them to trust the courts, trust their rights under the 14th amendment and to seek their remedies case by case in the Federal court system. Now suppose the women of America were required to do the same thing when they wanted the right to vote. Do you think they would have won the right to vote by going through the courts?

Senator Ervin: I think so, I don't think the Court now would hold the difference of voting rights between men and women on the basis of sex.

Mr. Edwards: Switzerland is quite a democracy, too, and some women in Switzerland still can't vote.

Senator Ervin: Switzerland does not have the equal protection clause. . . .

Mr. Conyers: . . . Your opposition to the proposed legislation, of course, casts a restraint upon us—perhaps maybe even more than the 15 members in the House who last year voted against the legislation that passed the House of Representatives but did not come to a vote, as I recall, in your body.

Senator Ervin: Notwithstanding the fact it had 82 cosponsors over there.

Mr. Conyers: Is that right? Maybe that is why it did not come to a vote.

Senator, I am interested in this statement which I think is particularly one of law and perhaps one of philosophy in which you say, "It is the better part of wisdom to recognize that discriminations not created by law cannot be abolished by law, they must be abolished by changed attitudes in the society which imposes them."

Now of course I must relate that statement to the struggle of why people in America—I realize this question has come up in matters in our society other than abolishing discrimination as relates to women. "Discriminations not created by law cannot be abolished by law."

But is it not true, would you not even consider the fact that the law creates the framework around the sanctions in our society? In other words, if there is a law against racial discrimination, that encourages law abiding citizens to conform their conduct to that legislation which we have prescribed as reasonable and wise. So in the case involving race or sex or opportunity we must necessarily turn to the law as it is now and the members of a society that consider the law to be that base and bulwark upon which all of our conduct and inevitably our attitudes emanate from. . . .

Is that the peril, Senator, making men and women equal human beings?

Senator Ervin: Identical legal beings.

Mr. Conyers: Identical?

Senator Ervin: Yes.

Mr. Conyers: What do you mean by that?

Senator Ervin: I mean make them have exactly the same rights and the same responsibilities. There is quite a difference between that and the equality because there are greater values in equality.

Mr. Conyers: Could I just pursue that one point further. What different right and responsibilities do you envision?

Senator Ervin: Well, if you give men and women the same rights and responsibilities, the husband has no longer any primary duty to support his wife or his children, the wife has exactly the same responsibilities in this field.

Mr. Conyers: Of course for 38 percent of the women that is precisely the case now.

Senator Ervin: You know, sometimes we are prone to claim we are speaking for a lot of old people. My experience is that outside of business women, business professional women in the United States, and only part of them, the great majority of the women in this country don't want the amendment. . . .

Mrs. Shriver: The National Federation of Business and Professional Women's Clubs, Inc. presents this statement in support of House Joint Resolution 208, the equal rights amendment . . . We support this joint resolution completely and urge the committee to report it favorably . . .

BPW has no illusion that the equal rights amendment will irrevocably remove the inequities practiced against women; nor that the amendment will elevate women to their proper political and economic role in a democratic society, as many reformers had hoped.

We do believe, however, that this is a Nation of laws, not men; and that although we cannot change a person's prejudice or ill will, we can and should put this Nation on record in support of woman's right to full economic, legal, and social responsibility to full citizenship. . . .

[State Labor laws] establish maximum daily or weekly working hours, require certain lunch and rest periods and seating facilities, establish weight lifting limitations, restrict the kinds and places of employment.

We believe that the term "protective" no longer applies to this kind of legislation. Certainly at one time special labor regulations for women were protective because they were the only labor laws on the books; there were no Federal or State laws protecting a worker as to the hours of employment, wages due, or healthy and safe working conditions . . .

We believe that protective legislation for women has become restrictive, burdensome, and discriminatory. We support passage of the equal rights amendment to eliminate such laws for women only. Protective laws will prohibit women from being bartenders but allow them to be barmaids, to serve the drinks they cannot mix, and at a lower pay.

In some States, women cannot work overtime in factories but laundry, hotel, and restaurant workers, agricultural and domestic laborers are often exempt from the hours limitation. Special labor legislation for women restricts as fully as it was originally intended to protect.

These laws operate to prevent millions of women from competing on equal terms with men; they prevent women from providing themselves and their dependents with the proper support and care.

Instead of protecting, they impede and they deny equal employment opportunity to those women who need it the most.

Obviously, if all other factors are equal and if an employer has to supply additional benefits to women workers, he will be more hesitant to hire her, promote her, and give her options open to men.

Given current employment practice and health standards, many of these laws only create an expense to the employer and no benefit that is not as desirable for men and women. There can be no doubt that a problem does exist with respect to employment discrimination based on sex, a good measure of which has as its excuse State protective legislation.

A Department of Labor report released last year indicated a substantial earnings gap between men and women. In 1960, women made 60.8 percent of the salaries men made; in 1968, the percentage was 58.2 percent of what men made.

This discrepancy existed in spite of the fact that women are today better educated than ever before and constitute 38 percent of the work force. In 1968, 8 percent of full-time male workers earned less than $3,000, while 20 percent of full-time female workers were at that level.

Sixty percent of female full-time workers earned less than $5,000 compared to 20 percent of male full-time workers who earned less than $5,000. Only 3 percent of women earned more than $10,000, whereas 28 percent of men earned more than that.

It has been stated that the lesser position of women in the employment area stems largely from an employer's higher costs in employing them. Factors in addition to compliance with state protective laws such as greater absenteeism, turnover, and decreased job tenure are cited.

A recent study of the Department of Labor discredited all these additional factors. The study concluded: "The cost differentials are shown to be insignificant. The favorable findings for women workers emphasize the importance of judging work performance on the basis of individual achievement rather than on sex"...

The obvious fact that women are different from men does not justify legal restrictions imposed on women. What must be demonstrated is that a particular weakness in women requires the particular kind of restraint which is being imposed...

We would like to point out, Mr. Chairman, that during wartime, women loaded and unloaded heavy materials, labored in munition plants, worked at unskilled manual labor. "Rosie the Riveter" was not protected from heavy, grueling labor, nor does our population, in terms of

Pro-Equal Rights Amendment demonstrators crowd downtown Richmond, Virginia, for a January 1980 rally. As of 2009, Virginia was one of 15 states that had not yet ratified the amendment. (AP Photo)

those women who did this work or their offspring, seem to have been adversely affected by the work.

An exception is made whenever sex is a bona fide occupational qualification necessary to the normal operation of a particular business or enterprise. The Equal Employment Opportunity Commission, charged with implementing title VII, believes also that an irreconcilable conflict exists between the sex discrimination provisions of title VII and State labor regulations for women. . . .

We respectively submit, Mr. Chairman, that passage of this equal rights amendment will significantly help to begin the job of erasing all these pockets of legal and social inequality between the sexes. We therefore urge its passage . . .

Document 2.4: Guaranteeing Constitutional Equality

- *Document:* The full text of the federal Equal Rights Amendment, with Congressional and state actions, plus texts of several state equal rights amendments
- *Date:* March 22, 1972
- *Where:* Washington, DC
- *Significance:* First proposal in the early twentieth century, a prospective amendment to safeguard equal rights among men and women was sent to the several states for ratification in 1972. Although the ERA fell short at the federal level, a number of states incorporated a version of the ERA into their state constitutions, including the examples below from Alaska, California, Colorado, Hawaii, New Mexico, Texas, and Utah.

Proposed Federal Equal Rights Amendment

Section 1. Equality of rights under the law shall not be denied or abridged by the United States or by any State on account of sex.

Section 2. The Congress shall have the power to enforce, by appropriate legislation, the provisions of this article.

Section 3. This amendment shall take effect two years after the date of ratification.

Congressional Actions

U.S. House Vote, October 12, 1971 H J Res. 208, Equal Rights Amendment

Party /	Seats	Yeas		Nays		Other	
D	253	216	(85.38%)	12	(4.74%)	25	(9.88%)
R	180	138	(76.67%)	12	(6.67%)	30	(16.67%)
Totals	433	354	(81.76%)	24	(5.54%)	55	(12.70%)

Passage of the resolution approving a constitutional amendment guaranteeing equal rights for men and women. Passed 354–24: Republicans 137–12; Democrats 217–12), Oct. 12, 1971. A two-thirds majority vote (252 in this case) is needed for approval of a constitutional amendment.

U.S. Senate Vote, March 22, 1972

Party /	Seats	Yeas		Nays		Other	
C	1	0	(0.00%)	1	(100.00%)	0	(0.00%)
D	54	46	(85.19%)	2	(3.70%)	6	(11.11%)
I	1	1	(100.00%)	0	(0.00%)	0	(0.00%)
R	44	37	(84.09%)	5	(11.36%)	2	(4.55%)
Totals	100	84	(84.00%)	8	(8.00%)	8	(8.00%)

Equal Rights Amendment (in Sen.) H J Res 208

H J Res 208 Passage of the resolution containing a constitutional amendment guaranteeing equal rights for men and women. A two-thirds majority vote (62 in this case) is required for adoption of a constitutional amendment. Passed 84–8: R 37–6; D 47–2, March 22, 1972. A "yea" was a vote supporting the President's position.

Actions in the State Legislatures:

Unratified States

Alabama, Arizona, Arkansas, Florida, Georgia, Illinois, Louisiana, Mississippi, Missouri, Nevada, North Carolina, Oklahoma, South Carolina, Utah, Virginia

Ratified States

Alaska, California, Colorado, Connecticut, Delaware, Hawaii, Idaho*, Indiana, Iowa, Kansas, Kentucky*, Maine, Maryland, Massachusetts, Michigan, Minnesota, Montana, Nebraska*, New Hampshire, New Jersey, New Mexico, New York, North Dakota, Ohio, Oregon, Pennsylvania, Rhode Island, South Dakota*, Tennessee*, Texas, Vermont, Washington, West Virginia, Wisconsin, Wyoming.

*=legislature later rescinded its vote

Equal Rights Amendments Ratified as Part of State Constitutions

Alaska Constitution, Article I, S3 (1972)

No person is to be denied the enjoyment of any civil or political right because of race, color, creed, sex or national origin.

> "Equality of rights under the law shall not be denied or abridged by the United States or by any State on account of sex."

California Constitution, Article I, S8 (1979)

A person may not be disqualified from entering or pursuing a business, profession, vocation, or employment because of sex, race, creed, color, or national or ethnic origin.

Colorado Constitution, Article II, S29 (1973)

Equality of rights under the law shall not be denied or abridged by the state of Colorado or any of its political subdivisions because of sex.

Hawaii Constitution Article I, S5 (1978):

No person shall be deprived of life, liberty, or property without due process of law, nor be denied the equal protection of the laws, nor be denied the enjoyment of the person's civil rights or be discriminated against in the exercise thereof because of race, religion, sex or ancestry.

New Mexico Constitution, Article II, S18 (1973)

No person shall be deprived of life, liberty or property without due process of law. Equality of rights under the law shall not be denied on account of the sex of any person.

Texas Constitution, Article I, S3a (1972)

Equality under the law shall not be denied or abridged because of sex, race, color, creed, or national origin.

Utah Constitution, Article IV, S1 (1896).

The rights of citizens in the State of Utah to vote and hold office shall not be denied or abridged on account of sex. Both male and female citizens of this State shall enjoy all civil, political and religious rights and privileges.

Document 2.5: Establishing "Intermediate Scrutiny" for Women's Issues

- **Document:** Excerpt from the Supreme Court case *Craig v. Boren*
- **Date:** December 20, 1976
- **Where:** U.S. Supreme Court, Washington, DC
- **Significance:** The Supreme Court struck down a discriminatory age law in Oklahoma for purchase of beer, ruling that the statutes constituted sex-based discrimination. With this ruling, the Court created a new "intermediate scrutiny" standard for sex, significantly increasing women's constitutional equality protections.

CRAIG ET AL. v. BOREN, GOVERNOR OF OKLAHOMA, ET AL., ante, p. 190.

SUPREME COURT OF THE UNITED STATES

429 U.S. 1124; 97 S. Ct. 1161; 51 L. Ed. 2d 574;

Argued October 5, 1976
Decided December 20, 1976

BRENNAN, J., delivered the opinion of the Court

The interaction of two sections of an Oklahoma statute, and 245 prohibits the sale of "nonintoxicating" 3.2% beer to males under the age of 21 and to females under the age of 18. The question to be decided is whether such a gender-based differential constitutes a denial to males 18–20 years of age of the equal protection of the laws in violation of the Fourteenth Amendment.

This action was brought in the District Court for the Western District of Oklahoma on December 20, 1972, by appellant Craig, a male then between 18 and 21 years of age, and by appellant Whitener, a licensed vendor of 3.2% beer. The complaint sought declaratory and injunctive relief against enforcement of the gender-based differential on the ground that it constituted invidious discrimination against males 18–20 years of age. A three-judge court convened under *28 U.S.C. § 2281* sustained the constitutionality of the statutory differential and dismissed the action. We noted probable jurisdiction of appellants' appeal. We reverse . . .

> "To withstand constitutional challenge, previous cases establish that classifications by gender must serve important governmental objectives and must be substantially related to achievement of those objectives."

Analysis may appropriately begin with the reminder that Reed emphasized that statutory classifications that distinguish between males and females are "subject to scrutiny under the Equal Protection Clause." To withstand constitutional challenge, previous cases establish that classifications by gender must serve important governmental objectives and must be substantially related to achievement of those objectives. Thus, in Reed, the objectives of "reducing the workload on probate courts," and "avoiding intrafamily controversy," were deemed of insufficient importance to sustain use of an overt gender criterion in the appointment of administrators of intestate decedents' estates. Decisions following Reed similarly have rejected administrative ease and convenience as sufficiently important objectives to justify gender-based classifications. And only two Terms ago expressly stating that Reed v. Reed was "controlling," held that Reed required invalidation of a Utah differential age-of-majority statute, notwithstanding the statute's coincidence with and furtherance of the State's purpose of fostering "old notions" of role typing and preparing boys for their expected performance in the economic and political worlds . . .

Reed v. Reed has also provided the underpinning for decisions that have invalidated statutes employing gender as an inaccurate proxy for other, more germane bases of classification. Hence, "archaic and overbroad" generalizations, concerning the financial position of servicewomen, and working women, could not justify use of a gender line in determining eligibility for certain governmental entitlements. Similarly, increasingly outdated misconceptions concerning the role of females in the home rather than in the "marketplace and world of ideas" were rejected as loose-fitting characterizations incapable of supporting state statutory schemes that were premised upon their accuracy. In light of the weak congruence between gender and the characteristic or trait that gender purported to represent, it was necessary that the legislatures choose either to realign their substantive laws in a gender-neutral fashion, or to adopt procedures for identifying those instances where the sex-centered generalization actually comported with fact . . .

We conclude that the gender-based differential contained in *Okla. Stat., Tit. 37, § 245* constitutes a denial of the equal protection of the laws to males aged 18–20 and reverse the judgment of the District Court.

JUSTICE POWELL, with whom STEVENS, BLACKMUN (in part) and STEWART join, concurring,

With respect to the equal protection standard, I agree that Reed v. Reed, 404 U.S. 71 (1971), is the most relevant precedent. But I find it unnecessary, in deciding this case, to read that decision as broadly as some of the Court's language may imply. Reed and subsequent cases involving gender-based classifications make clear that the Court subjects such classifications to a more critical examination than is normally applied when "fundamental" constitutional rights and "suspect classes" are not present.

I view this as a relatively easy case. No one questions the legitimacy or importance of the asserted governmental objective: the promotion of highway safety. The decision of the case turns on whether the state legislature, by the classification it has chosen, has adopted a means that bears a "fair and substantial relation" to this objective. It seems to me that the statistics offered by appellees and relied upon by the District Court do tend generally to support the view that young men drive more, possibly are inclined to drink more, and—for various reasons—are involved in more accidents than young women. Even so, I am not persuaded that these facts and the inferences fairly drawn from them justify this classification based on a three-year age differential between the sexes, and especially one that is so easily circumvented as to be virtually meaningless. Putting it differently, this gender-based classification does not bear a fair and substantial relation to the object of the legislation.

JUSTICE STEVENS, concurring.

. . . I am inclined to believe that what has become known as the two-tiered analysis of equal protection claims does not describe a completely logical method of deciding cases, but rather is a method the Court has employed to explain decisions that actually apply a single standard in a reasonably consistent fashion. I also suspect that a careful explanation of the reasons motivating particular decisions may contribute more to an identification of that standard than an attempt to articulate it in all-encompassing terms. It may therefore be appropriate for me to state the principal reasons which persuaded me to join the Court's opinion.

. . . The classification is not totally irrational. For the evidence does indicate that there are more males than females in this age bracket who drive and also more who drink. Nevertheless, there are several reasons why I regard the justification as unacceptable. It is difficult to believe that the statute was actually intended to cope with the problem of traffic safety, since it has only a minimal effect on access to a not very intoxicating beverage and does not prohibit its consumption.

CHIEF JUSTICE BURGER, with whom JUSTICE REHNQUIST joins, dissenting.

. . . On the merits, we have only recently recognized that our duty is not "to create substantive constitutional rights in the name of guaranteeing equal protection of the laws." Thus, even interests of such importance in our society as public education and housing do not qualify as "fundamental rights" for equal protection purposes because they have no [*217] textually independent constitutional status. Though today's decision does not go so far as to make gender-based classifications "suspect," it makes gender a disfavored classification. Without an independent constitutional basis supporting the right asserted or disfavoring the classification adopted, I can justify no substantive constitutional protection other than the normal protection afforded by the Equal Protection Clause. The means employed by the Oklahoma Legislature to achieve the objectives sought may not be agreeable to some judges, but since eight Members of the Court think the means not irrational, I see no basis for striking down the statute as violative of the Constitution simply because we find it unwise, unneeded, or possibly even a bit foolish.

JUSTICE REHNQUIST, with whom CHIEF JUSTICE BURGER joins, dissenting.

The Court's conclusion that a law which treats males less favorably than females "must serve important governmental objectives and must be substantially related to achievement of those objectives" apparently comes out of thin air. The Equal Protection Clause contains no such language, and none of our previous cases adopt that standard. I would think we have had enough difficulty with the two standards of review which our cases have recognized—the norm of "rational basis," and the "compelling state interest" required where a "suspect classification" is involved—so as to counsel weightily against the insertion of still another "standard" between those two. How is this Court to divine what objectives are important? How is it to determine whether a particular law is "substantially" related to the achievement of such objective, rather than related in some other way to its achievement? Both of the phrases used are so diaphanous and elastic as to invite subjective judicial preferences or prejudices relating to particular types of legislation, masquerading as judgments whether such legislation is directed at "important" objectives or, whether the relationship to those objectives is "substantial" enough . . .

The Oklahoma Legislature could have believed that 18–20-year-old males drive substantially more, and tend more often to be intoxicated than their female counterparts; that they prefer beer and admit to drinking and driving at a higher rate than females; and that they suffer traffic injuries out of proportion to the part they make up of the population. Under the appropriate rational-basis test for equal protection, it is neither irrational nor arbitrary to bar them from making purchases of 3.2% beer, which purchases might in many cases be made by a young man who immediately returns to his vehicle with the beverage in his possession. The record does not give any good indication of the true proportion of males in the age group who drink and drive (except that it is no doubt greater than the 2% who are arrested), but whatever it may be I cannot see that the mere purchase right involved could conceivably raise a due process question. There being no violation of either equal protection or due process, the statute should accordingly be upheld.

"It is the policy of the United States
Government to provide equal opportunity."

Making Women's Equality a Reality

As seen in the prior section, the struggle over the Constitutional equality of women has been conducted on many levels: through the federal Constitutional amendment process, through inclusion into state constitutions, and through judicial interpretation. But even the most thorough-going legal or theoretical acceptance of women's equality may not be enough to deter the practical reality that discrimination, assault, harassment, and other forms of bias against women persist.

Thus, beyond enshrining the principle of equality, both the federal and state governments have taken a variety of steps toward enacting public policies designed to make women's equality a reality. Some have taken place through the use of executive power, by either presidents or governors. One of the most important of these was Executive Order 11375 (Document 2.6), issued by Lyndon Johnson in 1967. The order builds upon the equally important Executive Order 10925 by Johnson's predecessor, John F. Kennedy, which not only established the principle of "equal opportunity on the basis of race" but also recognized the reality that sometimes extra steps—"affirmative actions"—are needed to be taken to overcome the legacy of discrimination. Johnson's order extends and expands Kennedy's, explicitly citing the need to prevent sex discrimination and to allow women to benefit from affirmative action programs.

By the time Johnson enacted his Executive Order, he had seen through a landmark piece of legislation, the Civil Rights Act of 1964, which represented a major effort to enforce the Fourteenth Amendment through statutory law. The law prohibited discrimination in a wide range of areas, including housing, education, employment, and public accommodations. In a cynical attempt to stop the legislation, conservative lawmakers added provisions that employment discrimination on the basis of "sex" would also be banned—assuming that this would cause the bill to lose supporters. To their chagrin, it passed with the sex discrimination provision intact, substantially expanding the reach of the bill, which also covers "color," religion, and national origin.

In 1978, the Civil Rights Act was further amended to include protections on the basis of the uniquely female biological attribute of pregnancy. Its relevant portion reads as follows: "the terms 'because of sex' or 'on the basis of sex' include, but are not limited to, because of or on the basis of pregnancy, childbirth, or related medical conditions; and women affected by pregnancy, childbirth, or related medical conditions shall be treated the same for all employment-related purposes, including receipt of benefits under fringe benefit programs, as other persons not so affected but similar in their ability or inability to work." In 1993, the Family and Medical Leave Act further extended opportunities for unpaid work leaves for the parents of newborn or newly adopted children.

A related area of concern in the workplace involves sexual harassment. This issue burst onto the public stage with dramatic "he said, she said" testimony during the 1990 Senate confirmation hearings for Supreme Court Justice Clarence Thomas (see Documents 6.1 and 6.2). In one of the most public forums imaginable, Thomas was accused of a long and repeated pattern of sexual harassment by his former employee Anita Hill.

Since that time, the United States has witnessed a wide-scale growth of awareness about appropriate sexual behavior in the workplace, most notably regarding harassment of women by men, but also vice versa and among members of the same sex. Behaviors that might have once been considered acceptable—or at least unremarkable—in the workplace, such as lewd comments, sexual propositions, or unwanted physical contact, are now more widely understood to be both offensive as well as illegal. Sexual harassment can occur either on an interpersonal level or through the cultivation of a "hostile work environment," both of which are reflected in the sexual harassment policy of the U.S. Equal Employment Opportunity Commission (EEOC; Document 2.8). (Ironically the EEOC was the very agency that Thomas headed when he allegedly harassed Hill.)

Equal educational opportunity, the stepping stone toward better employment and higher income, has also been an area of concern. Recognizing that women had traditionally been disadvantaged in educational settings, Congress in 1972 acted to ensure equal access for women to schools that receive federal funds (Document 2.7). Although the law applies to the full panoply of educational facilities, and makes no specific mention of athletics, it has had its greatest impact in that area. In enforcing the law, the federal bureaucracy established that educational institutions must provide athletic opportunities that are substantially proportionate to the student enrollment, or that at least demonstrate a continual expansion of athletic opportunities for the underrepresented sex. In a debate that parallels the larger controversies over affirmative action, critics have charged that Title IX effectively creates a "quota system" for women in sports. However, the law also allows institutions to demonstrate "full and effective accommodation of the interest and ability of underrepresented sex," which may allow for smaller women's sports programs if surveys demonstrate less interest among female students.

Unfortunately, invidious discrimination against women goes beyond the workplace and right into women's homes and relationships in the form of various types of violence and abuse. Although this falls primarily under the purview of the "police power" of individual states, Congress has also acted in this area to attempt to redress society-wide means by which women, particularly young women, are subjected to violence. Its most notable effort has been the Violence Against Women Act (1994), which provides funds for intervention and awareness campaigns. Focused on such areas as domestic violence, stalking, and sexual assault, the Act establishes and funds programs to provide services to victims, to encourage the prosecution of abusers, and to promote prevention of violence through cooperation among police, law courts, and victims' rights groups.

Document 2.6: Equal Employment Opportunities for Women

- *Document:* Text of President Lyndon B. Johnson's famous Civil Rights Executive Order
- *Date:* October 13, 1967
- *Where:* Washington, DC
- **Significance:** President Lyndon B. Johnson secured the protections of the Civil Rights Act of 1964, especially with regard to sex discrimination, to federal employment opportunities.

Amending Executive Order No. 11246, Relating to Equal Employment Opportunity

It is the policy of the United States Government to provide equal opportunity in Federal employment and in employment by Federal contractors on the basis of merit and without discrimination because of race, color, religion, sex or national origin.

The Congress, by enacting Title VII of the Civil Rights Act of 1964, enunciated a national policy of equal employment opportunity in private employment, without discrimination because of race, color, religion, sex or national origin.

EXECUTIVE ORDER No. 11246 1 of September 24, 1965, carried forward a program of equal employment opportunity in Government employment, employment by Federal contractors and subcontractors and employment under Federally assisted construction contracts regardless of race, creed, color or national origin.

It is desirable that the equal employment opportunity programs provided for in EXECUTIVE ORDER No. 11246 expressly embrace discrimination on account of sex.

"It is desirable that the equal employment opportunity programs expressly embrace discrimination on account of sex."

NOW, THEREFORE, by virtue of the authority vested in me as President of the United States by the Constitution and statutes of the United States, it is ordered that EXECUTIVE ORDER No. 11246 of September 24, 1965, be amended as follows:

(1) Section 101 of Part I, concerning nondiscrimination in Government employment, is revised to read as follows:

"Sec. 101. It is the policy of the Government of the United States to provide equal opportunity in Federal employment for all qualified persons, to prohibit discrimination in employment because of race, color, religion, sex or national origin, and to promote the full realization of equal employment opportunity through a positive, continuing program in each EXECUTIVE department and agency. The policy of equal opportunity applies to every aspect of Federal employment policy and practice."

(2) Section 104 of Part I is revised to read as follows:

"Sec. 104. The Civil Service Commission shall provide for the prompt, fair, and impartial consideration of all complaints of discrimination in Federal employment on the basis of race, color, religion, sex or national origin. Procedures for the consideration of complaints shall include at least one impartial review within the EXECUTIVE department or agency and shall provide for appeal to the Civil Service Commission."

(3) Paragraph (1) and (2) of the quoted required contract provisions in section 202 of Part II, concerning nondiscrimination in employment by Government contractors and subcontractors, are revised to read as follows:

"(1) The contractor will not discriminate against any employee or applicant for employment because of race, color, religion, sex, or national origin. The contractor will take affirmative action to ensure that applicants are employed, and that employees are treated during employment, without regard to their race, color, religion, sex or national origin. Such action shall include, but not be limited to the following: employment, upgrading, demotion, or transfer; recruitment or recruitment advertising; layoff or termination; rates of pay or other forms of compensation; and selection for training, including apprenticeship. The contractor agrees to post in conspicuous places, available to employees and applicants for employment, notices to be provided by the contracting officer setting forth the provisions of this nondiscrimination clause.

"(2) The contractor will, in all solicitations or advertisements for employees placed by or on behalf of the contractor, state that all qualified applicants will receive consideration for employment without regard to race, color, religion, sex or national origin." (4) Section 203 (d) of Part II is revised to read as follows:

"(d) The contracting agency or the Secretary of Labor may direct that any bidder or prospective contractor or subcontractor shall submit, as part of his Compliance Report, a statement in writing, signed by an authorized officer or agent on behalf of any labor union or any agency referring workers or providing or supervising apprenticeship or other training, with which the bidder or prospective contractor deals, with supporting information, to the effect that the signer's

Historical View: The Seneca Falls Convention and the Declaration of Sentiments

One of the best known, and most ringing statements of the Declaration of Independence is that "all men are created equal." But what in practice did this stirring phrase mean? At the time of the founding, some men, especially those of Native American and African ancestry, were manifestly not equal before the law. And what of women? They were citizens, but how great was their political claim to equality with men?

More than 70 years after 1776, a group of women political activists met in Seneca Falls, New York, to declare their equality. Much as Abraham Lincoln would turn to the Declaration of Independence as an argument against the abomination of slavery, the attendees in Seneca Falls issued their own "Declaration of Sentiments" which paralleled Jefferson's great work by stating:

> We hold these truths to be self-evident: that all men and women are created equal; that they are endowed by their Creator with certain inalienable rights; that among these are life, liberty, and the pursuit of happiness; that to secure these rights governments are instituted, deriving their just powers from the consent of the governed.

The drafters then turned to paraphrasing the Declaration of Independence's long list of grievances against the King of England to level their indictment against men's treatment of women.

Elizabeth Cady Stanton drafted the Declaration of Sentiments and Resolutions with Lucretia Mott and presented the document to the Seneca Falls Convention in July 1848. In that year she was photographed with two of her sons, Daniel and Henry. (Library of Congress Prints & Photographs Division/LC-USZ62-50821)

> When a long train of abuses and usurpations, pursuing invariably the same object, evinces a design despotism, it is their duty to throw off such government, and to provide new guards for their future security. Such has been the patient sufferance of the women under this government, and such is now the necessity which constrains them to demand the equal station to which they are entitled. The history of mankind is a history of repeated injuries and usurpations on the part of man toward woman, having in direct object the establishment of an absolute tyranny over her.

Their specifics included the following:

- "He has never permitted her to exercise her inalienable right to the elective franchise."
- "He has compelled her to submit to laws, in the formation of which she had no voice."
- "He has made her, if married, in the eye of the law, civilly dead."
- "He has taken from her all right in property, even to the wages she earns."
- "After depriving her of all rights as a married woman, if single and the owner of property, he has taxed her to support a government which recognizes her only when her property can be made profitable to it."

Although the Declaration of Sentiments did not lead to a revolution, it did spark a growing awareness that women could and should assert their equal rights. "Because women do feel themselves aggrieved, oppressed, and fraudulently deprived of their most sacred rights," they wrote, "we insist that they have immediate admission to all the rights and privileges which belong to them as citizens of these United States."

The Democratic Party Platform, 2008: Women's Equality

We, the Democratic Party, are the party that has produced more women Governors, Senators, and Members of Congress than any other. We have produced the first woman Secretary of State, the first woman Speaker of the House of Representatives, and, in 2008, Hillary Rodham Clinton, the first woman in American history to win presidential primaries in our nation. We believe that our daughters should have the same opportunities as our sons; our party is proud that we have put eighteen million cracks in the highest glass ceiling. We know that when America extends its promise to women, the result is increased opportunity for families, communities, and aspiring people everywhere.

When women still earn 76 cents for every dollar that a man earns, it doesn't just hurt women; it hurts families and children. We will pass the "Lilly Ledbetter" Act, which will make it easier to combat pay discrimination; we will pass the Fair Pay Act; and we will modernize the Equal Pay Act. We will invest in women-owned small businesses and remove the capital gains tax on startup small businesses. We will support women in math and science, increasing American competitiveness by retaining the best workers in these fields, regardless of gender. We recognize that women still carry the majority of childrearing responsibilities, so we have created a comprehensive work and family agenda. We recognize that women are the majority of adults who make the minimum wage, and are particularly hard-hit by recession and poverty; we will protect Social Security, increase the minimum wage, and expand programs to combat poverty and improve education so that parents and children can lift themselves out of poverty. We will work to combat violence against women.

We believe that standing up for our country means standing up against sexism and all intolerance. Demeaning portrayals of women cheapen our debates, dampen the dreams of our daughters, and deny us the contributions of too many. Responsibility lies with us all . . .

We are committed to ensuring full equality for women: we reaffirm our support for the Equal Rights Amendment, recommit to enforcing Title IX, and will urge passage of the Convention on the Elimination of All Forms of Discrimination Against Women. We will pursue a unified foreign and domestic policy that promotes civil rights and human rights, for women and minorities, at home and abroad.

On January 29, 2009, President Barack Obama signed the Lilly Ledbetter Fair Pay Act in the East Room of the White House. With the president are, from left, Senator Barbara Mikulski (D-Maryland), House Majority Leader Steny Hoyer (D-Maryland), and Lilly Ledbetter. (AP Photo/Charles Dharapak)

practices and policies do not discriminate on the grounds of race, color, religion, sex or national origin, and that the signer either will affirmatively cooperate in the implementation of the policy and provisions of this ORDER or that it consents and agrees that recruitment, employment, and the terms and conditions of employment under the proposed contract shall be in accordance with the purposes and provisions of the ORDER. In the event that the union, or the agency shall refuse to execute such a statement, the Compliance Report shall so certify and set forth what efforts have been made to secure such a statement and such additional factual material as the contracting agency or the Secretary of Labor may require."

The amendments to Part I shall be effective 30 days after the date of this ORDER. The amendments to Part II shall be effective one year after the date of this ORDER.

THE WHITE HOUSE, October 13, 1967.

Document 2.7: Curbing Gender-Based Violence

- *Document:* Excerpts from the U.S. Violence against Women Act
- *When:* September 13, 1994
- *Where:* U.S. Capitol Building, Washington, DC
- *Significance:* The Violence Against Women Act imposes federal penalties on perpetrators of sexual violence, outlines the benefits of programs that aid women victims of sexual violence, and appropriates funds for prevention programs. With this, the federal government added its resources to an area mostly under the purview of the states.

TITLE III—SERVICES, PROTECTION, AND JUSTICE FOR YOUNG VICTIMS OF VIOLENCE

SEC. 301. FINDINGS.

Congress finds the following:

(1) Youth, under the age of 18, account for 67 percent of all sexual assault victimizations reported to law enforcement officials.

(2) The Department of Justice consistently finds that young women between the ages of 16 and 24 experience the highest rate of non-fatal intimate partner violence.

(3) In 1 year, over 4,000 incidents of rape or sexual assault occurred in public schools across the country.

(4) Young people experience particular obstacles to seeking help. They often do not have access to money, transportation, or shelter services. They must overcome issues such as distrust of adults, lack of knowledge about available resources, or pressure from peers and parents . . .

(7) Many youth are involved in dating relationships, and these relationships can include the same kind of domestic violence and dating violence seen in the adult population. In fact, more than 40 percent of all incidents of domestic violence involve people who are not married.

(8) 40 percent of girls ages 14 to 17 report knowing someone their age who has been hit or beaten by a boyfriend, and 13 percent of college women report being stalked.

(9) Of college women who said they had been the victims of rape or attempted rape, 12.8 percent of completed rapes, 35 percent of attempted rapes, and 22.9 percent of threatened rapes took place on a date. Almost 60 percent of the completed rapes that occurred on campus took place in the victim's residence . . .

TITLE IV—STRENGTHENING AMERICA'S FAMILIES BY PREVENTING VIOLENCE

SEC. 401. PREVENTING VIOLENCE AGAINST WOMEN AND CHILDREN.

The Violence Against Women Act of 1994 (108 Stat. 1902 et seq.) is amended by adding at the end the following:

"**Subtitle M—Strengthening America's Families by Preventing Violence Against Women and Children**

"**SEC. 41301. FINDINGS.**

"Congress finds that—H. R. 3402—59

"(1) the former United States Advisory Board on Child Abuse suggests that domestic violence may be the single major precursor to child abuse and neglect fatalities in this country;

"(2) studies suggest that as many as 10,000,000 children witness domestic violence every year;

"(3) studies suggest that among children and teenagers, recent exposure to violence in the home was a significant factor in predicting a child's violent behavior;

"(4) a study by the Nurse-Family Partnership found that children whose parents did not participate in home visitation programs that provided coaching in parenting skills, advice and support, were almost 5 times more likely to be abused in their first 2 years of life;

"(5) a child's exposure to domestic violence seems to pose the greatest independent risk for being the victim of any act of partner violence as an adult;

"(6) children exposed to domestic violence are more likely to believe that using violence is an effective means of getting one's needs met and managing conflict in close relationships;

"(7) children exposed to abusive parenting, harsh or erratic discipline, or domestic violence are at increased risk for juvenile crime; and

"(8) in a national survey of more than 6,000 American families, 50 percent of men who frequently assaulted their wives also frequently abused their children.

"SEC. 41302. PURPOSE.

"The purpose of this subtitle is to—

"(1) prevent crimes involving violence against women, children, and youth;

"(2) increase the resources and services available to prevent violence against women, children, and youth;

"(3) reduce the impact of exposure to violence in the lives of children and youth so that the intergenerational cycle of violence is interrupted;

"(4) develop and implement education and services programs to prevent children in vulnerable families from becoming victims or perpetrators of domestic violence, dating violence, sexual assault, or stalking;

"(5) promote programs to ensure that children and youth receive the assistance they need to end the cycle of violence and develop mutually respectful, nonviolent relationships; and

"(6) encourage collaboration among community-based organizations and governmental agencies serving children and youth, providers of health and mental health services and providers of domestic violence, dating violence, sexual assault, and stalking victim services to prevent violence against women and children . . .

"SEC. 41304. DEVELOPMENT OF CURRICULA AND PILOT PROGRAMS FOR HOME VISITATION PROJECTS.

"(a) GRANTS AUTHORIZED—

"(1) IN GENERAL—The Attorney General, acting through the Director of the Office on Violence Against Women, and in collaboration with the Department of Health and Human Services, shall award grants on a competitive basis to home visitation programs, in collaboration with victim service providers, for the purposes of developing and implementing model policies and procedures to train home visitation service providers on addressing domestic violence, dating violence, sexual assault, and stalking in families experiencing violence, or at risk of violence, to reduce the impact of that violence on children, maintain safety, improve parenting skills, and break intergenerational cycles of violence . . .

"SEC. 41305. ENGAGING MEN AND YOUTH IN PREVENTING DOMESTIC VIOLENCE, DATING VIOLENCE, SEXUAL ASSAULT, AND STALKING.

"(a) GRANTS AUTHORIZED—

(1) IN GENERAL—The Attorney General, acting through the Director of the Office on Violence Against Women, and in collaboration with the Department of Health and Human Services, shall award grants on a competitive basis to eligible entities for the purpose of developing or enhancing programs related to engaging men and youth in preventing domestic

violence, dating violence, sexual assault, and stalking by helping them to develop mutually respectful, nonviolent relationships.

"The purpose of this subtitle is to prevent crimes involving violence against women, children, and youth."

SEC. 403. PUBLIC AWARENESS CAMPAIGN.

(a) IN GENERAL—The Attorney General, acting through the Office on Violence Against Women], shall make grants to States for carrying out a campaign to increase public awareness of issues regarding domestic violence against pregnant women.

Document 2.8: Advancing Educational Opportunity

- **Document:** Excerpts from Title IX, Education Amendments of 1972 to the Civil Rights Act of 1964
- **Date:** June 23, 1972
- **Where:** U.S. Congress, Washington, DC
- **Significance:** Expanding the reach of the Civil Rights Act, this act—titled the "Patsy T. Mink Equal Opportunity in Education Act" to recognize the House member who authored it—has been particularly important in providing equal access to athletic and other facilities and opportunities for women.

Title IX, Education Amendments of 1972

(Title 20 U.S.C. Sections 1681-1688)

Section 1681. Sex

(a) Prohibition against discrimination; exceptions. No person in the United States shall, on the basis of sex, be excluded from participation in, be denied the benefits of, or be subjected to discrimination under any education program or activity receiving Federal financial assistance, except that:

(1) Classes of educational institutions subject to prohibition

In regard to admissions to educational institutions, this section shall apply only to institutions of vocational education, professional education, and graduate higher education, and to public institutions of undergraduate higher education . . .

(3) Educational institutions of religious organizations with contrary religious tenets

This section shall not apply to any educational institution which is controlled by a religious organization if the application of this subsection would not be consistent with the religious tenets of such organization;

> "No person in the United States shall, on the basis of sex, be excluded from participation in, be denied the benefits of, or be subjected to discrimination under any education program or activity receiving Federal financial assistance."

(4) Educational institutions training individuals for military services or merchant marine

This section shall not apply to an educational institution whose primary purpose is the training of individuals for the military services of the United States, or the merchant marine;

(5) Public educational institutions with traditional and continuing admissions policy

In regard to admissions this section shall not apply to any public institution of undergraduate higher education which is an institution that traditionally and continually from its establishment has had a policy of admitting only students of one sex . . .

(b) Preferential or disparate treatment because of imbalance in participation or receipt of Federal benefits; statistical evidence of imbalance.

Nothing contained in subsection (a) of this section shall be interpreted to require any educational institution to grant preferential or disparate treatment to the members of one sex on account of an imbalance which may exist with respect to the total number or percentage of persons of that sex participating in or receiving the benefits of any federally supported program or activity, in comparison with the total number or percentage of persons of that sex in any community, State, section, or other area: Provided, that this subsection shall not be construed to prevent the consideration in any hearing or proceeding under this chapter of statistical evidence tending to show that such an imbalance exists with respect to the participation in, or receipt of the benefits of, any such program or activity by the members of one sex.

Section 1687. Interpretation of "program or activity"

For the purposes of this title, the term "program or activity" and "program" mean all of the operations of—

(1)(A) a department, agency, special purpose district, or other instrumentality of a State or of a local government; or

(B) the entity of such State or local government that distributed such assistance and each such department or agency (and each other State or local government entity) to which the assistance is extended, in the case of assistance to a State or local government;

(2)(A) a college, university, or other postsecondary institution, or a public system of higher education; or

(B) a local educational agency, system of vocational education, or other school system . . .

Document 2.9: Preventing Sexual Harassment

- **Document:** Excerpts from the U.S. Equal Employment Opportunity Commission's (EEOC) regulations on sexual harassment
- **Date:** Revised as of July 1, 2006
- **Where:** U.S. Equal Employment Opportunity Commission, Washington, DC
- **Significance:** Drawing on Title VII of the Civil Rights Act, the EEOC establishes and enforces federal regulations regarding sexual harassment. The growth of awareness about sexual harassment as an unacceptable activity has underscored that once-common behavior in the workplace has become unacceptable.

Title VII of the Civil Rights Act

TITLE 29—LABOR

CHAPTER XIV—EQUAL EMPLOYMENT OPPORTUNITY COMMISSION

Sec. 1604.11 Sexual harassment.

(a) Harassment on the basis of sex is a violation of section 703 of title VII. \1\ Unwelcome sexual advances, requests for sexual favors, and other verbal or physical conduct of a sexual nature constitute sexual harassment when (1) submission to such conduct is made either explicitly or implicitly a term or condition of an individual's employment, (2) submission to or rejection of such conduct by an individual is used as the basis for employment decisions affecting such individual, or (3) such conduct has the purpose or effect of unreasonably interfering with an individual's work performance or creating an intimidating, hostile, or offensive working environment . . .

(b) In determining whether alleged conduct constitutes sexual harassment, the Commission will look at the record as a whole and at the totality of the circumstances, such as the nature of the sexual advances and the context in which the alleged incidents occurred. The determination of the legality of a particular action will be made from the facts, on a case by case basis . . .

> "Unwelcome sexual advances, requests for sexual favors, and other verbal or physical conduct of a sexual nature constitute sexual harassment."

(d) With respect to conduct between fellow employees, an employer is responsible for acts of sexual harassment in the workplace where the employer (or its agents or supervisory employees) knows or should have known of the conduct, unless it can show that it took immediate and appropriate corrective action.

(e) An employer may also be responsible for the acts of non-employees, with respect to sexual harassment of employees in the workplace, where the employer (or its agents or supervisory employees) knows or should have known of the conduct and fails to take immediate and appropriate corrective action. In reviewing these cases the Commission will consider the extent of the employer's control and any other legal responsibility which the employer may have with respect to the conduct of such non-employees.

(f) Prevention is the best tool for the elimination of sexual harassment. An employer should take all steps necessary to prevent sexual harassment from occurring, such as affirmatively raising the subject, expressing strong disapproval, developing appropriate sanctions, informing employees of their right to raise and how to raise the issue of harassment under title VII, and developing methods to sensitize all concerned.

(g) Other related practices: Where employment opportunities or benefits are granted because of an individual's submission to the employer's sexual advances or requests for sexual

---

Comparative View: The United Nations Convention on the Elimination of All Forms of Discrimination Against Women (CEDAW)

More than three decades after the General Assembly of the United Nations created the Universal Declaration of Human Rights, member states passed the Convention on the Elimination of All Forms of Discrimination Against Women (CEDAW). Often called an international Bill of Rights for women, the Convention defines discrimination against women as "any distinction, exclusion or restriction made on the basis of sex which has the effect or purpose of impairing or nullifying the recognition, enjoyment or exercise by women, irrespective of their marital status, on a basis of equality of men and women, of human rights and fundamental freedoms in the political, economic, social, cultural, civil or any other field."

Ratification of the Convention obliges States to incorporate the principle of gender equality of men and women into their legal system, such as by abolishing discriminatory law and enacting laws to prohibit further discrimination. Governments are further required to actively pursue the elimination of gender discrimination throughout their countries. Such laws must also receive the effective support of the legal system, to which women must have equal access and standing. Further, women must be guaranteed the right to participate in public and political life, including voting and office holding.

CEDAW also guarantees a range of social and economic rights with regard to equality of opportunity in employment, access to services, and social security programs. Perhaps most controversially, CEDAW affirm women's reproductive rights, including access to contraception and equal power within marriage relationships. These social and economic rights have alienated some conservatives in the United States. While the Convention was signed by the United States in 1980, during the presidency of Jimmy Carter, it has never been ratified—making the United States the *only* industrialized country that is not bound by its conventions.

To oversee CEDAW, the United Nations established an expert body called the Committee on the Elimination of Discrimination against Women (CEDAW), composed of 23 experts on women's issues from around the world. The Committee monitors the progress made regarding women in countries that are party to the Convention and makes recommendations. However, as with most international agreements, CEDAW has no enforcement mechanism. As of 2008, 185 countries have ratified the Convention, making it technically a binding part of their national law, but these include such nations as Saudi Arabia, Yemen, and Libya, where women's rights are severely curtailed. As with most UN initiatives, CEDAW is only as effective as states choose to make it.

From the Right: Concerned Women for America (CWA)

For the past three decades, Concerned Women for America (CWA) have been "helping our members across the country bring Biblical principles into all levels of public policy." The group focuses on six core issues: definition of family, sanctity of life, education, pornography, religious liberty, and national sovereignty. The group believes that, "at its root, each of these issues is a battle over worldviews."

In contrast to the left-leaning tendencies of many women's organizations affiliated with the feminist movement, CWA takes profoundly conservative views on numerous issues of concern to women. It opposes abortion, emphasizing "the physical, emotional and spiritual harm to women, men and their families resulting from abortion." It advocates for traditional patriarchal family structures, arguing that it esteems the nuclear family as "the bedrock institution of society consisting of individuals related by blood, marriage (the legal union of one man and one woman), birth, or adoption [with] respect for the distinctiveness of men and women." The group also takes stands against "sexual promiscuity, cohabitation and sexually transmitted diseases," promoting abstinence-based sex education and coercive public health approaches to people with HIV/AIDS.

Notably, some of CWA's areas of focus overlap with those of the feminist movement, including "an end to violence within households, especially the sexual abuse of children," as well as "prostitution that feeds the sex trafficking industry worldwide-endangering the well-being and lives of thousands of girls, boys and women" and "the consistent strict enforcement of laws regulating the use and distribution of pornography."

Overall, "the vision of CWA is for women and like-minded men, from all walks of life, to come together and restore the family to its traditional purpose and thereby allow each member of the family to realize their God-given potential and be more responsible citizens."

---

favors, the employer may be held liable for unlawful sex discrimination against other persons who were qualified for but denied that employment opportunity or benefit. . . .

The U.S. Equal Employment Opportunity Commission—Policy Statement on Sexual Harassment

Sexual harassment is a form of sex discrimination that violates Title VII of the Civil Rights Act of 1964. Title VII applies to employers with 15 or more employees, including state and local governments. It also applies to employment agencies and to labor organizations, as well as to the federal government.

Unwelcome sexual advances, requests for sexual favors, and other verbal or physical conduct of a sexual nature constitute sexual harassment when this conduct explicitly or implicitly affects an individual's employment, unreasonably interferes with an individual's work performance, or creates an intimidating, hostile, or offensive work environment.

Sexual harassment can occur in a variety of circumstances, including but not limited to the following:

- The victim as well as the harasser may be a woman or a man. The victim does not have to be of the opposite sex.
- The harasser can be the victim's supervisor, an agent of the employer, a supervisor in another area, a co-worker, or a non-employee.
- The victim does not have to be the person harassed but could be anyone affected by the offensive conduct.
- Unlawful sexual harassment may occur without economic injury to or discharge of the victim.
- The harasser's conduct must be unwelcome.

From the Left: The National Organization for Women (NOW)

As the flagship organization of the feminist movement, the purpose of the National Organization for Women (NOW) "is to take action to bring women into full participation in society—sharing equal rights, responsibilities and opportunities with men, while living free from discrimination." NOW identifies six top priority issues: advancing reproductive freedom, promoting diversity and ending racism, stopping violence against women, winning lesbian rights, achieving constitutional equality, and ensuring economic justice.

Supporters of the women's rights movement pass a torch that had been carried from New York City to Houston, where the November 1977 National Women's Convention was to be held. Leading the marchers were tennis star Billie Jean King (second row, far left), former congresswoman Bella Abzug (center front, in her trademark hat), and Betty Friedan (far right), cofounder and first president of the National Organization for Women. (AP Photo/Greg Smith)

By its own description, "NOW is one of the few multi-issue progressive organizations in the United States. NOW stands against all oppression, recognizing that racism, sexism and homophobia are interrelated, that other forms of oppression such as classism and ableism work together with these three to keep power and privilege concentrated in the hands of a few."

NOW frames reproductive rights as "issues of life and death for women, not mere matters of choice," and supports "access to safe and legal abortion, to effective birth control and emergency contraception, to reproductive health services and education for all women." The group "is committed to fighting discrimination based on sexual orientation or gender identity in all areas" through education, civil rights protections, and marriage equality. With regard to social justice, NOW emphasizes a "wide range of economic justice issues affecting women, from the glass ceiling to the sticky floor of poverty," with its emphasis on equality extending to other forms of sex discrimination as well, including racial diversity and prevention of domestic violence.

In summation, NOW argues that "government, our judicial system, big business, mainstream media and other institutions treat many groups in our society like second-class citizens. Pitting us against each other is an essential mechanism for maintaining the status quo. Together, we can create the change we've been dreaming of—our unity is our strength."

It is helpful for the victim to inform the harasser directly that the conduct is unwelcome and must stop. The victim should use any employer complaint mechanism or grievance system available.

When investigating allegations of sexual harassment, EEOC looks at the whole record: the circumstances, such as the nature of the sexual advances, and the context in which the alleged incidents occurred. A determination on the allegations is made from the facts on a case-by-case basis.

Prevention is the best tool to eliminate sexual harassment in the workplace. Employers are encouraged to take steps necessary to prevent sexual harassment from occurring. They should clearly communicate to employees that sexual harassment will not be tolerated. They can do so by providing sexual harassment training to their employees and by establishing an effective complaint or grievance process and taking immediate and appropriate action when an employee complains.

It is also unlawful to retaliate against an individual for opposing employment practices that discriminate based on sex or for filing a discrimination charge, testifying, or participating in any way in an investigation, proceeding, or litigation under Title VII.

BIBLIOGRAPHY

Abelson, Reed. "A Push from the Top Shatters a Glass Ceiling." *New York Times*, August 20, 1999, 1.

Bailyn, Lotte. "Chapter 3: Individual Constraints: Occupational Demands and Private Life." In *Breaking the Mold: Women, Men and Time in the New Corporate World*. New York: Free Press, A Division of Macmillan, Inc., 1993, 40–54.

Cook, Rebecca J., ed. *Human Rights of Women: National and International Perspectives*. Philadelphia: University of Pennsylvania Press, 1994.

Cott, Nancy F. *The Grounding of Modern Feminism*. New Haven, CT: Yale University Press, 1987.

Dalton, Clare. "Discrimination at Its Most Dangerous." *Boston Globe*, October 3, 1993, A1.

DuBois, Ellen Carol. *Woman Suffrage and Women's Rights*. New York: New York University Press, 1998.

Estrich, Susan. *Sex and Power*. New York: Riverhead Books (Penguin Putnam), 2000.

Evans, Sara M. *Born for Liberty: A History of Women in America*. New York: Free Press, 1989.

Goldin, Claudia, and Lawrence F. Katz. "The Power of the Pill: Contraceptives and Women's Career and Marriage Decisions." *Journal of Political Economy* 110 (August 2002): 731.

Jacobs, Jerry. *Gender Inequality at Work*. Thousand Oaks, CA: SAGE Publications, 1995.

————. and Kathleen Gerson. *The Time Divide: Work, Family, and Gender Inequality*. Cambridge, MA: Harvard University Press, 2004.

Massey, Douglas. *Categorically Unequal: The American Stratification System*. New York: Russell Sage Foundation, 2007.

Valian, Virginia. *Why So Slow? The Advancement of Women*. Cambridge, MA: MIT Press, 1998.

Vianello, Mino, and Renata Siemienska. *Gender Inequality: A Comparative Study of Discrimination and Participation*. Newbury Park, CA: SAGE Publications Ltd., 1990.

Walter, Lynn, ed. *Women's Rights: A Global View*. Westport, CT: Greenwood Press, 2001.

3

SEXUAL EXPRESSION AND SEX EDUCATION: CONTRACEPTION AND ABORTION

"I know it when I see it . . ."

REGULATIONS OF OBSCENITY AND INDECENCY

3.1 The Difficulty of Defining Obscenity: Supreme Court ruling in *Miller v. California* (1973)

3.2 Attempting to Apply Obscenity Standards: Ohio Statute on "Pandering Obscenity" (1974)

3.3 Determining the "Harm" of Pornography: Report of the Attorney General's Commission on Pornography (1986)

3.4 The George Carlin "Seven Dirty Words" Case: Supreme Court ruling in *FCC v. Pacifica Foundation* (1978)

3.5 Preventing "Indecency" on the Airwaves: The Federal Communications Commission (FCC) ruling "In the Matter of Complaints against Various Broadcast Licensees Regarding Their Airing of 'The Golden Globe Awards'" (2003)

3.6 Indecency on the Internet: Supreme Court ruling in the case of *Reno v. ACLU* (1997)

"Abstinence from sexual activity outside marriage is the expected standard."

APPROACHES TO SEX EDUCATION

3.7 Promoting "Abstinence-Only" Education: The Federal Social Security Act (1996)

3.8 Critiquing "Abstinence-Only" Approaches: Report of a House Committee on Government Oversight and Reform (2004)

3.9 Critiquing "Comprehensive" Sex Education: Report by the Department of Health and Human Services (2007)

3.10 Exporting the Abstinence Debate Abroad: The "ABC" Approach to Global HIV Prevention (2005)

Introduction

Among the most sweeping civil liberties guaranteed to Americans by the Bill of Rights are those protecting freedom of speech and of the press under the First Amendment. Indeed, government censorship of nearly all types has been repeatedly banned in the United States, particularly with regard to expression that is political in nature. Thus, newspapers and magazines may print what they wish, subject only to extremely narrow (and thus rarely invoked) national security exceptions. Similarly, "speech" has been construed to broadly protect "expression," so that, for instance, the courts have held that the public burning of the American flag cannot be outlawed because such an act is a potent, and protected, form of political expression.

Despite these broad protections of free expression, the discussion of topics related to human sexuality has remained controversial. Indeed, for the better part of a century, the Comstock Act of 1873 effectively squelched most explicit discussion and depiction of sexuality (see "Historical View" sidebar in this chapter). However, the 1972 case of *Miller v. California* (Document 3.1) set the modern standard for the concept of "obscenity." On the one hand, *Miller* upheld the principle that some depictions of sexuality are beyond the bounds of the protection of the First Amendment. On the other hand, *Miller* established a test for identifying obscenity that can be difficult to meet. Most states have incorporated the *Miller* test into their laws (see Ohio's example in Document 3.2). Another approach to regulating sexually explicit material has been to argue against it not on freedom of speech grounds, but instead by trying to link it to other social ills. One prominent example of this was a report by the U.S. Attorney General in 1986 (Document 3.3), which claimed that pornography was socially harmful. Today, government authority to regulate obscenity has clearly declined, but its exact nature and scope remains vaguely undefined.

The power of the government to limit "indecency" (as opposed to "obscenity") is clearer, at least with specific regard to radio and television broadcasts. In a landmark case involving comedian George Carlin's "seven dirty words," the Supreme Court upheld the government's right to control expression about sexual and excretory functions on public airwaves (see Document 3.4). This power was reasserted by the Federal Communications Commission as recently as 2003 (see Document 3.5). However, the significance of this power is declining as more and more communication is occurring through new means such as cable and satellite TV and, particularly, the Internet, which has been deemed by the Supreme Court to be subject to very limited government censorship (see Document 3.6).

Although not subject to the same level of constitutional scrutiny, major public policy debates have raged over the propriety and even morality of sex education programs for children and adolescents. Some disagreements are empirical in nature, such as the age at which sex education should commence and the degree of explicitness and detail that should be provided. Other disagreements, however, are more overtly ideological and thus acrimonious. Should sex education be primarily *descriptive* by providing comprehensive factual information about a broad array of themes in human sexuality? Or should it be *prescriptive* by promoting traditional values relating to abstinence until and lifelong monogamy within (heterosexual) marriage. Document 3.7 offers the federal definition of "abstinence-only" sex education, while Documents 3.8 and 3.9 present Congressionally initiated criticisms of both the abstinence-only and comprehensive approaches to sex education. The issue Document 3.10 reflects how these debates have been translated into U.S. foreign policy through aid programs for HIV prevention that prioritize abstinence and marital fidelity.

"I know it when I see it . . ."

Regulations of Obscenity and Indecency

INTRODUCTION

Despite the sweeping protections of the First Amendment, the U.S. federal and state governments have long claimed—and still claim—the right to prohibit expression that is "obscene." The legal conundrum has been to define exactly what constitutes "obscenity," a concept that is notoriously subjective. What may be a moral outrage to one person may reflect artistic erotica to another; what is disgusting to one person may be appealing to someone else; and what in one community might seem shocking or depraved might be bland and "vanilla" in another. A famous statement by Supreme Court Justice Potter Stewart perhaps best epitomizes this ambiguity: "I shall not today attempt further to define the kinds of material I understand to be [obscene]; and perhaps I could never succeed in intelligibly doing so. But I know it when I see it . . ."

The critical modern legal case in defining the concept of obscenity was that of *Miller v. California* (Document 3.1) in 1973. This case created the "Miller Test," which indicates that a form of expression cannot be regulated unless it appeals to the "prurient interest in sex," portrays "patently offensive" sexual conduct, and, taken as a whole, lacks serious literary, artistic, political, or scientific value. The prevailing standard was to be that of "the average person applying contemporary standards" in any given community. With this many legal hurdles to cross, each fraught with ambiguity and subjective interpretation, the ability of the government to regulate obscenity has become more theoretical rather than practical.

Perhaps the most high-profile court challenge under the *Miller* precedent was brought in 1990 against the Cincinnati Contemporary Arts Center for violating the Ohio statute prohibiting "pandering of obscenity" (Document 3.2). The museum was exhibiting "The Perfect Moment," a collection of images by renowned photographer Robert Mapplethorpe, several of which included highly explicit depictions of homosexual and sadomasochistic behavior. In an extraordinary scene, sheriff's deputies raided the well-respected museum, seized the offending photos, and shut down the exhibition. The subsequent prosecution of Dennis Barrie, the curator, was widely interpreted as a challenge to the autonomy of arts institutions across the country. After viewing the images in question, the jury acquitted Barrie in a short-term victory for freedom of expression. But the very fact that the prosecution was brought at all had an enduring and chilling effect on the public display of potentially obscene materials.

Another approach to curbing pornography has been to argue that it demands regulation because it causes broader societal ills. As is sometimes the case in politics, this issue has created "strange bedfellows," with right-wing "family values" advocates declaring pornography harmful to the social fabric and coarsening of the culture, while left-wing feminists deem pornography to be demeaning and exploitative of women. A 1970 attorney general's commission on pornography shortly before the *Miller* decision found that pornography did not have harmful effects. But in the more conservative 1980s, another report by a similar commission found that it was harmful (Document 3.3).

Nonetheless, since the 1990s, the private viewing of sexually explicit imagery has grown explosively via new technologies such as videotapes, DVDs, cable television, and the Internet. As a result, "community standards" are widely understood to have changed, and relatively few prosecutions have been brought in recent decades for the production of obscene materials. However, in the mid-2000s, the U.S. Department of Justice successfully brought several prosecutions against the producers of "extreme" images, usually involving sexually explicit scenes that are unusually violent or degrading in nature. Upheld by the courts, these more recent prosecutions have rendered the outer border of "obscenity" as obscure and undefined as ever. Government officials do, however, actively pursue producers of pornographic materials that involve children or adolescents, although not necessarily on grounds of obscenity but because of the exploitation of those too young to provide their willing consent.

The regulatory power of the government is more fully developed in the closely related area of "indecency" in broadcast media. Since the radio and television airwaves include only a limited number of usable frequencies, these are regulated by the government via the Federal Communications Commission (FCC). The result is that a wide variety of "indecent" words and images cannot be publicly broadcast, particularly during the period 6 AM to 10 PM, which are considered hours when children might be watching or listening. (Obscene images and words, whatever exactly those may be, are always banned.)

Thus, commonly used words relating to sexual or excretory functions, such as "fuck" or "shit," can be freely expressed in conversation or in print but may not be spoken on broadcast radio or television. The signature case in this area involves the "seven dirty words" discussed by comedian George Carlin in a 1972 stage act, which were recorded and broadcast on Pacifica radio, eventually resulting in a Supreme Court ruling in the case of *FCC vs. Pacifica Foundation* (Document 3.3).

The FCC continues to regulate indecency on broadcast television, such as through a 2001 "industry guidance" (Document 3.4). However, its regulatory power has in practice shrunk considerably, due to the increasing prevalence of cable and satellite television and radio. FCC indecency rules are based on the premise that citizens should be shielded from having unwelcome language and images come into their homes via free broadcasts, but that they consent to receiving such images when they pay to subscribe to a cable or satellite provider, which also does not use the public airwaves.

Similar issues have been raised with regard to the Internet but the Supreme Court has distinguished this technology from that of traditional broadcast media. The Communications Decency Act (CDA) of 1996 had sought to regulate the then new technology of the Internet. Although it raised the complex issue of obscenity, its major target was to prevent children from viewing pornographic or other indecent materials. The Act stated established criminal penalties for anyone who "knowingly (A) uses an interactive computer service to send to a specific person or persons under 18 years of age, or (B) uses any interactive computer service to display in a manner available to a person under 18 years of age, any comment, request, suggestion, proposal, image, or other communication that, in context, depicts or describes, in terms patently offensive as measured by contemporary community standards, sexual or excretory activities or organs."

In the 1997 *Reno v. ACLU* ruling (Document 3.5), the Supreme Court found that this portion of the Communications Decency Act to be overly broad. Because the Internet is universally available, the CDA had the potentially of severely curtailing access by all, adults included, to material that might be considered indecent by some potential viewers. As a still-developing technology, the Internet remains likely to be a site of contestation over the nature and extent of free speech.

Document 3.1: The Difficulty of Defining Obscenity

- **Document:** Excerpts from the Supreme Court ruling in *Miller v. California*, including portions of the syllabus (summary), the majority opinion, and the dissenting opinion
- **Date:** June 21, 1973
- **Where:** The U.S. Supreme Court, Washington, DC
- **Significance:** This case established the three-pronged "Miller test" to determine whether a work of expression can be considered "obscene" and thus subject to government regulation. The Miller test sets a very high threshold for prosecutions.

SUPREME COURT OF THE UNITED STATES

413 U.S. 15

Miller v. California

APPEAL FROM THE APPELLATE DEPARTMENT, SUPERIOR COURT OF
CALIFORNIA, COUNTY OF ORANGE

No. 70-73

Argued: January 18–19, 1972—Decided: June 21, 1973

Syllabus

Appellant was convicted of mailing unsolicited sexually explicit material in violation of a California statute that approximately incorporated the obscenity test formulated in *Memoirs v. Massachusetts*, 383 U.S. 413, 418. The trial court instructed the jury to evaluate the materials by the contemporary community standards of California. Appellant's conviction was affirmed on appeal. In lieu of the obscenity criteria enunciated by the *Memoirs* plurality, it is *held:*

1. Obscene material is not protected by the **First Amendment**. *Roth v. United States*, **354 U.S. 476**, reaffirmed. A work may be subject to state regulation where that work, taken as a whole, appeals to the prurient interest in sex; portrays, in a patently offensive way, sexual conduct specifically defined by the applicable state law; and, taken as a whole, does not have serious literary, artistic, political, or scientific value.

3. The basic guidelines for the trier of fact must be: (a) whether "the average person, applying contemporary community standards" would find that the work, taken as a whole, appeals to the prurient interest, *Roth, supra*, at 489, (b) whether the work depicts or describes, in a patently offensive way, sexual conduct specifically defined by the applicable state law, and (c) whether the work, taken as a whole, lacks serious literary, artistic, political, or scientific value. If a state obscenity law is thus limited, **First Amendment** values are adequately protected by ultimate independent appellate review of constitutional claims when necessary. Pp. 24-25.

3. The test of "utterly without redeeming social value" articulated in *Memoirs, supra*, is rejected as a constitutional standard. Pp. 24-25.

4. The jury may measure the essentially factual issues of prurient appeal and patent offensiveness by the standard that prevails in the forum community, and need not employ a "national standard." Pp. 30-34.

Vacated and remanded. **[p16]**

BURGER, C.J., delivered the opinion of the Court, in which WHITE, BLACKMUN, POWELL, and REHNQUIST, JJ., joined. DOUGLAS, J., filed a dissenting opinion, *post*, p. 37. BRENNAN, J., filed a dissenting opinion, in which STEWART and MARSHALL, JJ., joined, *post*, p. 47.

BURGER, C.J., Opinion of the Court

SUPREME COURT OF THE UNITED STATES

_____

413 U.S. 15

Miller v. California

APPEAL FROM THE APPELLATE DEPARTMENT, SUPERIOR COURT OF
CALIFORNIA, COUNTY OF ORANGE

No. 70-73 Argued: January 18-19, 1972—Decided: June 21, 1973

MR. CHIEF JUSTICE BURGER delivered the opinion of the Court.

This much has been categorically settled by the Court, that obscene material is unprotected by the First Amendment. "The First and Fourteenth Amendments have never been treated as absolutes." We acknowledge, however, the inherent dangers of undertaking to regulate any form of expression. State statutes designed to regulate obscene materials must be carefully limited. As a result, we now confine the permissible scope of such regulation to works which depict or describe sexual conduct. That conduct must be specifically defined by the applicable state law, as written or authoritatively construed. A state offense must also be limited to works which, taken as a whole, appeal to the prurient interest in sex, which portray sexual conduct in a patently offensive way, and which, taken as a whole, do not have serious literary, artistic, political, or scientific value.

The basic guidelines for the trier of fact must be: (a) whether "the average person, applying contemporary community standards" would find that the work, taken as a whole, appeals to the prurient interest; (b) whether the work depicts or describes, in a patently offensive way, sexual conduct specifically defined by the applicable state law; and (c) whether the work, taken as a whole, lacks serious literary, artistic, political, or scientific value . . .

This may not be an easy road, free from difficulty. But no amount of "fatigue" should lead us to adopt a convenient "institutional" rationale—an absolutist, "anything goes" view of the First Amendment—because it will lighten our burdens." Such an abnegation of judicial supervision in this field would be inconsistent with our duty to uphold the constitutional guarantees."

We conclude that neither the State's alleged failure to offer evidence of "national standards," nor the trial court's charge that the jury consider state community standards, were constitutional errors. Nothing in the First Amendment requires that a jury must consider hypothetical and unascertainable "national standards" when attempting to determine whether certain materials are obscene as a matter of fact. Mr. Chief Justice Warren pointedly commented in his dissent in *Jacobellis v. Ohio, supra,* at 200:

It is my belief that, when the Court said in *Roth* that obscenity is to be defined by reference to "community standards," it meant community standards—not a national standard, as is sometimes argued. I believe that there is no provable "national standard." . . . At all events, this Court has not been able to enunciate one, and it would be unreasonable to expect local courts to divine one.

It is neither realistic nor constitutionally sound to read the First Amendment as requiring that the people of Maine or Mississippi accept public depiction of conduct found tolerable in Las Vegas, or New York City . . . People in different States vary in their tastes and attitudes, and this diversity is not to be strangled by the absolutism of imposed uniformity. As the Court made clear in *Mishkin v. New York,* the primary concern with requiring a jury to apply the standard of

> "A work may be subject to state regulation where that work, taken as a whole, appeals to the prurient interest in sex; portrays, in a patently offensive way, sexual conduct specifically defined by the applicable state law; and, taken as a whole, does not have serious literary, artistic, political, or scientific value."

"the average person, applying contemporary community standards" is to be certain that, so far as material is not aimed at a deviant group, it will be judged by its impact on an average person, rather than a particularly susceptible or sensitive person—or indeed a totally insensitive one. We hold that the requirement that the jury evaluate the materials with reference to "contemporary standards of the State of California" serves this protective purpose and is constitutionally adequate.

IV

The dissenting Justices sound the alarm of repression. But, in our view, to equate the free and robust exchange of ideas and political debate with commercial exploitation of obscene material demeans the grand conception of the First Amendment and its high purposes in the historic struggle for freedom. It is a "misuse of the great guarantees of free speech and free press . . ." The First Amendment protects works which, taken as a whole, have serious literary, artistic, political, or scientific value, regardless of whether the government or a majority of the people approve of the ideas these works represent.

The protection given speech and press was fashioned to assure unfettered interchange of *ideas* for the bringing about of political and social changes desired by the people,

In sum, we (a) reaffirm the *Roth* holding that obscene material is not protected by the First Amendment; (b) hold that such material can be regulated by the States, subject to the specific safeguards enunciated above, without a showing that the material is "utterly without redeeming social value"; and (c) hold that obscenity is to be determined by applying "contemporary community standards," not "national standards." The judgment of the Appellate Department of the Superior Court, Orange County, California, is vacated and the case remanded to that court for further proceedings not inconsistent with the First Amendment standards established by this opinion.

Vacated and remanded.

BRENNAN, J., Dissenting Opinion

MR. JUSTICE BRENNAN, with whom MR. JUSTICE STEWART and MR. JUSTICE MARSHALL join, dissenting.

In my dissent in *Paris Adult Theatre I v. Slaton, post,* p. 73, decided this date, I noted that I had no occasion to consider the extent of state power to regulate the distribution of sexually oriented material to juveniles or the offensive exposure of such material to unconsenting adults. In the case before us, appellant was convicted of distributing obscene matter in violation of California Penal Code § 311.2, on the basis of evidence that he had caused to be mailed unsolicited brochures advertising various books and a movie. I need not now decide whether a statute might be drawn to impose, within the requirements of the First Amendment, criminal penalties for the precise conduct at issue here. For it is clear that, under my dissent in *Paris Adult Theatre I,* the statute under which the prosecution was brought is unconstitutionally overbroad, and therefore invalid on its face.

[T]he transcendent value to all society of constitutionally protected expression is deemed to justify allowing attacks on overly broad statutes with no requirement that the person making the attack demonstrate that his own conduct could not be regulated by a statute drawn with the requisite narrow specificity.

In 1970 a theater marquee in New York City's then-notorious Times Square–area porn district advertised live entertainment by burlesque queens Lili St. Cyr and Tempest Storm as well as a bevy of "Nature's Sweethearts." (AP Photo/John Lent)

Document 3.2: Attempting to Apply Obscenity Standards

- **Document:** Excerpts of the Ohio state law prohibiting "pandering obscenity"
- **Date:** January 1, 1974 (amended in 1996)
- **Where:** The Ohio State Legislature, Columbus, Ohio
- **Significance:** After the *Miller* case, state obscenity law had to integrate the three prongs of the newly enunciated "*Miller* test" into their lawbooks. This document represents an example of Ohio's attempt (as amended through 1996) to adjust to *Miller*.

Ohio State Law § 2907.33.

TITLE XXIX CRIMES—PROCEDURE
§ 2907.01.
Definitions.

As used in sections 2907.01 to 2907.37 of the Revised Code:

(A) "Sexual conduct" means vaginal intercourse between a male and female; anal intercourse, fellatio, and cunnilingus between persons regardless of sex; and, without privilege to do so, the insertion, however slight, of any part of the body or any instrument, apparatus, or other object into the vaginal or anal cavity of another. Penetration, however slight, is sufficient to complete vaginal or anal intercourse.

(B) "Sexual contact" means any touching of an erogenous zone of another, including without limitation the thigh, genitals, buttock, pubic region, or, if the person is a female, a breast, for the purpose of sexually arousing or gratifying either person.

(C) "Sexual activity" means sexual conduct or sexual contact, or both.

(D) "Prostitute" means a male or female who promiscuously engages in sexual activity for hire, regardless of whether the hire is paid to the prostitute or to another.

(E) "Harmful to juveniles" means that quality of any material or performance describing or representing nudity, sexual conduct, sexual excitement, or sado-masochistic abuse in any form . . .

(F) When considered as a whole, and judged with reference to ordinary adults or, if it is designed for sexual deviates or other specially susceptible group, judged with reference to that group, any material or performance is "obscene" if any of the following apply:

(1) Its dominant appeal is to prurient interest;

(2) Its dominant tendency is to arouse lust by displaying or depicting sexual activity, masturbation, sexual excitement, or nudity in a way that tends to represent human beings as mere objects of sexual appetite;

(3) Its dominant tendency is to arouse lust by displaying or depicting bestiality or extreme or bizarre violence, cruelty, or brutality;

(4) Its dominant tendency is to appeal to scatological interest by displaying or depicting human bodily functions of elimination in a way that inspires disgust or revulsion in persons with ordinary sensibilities, without serving any genuine scientific, educational, sociological, moral, or artistic purpose;

(5) It contains a series of displays or descriptions of sexual activity, masturbation, sexual excitement, nudity, bestiality, extreme or bizarre violence, cruelty, or brutality, or human bodily functions of elimination, the cumulative effect of which is a dominant tendency to appeal to prurient or scatological interest, when the appeal to such an interest is primarily for its own sake or for commercial exploitation, rather than primarily for a genuine scientific, educational, sociological, moral, or artistic purpose.

(G) "Sexual excitement" means the condition of human male or female genitals when in a state of sexual stimulation or arousal.

(H) "Nudity" means the showing, representation, or depiction of human male or female genitals, pubic area, or buttocks with less than a full, opaque covering, or of a female breast with less than a full, opaque covering of any portion thereof below the top of the nipple, or of covered male genitals in a discernibly turgid state.

(I) "Juvenile" means an unmarried person under the age of eighteen.

(J) "Material" means any book, magazine, newspaper, pamphlet, poster, print, picture, figure, image, description, motion picture film, phonographic record, or tape, or other tangible thing capable of arousing interest through sight, sound, or touch and includes an image or text appearing on a computer monitor, television screen, liquid crystal display, or similar display device or an image or text recorded on a computer hard disk, computer floppy disk, compact disk, magnetic tape, or similar data storage device.

(K) "Performance" means any motion picture, preview, trailer, play, show, skit, dance, or other exhibition performed before an audience . . .

"[Obscenity's] dominant tendency is to appeal to scatological interest by displaying or depicting human bodily functions of elimination in a way that inspires disgust or revulsion in persons with ordinary sensibilities."

(P) "Sado-masochistic abuse" means flagellation or torture by or upon a person or the condition of being fettered, bound, or otherwise physically restrained.

Pandering obscenity.

(A) No person, with knowledge of the character of the material or performance involved, shall do any of the following:

(1) Create, reproduce, or publish any obscene material, when the offender knows that the material is to be used for commercial exploitation or will be publicly disseminated or displayed, or when the offender is reckless in that regard;

(2) Promote or advertise for sale, delivery, or dissemination; sell, deliver, publicly disseminate, publicly display, exhibit, present, rent, or provide; or offer or agree to sell, deliver, publicly disseminate, publicly display, exhibit, present, rent, or provide, any obscene material;

(3) Create, direct, or produce an obscene performance, when the offender knows that it is to be used for commercial exploitation or will be publicly presented, or when the offender is reckless in that regard;

(4) Advertise or promote an obscene performance for presentation, or present or participate in presenting an obscene performance, when the performance is presented publicly, or when admission is charged;

(5) Buy, procure, possess, or control any obscene material with purpose to violate division (A)(2) or (4) of this section.

(B) It is an affirmative defense to a charge under this section, that the material or performance involved was disseminated or presented for a bona fide medical, scientific, educational, religious, governmental, judicial, or other proper purpose, by or to a physician, psychologist, sociologist, scientist, teacher, person pursuing bona fide studies or research, librarian, clergyman, prosecutor, judge, or other person having a proper interest in the material or performance.

(C) Whoever violates this section is guilty of pandering obscenity, a felony of the fifth degree. If the offender previously has been convicted of a violation of this section or of *section 2907.31* of the Revised Code, then pandering obscenity is a felony of the fourth degree.

An exhibition staff worker at the Institute of Contemporary Art in Boston hangs works by the controversial photographer Robert Mapplethorpe for an August 1990 showing of the exhibition Robert Mapplethorpe: The Perfect Moment. The photographer had died of AIDS the previous year, yet the outcry over his erotic subject matter ended in attacks on public funding for the arts. (AP Photo/ Julia Malakie)

Document 3.3: Determining the "Harm" of Pornography

- **Document:** Excerpts from the Attorney General's Commission on Pornography
- **Date:** July 1986
- **Where:** Department of Justice, Washington, DC
- **Significance:** Unlike a similar commission in 1970, before the *Miller* case, the lengthy report of the 1986 Attorney General's Commission on Pornography argued that sexually explicit images caused societal harms, apart from any question of obscenity.

Part II, Chapter 1

The formal mandate of The Commission is contained in its Charter, which is attached to this Report in Appendix A. In accordance with that Charter, we were asked to "determine the nature, extent, and impact on society of pornography in the United States, and to make specific recommendations to the Attorney General concerning more effective ways in which the spread of pornography could be contained, consistent with constitutional guarantees." Our scope was undeniably broad, including the specific mandate to "study ... the dimensions of the problem of pornography," to "review ... the available empirical evidence on the relationship between exposure to pornographic materials and antisocial behavior," and to explore "possible roles and initiatives that the Department of justice and agencies of local, State, and federal government could pursue in controlling, consistent with constitutional guarantees, the production and distribution of pornography." ...

Part IV, Chapter 3

An Integration of the Research Findings

It is clear that the conclusion of "no negative effects" advanced by the 1970 Commission is no longer tenable . . . This is not to say, however, that the evidence as a whole is comprehensive enough or definitive enough. While we have learned much more since 1970, even more areas remain to be explored.

What do we know at this point?

- It is clear that many sexually explicit materials, particularly of the commercial variety, that are obviously designed to be arousing, are, in fact, arousing, both to offenders and nonoffenders.
- Rapists appear to be aroused by both forced as well as consenting sex depictions while non-offenders . . . are less aroused by depictions of sexual aggression. On the other hand, when these portrayals show the victim as "enjoying" the rape, these portrayals similarly elicit high arousal levels.
- Arousal to rape depictions appears to correlate with attitudes of acceptance of rape myths and sexual violence and both these measures likewise correlate with laboratory observed aggressive behaviors.
- Depictions of sexual violence also increase the likelihood that rape myths are accepted and sexual violence toward women condoned. Such attitudes have further been found to be correlated with laboratory aggression toward women. Finally, there is also some evidence that laboratory aggression toward women correlates with self-reported sexually aggressive behaviors.
- What we know about the effects of nonviolent sexually explicit material is less clear. There are tentative indications that negative effects in the areas of attitudes might also occur, particularly from massive exposure. The mechanics of such effects need to be elaborated more fully, however, particularly in light of more recent findings that suggest that degrading themes might have effects that differ from nonviolent, nondegrading sexually explicit materials. This is clearly an area that deserves further investigation.
- There are suggestions that pornography availability may be one of a nexus of sociocultural factors that has some bearing on rape rates in this country. Other cross-cultural data, however, offer mixed results as well, so these findings have to be viewed as tentative at best.
- We still know very little about the causes of deviancy and it is important to examine the developmental patterns of offenders, particularly patterns of early exposure. We do have some convergence on the data from some rapists and males in the general population in the areas of arousal and attitudes but again, this remains to be examined more closely.

Clearly, the need for more research remains as compelling as ever. The need for more research to also examine the efficacy of strategies for dealing with various effects is as compelling. If learning—both prosocial and antisocial—occurs from various depictions, and there certainly is clear evidence of both, the need for strategies that implicate the same learning principles must be evaluated. Educational and media strategies have been discussed elsewhere and found to be effective in such disparate areas as health and media violence. Researchers in the area of pornography have no less a responsibility.

Summary of Commission Findings of Harm from Pornography

The Commission divided pornography into four classifications and then analyzed each classification according to three tiers as set forth below:

I. Sexually Violent Materials

    A. Social Science Evidence.— Negative effects were found to have been demonstrated.

    B. Totality of Evidence.—Harm found in all subtiers:

        1. Acceptance of Rape Myths;

        2. Degradation of the Class/Status of Women;

        3. Modeling Effect;

        4. Family

        5. Society

    C. Moral, Ethical and Cultural. Harm found.

> "The Commission was chartered "to make specific recommendations to the Attorney General concerning more effective ways in which the spread of pornography could be contained, consistent with constitutional guarantees."

II. Sexual Activity Without Violence But with Degradation, Submission, Domination, or Humiliation

    A. Social Science Evidence.—Negative effects were found to have been demonstrated.

    B. Totality of Evidence.—Harm found in all subtiers:

        1. Acceptance of Rape Myths;

        2. Degradation of the Class/Status of Women;

        3. Modeling Effect;

        4. Family

        5. Society

    C. Moral, Ethical and Cultural.—Harm found.

III. Sexual Activity Without Violence, Degradation, Submission, Domination, or Humiliation

All Commissioners agreed that some materials in this classification may be harmful, some Commissioners agreed that not all materials in this classification are not harmful. It was determined that this classification is a very small percentage of the total universe of pornographic materials. See text for further discussion.

IV. Nudity Without Force, Coercion, Sexual Activity, or Degradation

All Commissioners agreed that some materials in this classification may be harmful, some Commissioners agreed that not all materials in this classification are not harmful.

Document 3.4: The George Carlin "Seven Dirty Words" Case

- *Document:* Excerpts from the Supreme Court case of *Federal Communications Commission vs. Pacifica Foundation* about a comedy routine deemed "indecent" that the Court had incorporated into its opinion as an appendix.
- *Date:* July 3, 1978
- *Where:* U.S. Supreme Court, Washington, DC
- *Significance:* Even as the Supreme Court made it more difficult to bring prosecutions for "obscenity," it upheld the government's power to prohibit "indecency" on broadcast airwaves. This case is commonly called the "Seven Dirty Words" case, based on an act by comedian George Carlin which was later broadcast in uncensored form on Pacifica Radio out of New York City.

SUPREME COURT OF THE UNITED STATES

438 U.S. 726 (1978)

FEDERAL COMMUNICATIONS COMMISSION v. PACIFICA FOUNDATION ET AL.

CERTIORARI TO THE UNITED STATES COURT OF APPEALS FOR THE DISTRICT OF COLUMBIA CIRCUIT

No. 77-528.

Argued April 18, 19, 1978—Decided July 3, 1978

MR. JUSTICE STEVENS delivered the opinion of the Court . . .

This case requires that we decide whether the Federal Communications Commission has any power to regulate a radio broadcast that is indecent but not obscene.

A satiric humorist named George Carlin recorded a 12-minute monologue entitled "Filthy Words" before a live audience in a California theater. He began by referring to his thoughts about "the words you couldn't say on the public, ah, airwaves, um, the ones you definitely wouldn't say, ever." He proceeded to list those words and repeat them over and over again in a variety of colloquialisms. The transcript of the recording, which is appended to this opinion, indicates frequent laughter from the audience.

At about 2 o'clock in the afternoon on Tuesday, October 30, 1973, a New York radio station, owned by respondent Pacifica Foundation, broadcast the "Filthy Words" monologue. A few weeks later a man, who stated that he had heard the broadcast while driving with his young son, wrote a letter complaining to the Commission. He stated that, although he could perhaps understand the "record's being sold for private use, I certainly cannot understand the broadcast of same over the air that, supposedly, you control."

The complaint was forwarded to the station for comment. In its response, Pacifica explained that the monologue had been played during a program about contemporary society's attitude toward language and that, immediately before its broadcast, listeners had been advised that it included "sensitive language which might be regarded as offensive to some." Pacifica characterized George Carlin as "a significant social satirist" who "like Twain and Sahl before him, examines the language of ordinary people. . . . Carlin is not mouthing obscenities, he is merely using words to satirize as harmless and essentially silly our attitudes towards those words." Pacifica stated that it was not aware of any other complaints about the broadcast.

On February 21, 1975, the Commission issued a declaratory order granting the complaint and holding that Pacifica "could have been the subject of administrative sanctions." The Commission did not impose formal sanctions, but it did state that the order would be "associated with the station's license file, and in the event that subsequent complaints are received, the Commission will then decide whether it should utilize any of the available sanctions it has been granted by Congress." . . .

The Commission characterized the language used in the Carlin monologue as "patently offensive," though not necessarily obscene, and expressed the opinion that it should be regulated by principles analogous to those found in the law of nuisance where the "law generally speaks to channeling behavior more than actually prohibiting it. . . . [T]he concept of 'indecent' is intimately connected with the exposure of children to language that describes, in terms patently offensive as measured by contemporary community standards for the broadcast medium, sexual or excretory activities and organs, at times of the day when there is a reasonable risk that children may be in the audience."

Applying these considerations to the language used in the monologue as broadcast by respondent, the Commission concluded that certain words depicted sexual and excretory activities in a patently offensive manner, noted that they "were broadcast at a time when children were undoubtedly in the audience (i.e., in the early afternoon)," and that the prerecorded language, with these offensive words "repeated over and over," was "deliberately broadcast." In summary, the Commission stated: "We therefore hold that the language as broadcast was indecent and prohibited by 18 U.S.C. . . .

II

The relevant statutory questions are whether the Commission's action is forbidden "censorship" within the meaning of 47 U.S.C. 326 and whether speech that concededly is not obscene may be restricted as "indecent" under the authority of 18 U.S.C. 1464 (1976 ed.). The questions are not unrelated, for the two statutory provisions have a common origin. Nevertheless, we analyze them separately.

Section 29 of the Radio Act of 1927 provided:

"Nothing in this Act shall be understood or construed to give the licensing authority the power of censorship over the radio communications or signals transmitted by any radio station, and no regulation or condition shall be promulgated or fixed by the licensing authority which shall interfere with the right of free speech by means of radio communications. No person within the jurisdiction of the United States shall utter any obscene, indecent, or profane language by means of radio communication." 44 Stat. 1173.

The prohibition against censorship unequivocally denies the Commission any power to edit proposed broadcasts in advance and to excise material considered inappropriate for the airwaves. The prohibition, however, has never been construed to deny the Commission the power to review the content of completed broadcasts in the performance of its regulatory duties. . . .

IV

Pacifica makes two constitutional attacks on the Commission's order. First, it argues that the Commission's construction of the statutory language broadly encompasses so much constitutionally protected speech that reversal is required even if Pacifica's broadcast of the "Filthy Words" monologue is not itself protected by the First Amendment. Second, Pacifica argues that inasmuch as the recording is not obscene, the Constitution forbids any abridgment of the right to broadcast it on the radio.

A

The first argument fails because our review is limited to the question whether the Commission has the authority to proscribe this particular broadcast. As the Commission itself emphasized, its order was "issued in a specific factual context." 59 F. C. C. 2d, at 893. That approach is appropriate for courts as well as the Commission when regulation of indecency is at stake, for indecency is largely a function of context—it cannot be adequately judged in the abstract . . .

B

When the issue is narrowed to the facts of this case, the question is whether the First Amendment denies government any power to restrict the public broadcast of indecent language in any circumstances. For if the government has any such power, this was an appropriate occasion for its exercise . . .

The question in this case is whether a broadcast of patently offensive words dealing with sex and excretion may be regulated because of its content. Obscene materials have been denied the protection of the First Amendment because their content is so offensive to contemporary moral standards. But the fact that society may find speech offensive is not a sufficient reason for suppressing it. Indeed, if it is the speaker's opinion that gives offense, that consequence is a reason for according it constitutional protection. For it is a central tenet of the First Amendment that the government must remain neutral in the marketplace of ideas. If there were any reason to believe that the Commission's characterization of the Carlin monologue as offensive could be traced to its political content—or even to the fact that it satirized contemporary attitudes about four-letter words—First Amendment protection might be required. But that is simply not this case. These words offend for the same reasons that obscenity offends . . .

The judgment of the Court of Appeals is reversed.

It is so ordered.

> "The prohibition against censorship has never been construed to deny the Commission the power to review the content of completed broadcasts in the performance of its regulatory duties."

Historical View: The Comstock Act

For nearly a century, U.S. law with regards to obscenity and indecency was shaped by the Comstock Act of 1873, which stated that no one "shall sell . . . or shall offer to sell, or to lend, or to give away, or in any manner to exhibit, or shall otherwise publish or offer to publish in any manner, or shall have in his possession, for any such purpose or purposes, an obscene book, pamphlet, paper, writing, advertisement, circular, print, picture, drawing or other representation, figure, or image on or of paper of other material, or any cast instrument, or other article of an immoral nature . . ." The Comstock Act (which also prohibited items that could cause contraception or abortion) specified a prison sentence at hard labor between six months and five years or a fine up to $2000.

While the Act was particularly concerned with use of the U.S. Postal Service, its impact was more far-reaching. Circumscribing the distribution of materials it defined as obscene, the Act had effectively banned a number of important progressive materials in the United States, especially information relating to family planning practices. Comstock, a moral crusader, further orchestrated the execution of the Act in New York under his Society for the Suppression of Vice (NYSSV). Through the organization, Comstock spearheaded a number of arrests, from purveyors of art deemed to be of a pornographic nature to the distributors of information on contraception. Comstock himself rallied around a banner used to represent the NYSSV: "MORALS, Not Art or Literature," which says it all.

Yet Comstock's most pronounced impact was on the greater degree of self- and state-sponsored censorship in the United States. The Act led to a number of now classic pieces of literature being banned from sale in a number of U.S. jurisdictions. Indeed, such works as *Candide*, *Ulysses*, *The Arabian Nights*, even Whitman's *Leaves of Grass*, were at some point banned in many locales throughout America because of illicit references, graphic language, or imagery deemed to appeal to "prurient" interests. George Bernard Shaw eventually coined this excessively prudish standard as "comstockery." Although the Comstock Act was codified into a number of state laws, known collectively as the Comstock Laws, roughly 48 states have currently diverse interpretations of "obscene."—*Brandon L. H. Aultman*

Document 3.5: Preventing "Indecency" on the Airwaves

- **Document:** The Federal Communications Commission (FCC) 2003 ruling "In the Matter of Complaints against Various Broadcast Licensees regarding Their Airing of 'The Golden Globe Awards'"
- **Date:** October 3, 2003
- **Where:** Federal Communications Commission, Washington, DC
- **Significance:** Based on the U.S. Supreme Court's ruling in *FCC vs. Pacifica Foundation*, the FCC continues to regulate "indecency" in broadcast media. As this document makes clear, context is important, and incidents must be judged on a case-by-case basis.

FEDERAL COMMUNICATIONS COMMISSION DA 03-3045
Before the
Federal Communications Commission
Washington, D.C. 20554

In the Matter of	)	
	)	
COMPLAINTS AGAINST VARIOUS	)	File No. EB-03-IH-0110
BROADCAST LICENSEES	)	
REGARDING THEIR AIRING OF	)	
THE "GOLDEN GLOBE AWARDS"	)	
PROGRAM	)	
	)	

MEMORANDUM OPINION AND ORDER

Adopted: October 3, 2003   **Released:** October 3, 2003

By the Chief, Enforcement Bureau:

I. INTRODUCTION

1. In this Memorandum Opinion and Order, issued pursuant to Section 0.111(a)(7) of the Commission's rules, we deny complaints received from the Parents Television Council and from certain individuals who have alleged that various television station licensees aired program material during the "Golden Globe Awards" program on January 19, 2003, that violates the federal restrictions regarding the broadcast of obscene and indecent material.

II. BACKGROUND

2. The complainants allege that the licensees named in their respective complaints aired the "Golden Globe Awards" program, during which the performer Bono uttered the phrase "this is really, really, fucking brilliant," or "this is fucking great." The complainants contend that such material is either obscene and/or indecent, and they request that the Commission levy sanctions against the licensees for the broadcast of the subject material.

III. DISCUSSION

3. The Federal Communications Commission is authorized to license radio and television broadcast stations and is responsible for enforcing the Commission's rules and applicable statutory provisions concerning the operation of those stations. The Commission's role in overseeing program content is very limited. The First Amendment to the United States Constitution and section 326 of the Communications Act of 1934, as amended, (the "Act") prohibit the Commission from censoring program material and from interfering with broadcasters' freedom of expression. The Commission does, however, have the authority to enforce statutory and regulatory provisions restricting indecency and obscenity. Specifically, it is a violation of federal law to broadcast obscene or indecent programming. Title 18 of the United States Code, Section 1464 prohibits the utterance of "any obscene, indecent or profane language by means of radio communication." In addition, section 73.3999 of the Commission's rules provides that radio and television stations shall not broadcast obscene material at any time, and shall not broadcast indecent material during the period 6 a.m. through 10 p.m. The Commission may impose a monetary forfeiture, pursuant to Section 503(b)(1) of the Act, upon a finding that a licensee has broadcast indecent material in violation of 18 U.S.C. § 1464 and section 73.3999 of the rules.

A. Indecency Analysis

4. Any consideration of government action against allegedly indecent programming must take into account the fact that such speech is protected under the First Amendment. The federal courts consistently have upheld Congress's authority to regulate the broadcast of indecent speech, as well [as] the Commission's interpretation and implementation of the governing statute. Nevertheless, the First Amendment is a critical constitutional limitation that demands that, in indecency determinations, we proceed cautiously and with appropriate restraint.

5. The Commission defines indecent speech as language that, in context, depicts or describes sexual or excretory activities or organs in terms patently offensive as measured by contemporary community standards for the broadcast medium.

Indecency findings involve at least two fundamental determinations. First, the material alleged to be indecent must fall within the subject matter scope of our indecency definition—that is, the material must describe or depict sexual or excretory organs or activities.... Second, the broadcast must be *patently offensive* as measured by contemporary community standards for the broadcast medium.

As a threshold matter, the material aired during the "Golden Globe Awards" program does not describe or depict sexual and excretory activities and organs. The word "fucking" may be crude and offensive, but, in the context presented here, did not describe sexual or excretory organs or activities. Rather, the performer used the word "fucking" as an adjective or expletive to emphasize an exclamation. Indeed, in similar circumstances, we have found that offensive language used as an insult rather than as a description of sexual or excretory activity or organs is not within the scope of the Commission's prohibition of indecent program content.

6. Moreover, we have previously found that fleeting and isolated remarks of this nature do not warrant Commission action. Thus, because the complained-of material does not fall within the scope of the Commission's indecency prohibition, we reject the claims that this program content is indecent, and we need not reach the second element of the indecency analysis.

B. Obscenity Analysis

6. To be obscene, material must meet a three-prong test: (1) the average person, applying contemporary community standards, must find that the material, as a whole, appeals to the prurient interest; (2) the material must depict or describe, in a patently offensive way, sexual conduct specifically defined by applicable law; and (3) the material, taken as a whole, must lack serious literary, artistic, political or scientific value. Applying that test, we find that the material broadcast during the "Golden Globe Awards" program was not obscene. The use of specific words, including expletives or other "four letter words" does not render material obscene. Moreover, the complained-of material does not depict or describe sexual conduct and thus does not meet the obscenity standard under Miller v. California. Because the broadcast does not meet the obscenity standard under Miller, we deny the complaints alleging that the broadcast was obscene.

IV. CONCLUSION

7. In view of the foregoing, we conclude that the various licensees that aired the "Golden Globe Awards" program on January 19, 2003, did not violate the law, and, therefore, no action is warranted.

V. ORDERING CLAUSES

8. Accordingly, IT IS ORDERED, pursuant to Section 0.111(a)(7) of the Commission's rules, 47 C.F.R. § 0.111(a)(7), that the complaints filed against the broadcasts of the "Golden Globe Awards" program on January 19, 2003, by the licensees listed in the attached appendix are hereby DENIED.

FEDERAL COMMUNICATIONS COMMISSION

David H. Solomon
Chief, Enforcement Bureau

Document 3.6: Indecency on the Internet

- **Document:** Excerpts from the Supreme Court ruling in *Reno v. American Civil Liberties Union*, including portions of the syllabus (summary), the majority opinion, and the dissenting opinion
- **Date:** June 26, 1997
- **Where:** U.S. Supreme Court, Washington, DC
- **Significance:** In striking down portions of the Communications Decency Act of 1996, the U.S. Supreme Court made its first statements about how "indecency" in "cyberspace" is to be regulated. The ruling required Congress to more narrowly tailor its attempts to regulate constitutionally protected speech.

Reno v. American Civil Liberties Union

SUPREME COURT OF THE UNITED STATES

521 U.S. 844

JANET RENO, ATTORNEY GENERAL OF THE UNITED STATES, et al.,
APPELLANTS *v.* AMERICAN CIVIL LIBERTIES UNION et al.

ON APPEAL FROM THE UNITED STATES DISTRICT COURT FOR THE EASTERN
DISTRICT OF PENNSYLVANIA

No. 96-511

Argued: March 19, 1997—Decided: June 26, 1997

JUSTICE STEVENS delivered the opinion of the Court.

At issue is the constitutionality of two statutory provisions enacted to protect minors from "indecent" and "patently offensive" communications on the Internet. Notwithstanding the legitimacy and importance of the congressional goal of protecting children from harmful materials, we agree with the three judge District Court that the statute abridges "the freedom of speech" protected by the First Amendment.

Sexually Explicit Material

Sexually explicit material on the Internet includes text, pictures, and chat and "extends from the modestly titillating to the hardest core." These files are created, named, and posted in the same manner as material that is not sexually explicit, and may be accessed either deliberately or unintentionally during the course of an imprecise search. "Once a provider posts its content on the Internet, it cannot prevent that content from entering any community." Thus, for example,

> "when the UCR/California Museum of Photography posts to its Web site nudes by Edward Weston and Robert Mapplethorpe to announce that its new exhibit will travel to Baltimore and New York City, those images are available not only in Los Angeles, Baltimore, and New York City, but also in Cincinnati, Mobile, or Beijing—wherever Internet users live. Similarly, the safer sex instructions that Critical Path posts to its Web site, written in street language so that the teenage receiver can understand them, are available not just in Philadelphia, but also in Provo and Prague."

Some of the communications over the Internet that originate in foreign countries are also sexually explicit . . .

[T]here are significant differences between the order upheld in Pacifica and the CDA. First, the order in Pacifica, issued by an agency that had been regulating radio stations for decades, targeted a specific broadcast that represented a rather dramatic departure from traditional program content in order to designate when—rather than whether—it would be permissible to air such a program in that particular medium. The CDA's broad categorical prohibitions are not limited to particular times and are not dependent on any evaluation by an agency familiar with the unique characteristics of the Internet. Second, unlike the CDA, the Commission's declaratory order was not punitive; we expressly refused to decide whether the indecent broadcast "would justify a criminal prosecution." Finally, the Commission's order applied to a medium which as a matter of history had "received the most limited First Amendment protection," in large part because warnings could not adequately protect the listener from unexpected program content. The Internet, however, has no comparable history . . .

Neither before nor after the enactment of the CDA have the vast democratic fora of the Internet been subject to the type of government supervision and regulation that has attended the broadcast industry. Moreover, the Internet is not as "invasive" as radio or television. The District Court specifically found that "[c]ommunications over the Internet do not 'invade' an individual's home or appear on one's computer screen unbidden. Users seldom encounter content 'by accident.'" It also found that "[a]lmost all sexually explicit images are preceded by warnings as to the content," and cited testimony that "'odds are slim' that a user would come across a sexually explicit sight by accident." . . .

Finally, unlike the conditions that prevailed when Congress first authorized regulation of the broadcast spectrum, the Internet can hardly be considered a "scarce" expressive commodity.

It provides relatively unlimited, low cost capacity for communication of all kinds. The Government estimates that "[a]s many as 40 million people use the Internet today, and that figure is expected to grow to 200 million by 1999." This dynamic, multifaceted category of communication includes not only traditional print and news services, but also audio, video, and still images, as well as interactive, real time dialogue. Through the use of chat rooms, any person with a phone line can become a town crier with a voice that resonates farther than it could from any soapbox. Through the use of Web pages, mail exploders, and newsgroups, the same individual can become a pamphleteer. As the District Court found, "the content on the Internet is as diverse as human thought." We agree with its conclusion that our cases provide no basis for qualifying the level of First Amendment scrutiny that should be applied to this medium . . .

> "In order to deny minors access to potentially harmful speech, the CDA effectively suppresses a large amount of speech that adults have a constitutional right to receive and to address to one another."

We are persuaded that the CDA lacks the precision that the First Amendment requires when a statute regulates the content of speech. In order to deny minors access to potentially harmful speech, the CDA effectively suppresses a large amount of speech that adults have a constitutional right to receive and to address to one another. That burden on adult speech is unacceptable if less restrictive alternatives would be at least as effective in achieving the legitimate purpose that the statute was enacted to serve.

It is true that we have repeatedly recognized the governmental interest in protecting children from harmful materials. But that interest does not justify an unnecessarily broad suppression of speech addressed to adults. As we have explained, the Government may not "reduc[e] the adult population . . . to . . . only what is fit for children." "[R]egardless of the strength of the government's interest" in protecting children, "[t]he level of discourse reaching a mailbox simply cannot be limited to that which would be suitable for a sandbox."

"Abstinence from sexual activity outside marriage is the expected standard."

Approaches to Sex Education

First Amendment battles over obscenity and indecency raise significant constitutional issues. Yet disagreements over another form of expression about sexuality, namely the most appropriate approach to sex education for children and adolescents, may be even more important as public policy issues. Despite the pervasiveness of sexual images and ideas in modern society, tremendous ambivalence remains about how, when, and on what subjects youths should be informed about human sexuality.

Knowledge and education about sexuality have traditionally been severely curtailed. Indeed, until the publication of Dr. Alfred Kinsey's famous reports about sexual behavior in the human male (1948) and human female (1953), the study of sexuality was a largely off-limits subject in the United States. What little discussion did occur, often through informal channels, was full of misconceptions and other inaccurate information.

Concurrent with the "Sexual Revolution" of the 1960s and 1970s, sex education programs began to expand in schools, beginning to replace stigmatization and mystification with scientific facts. In the 1980s and 1990s, however, there began a pendulum swing back toward "traditional family values" and a more morally focused normative approach. Significantly, this shift occurred about the time that a deadly new sexually transmitted disease, HIV/AIDS, began to proliferate. The epidemic emboldened proponents of both views: Liberals argued that the need was stronger than ever for young people to be able to protect themselves, while conservatives pointed to the Sexual Revolution as the root cause of the spread of disease, out-of-wedlock pregnancy, and other social ills.

Today, some subjects of sex education remained relatively uncontroversial, such as the explanation of basic sexual anatomy and biological processes of reproduction. Most students in the United States receive at least some education about these issues, and perhaps also about issues that are becoming immediately relevant to them, such as menstruation and ejaculation. Those advocating "comprehensive sex education" would go much further, presenting students with age-appropriate instruction about the full spectrum of sexual behaviors, including non-procreative activities such as masturbation, oral sex, and anal sex. Truly comprehensive sex education (which is common in Europe, as explained in the "Comparative View" sidebar in this chapter) may also include information about sexual orientation, contraception, and prevention of sexually transmitted diseases, up to and including condom availability programs, access to birth control, and referrals to abortion services.

Critics of this approach argue that by discussing such topics, educators may be planting ideas in the otherwise innocent minds of vulnerable youths. They also claim that teaching about sexuality serves to provide validation of, and even license for, sexual activity. Many conservatives believe that sex education must include a strongly normative component, pointing to (heterosexual) marriage as the only acceptable venue for the expression of sexuality. Ironically, it is the conservative opponents of providing information about sexuality and contraception who also tend to be the most opposed to abortion rights, whereas liberals tend to view abortion as a viable, if unfortunate, option for unintended pregnancy.

While these tensions are recurrent, the documents below reflect the most recent iterations of these controversies, beginning with a law in 1996 providing federal funding for state-run programs that exclusively teach abstinence until and monogamy within marriage (Document 3.7). Instilled with a strong moral base, it is argued, youths will be empowered to resist all sexual activity, and thus will have no need of other types of information about sex. Proponents of comprehensive approaches believe that it is naïve and ultimately counterproductive to limit sex education so sharply. In an era where youths live in a sex-saturated media era with fewer social controls than in the past, providing accurate and complete information will make youths more likely to avert unintended pregnancy and sexually transmitted diseases, and to overall be better adjusted sexually. Abstinence, then, becomes only one approach among many. Documents 3.8 and 3.9 offer contrasting critiques of abstinence-only and comprehensive approaches, reflecting the continuing policy battle in the U.S. Congress. Notably, a growing weight of evidence that abstinence-only programs are ineffective has begun to lead some states to reject federal funds for such programs.

The emphasis on abstinence and fidelity has affected U.S. foreign aid policy as well. Document 3.10 excerpts the "ABC Policy" requiring that foreign recipients of U.S. funds for HIV prevention heavily focus on abstinence ("A") and being faithful ("B"), deemphasizing (although not entirely eliminating) information about condoms ("C"). The ABC approach remains controversial. On the one hand, some research indicates that increased abstinence and monogamy may have helped to reduce the spread of HIV in some countries. Other evidence points out the continuing need for a central role for condom use, such as among monogamous women whose husbands are unfaithful to them.

Document 3.7: Promoting "Abstinence-Only" Education

- *Document:* Excerpt from the Social Security Act that provides a definition for "abstinence-only" education, setting stipulations for federally funded programs
- *Date:* August 22, 1996
- *Where:* U.S. Congress, Washington, DC
- *Significance:* This provision of a "welfare reform" bill was intended to promote personal responsibility by providing grants to states to promote sexual abstinence until marriage among students, without reference to birth control or other perspectives on sexuality.

SOCIAL SECURITY ACT
Title V-Maternal and Child Health Services Block Grant, Section 510, 42 U.S.C. 710

(b)(1) The purpose of an allotment under subsection (a) to a State is to enable the State to provide abstinence education, and at the option of the State, where appropriate, mentoring, counseling, and adult supervision to promote abstinence from sexual activity, with a focus on those groups which are most likely to bear children out-of-wedlock.

(2) For purposes of this section, the term "abstinence education" means an educational or motivational program which—

(A) has as its exclusive purpose, teaching the social, psychological, and health gains to be realized by abstaining from sexual activity;

(B) teaches abstinence from sexual activity outside marriage as the expected standard for all school age children;

"Abstinence from sexual activity is the only certain way to avoid out-of-wedlock pregnancy, sexually transmitted diseases, and other associated health problems."

(C) teaches that abstinence from sexual activity is the only certain way to avoid out-of-wedlock pregnancy, sexually transmitted diseases, and other associated health problems;

(D) teaches that a mutually faithful monogamous relationship in context of marriage is the expected standard of human sexual activity;

(E) teaches that sexual activity outside of the context of marriage is likely to have harmful psychological and physical effects;

(F) teaches that bearing children out-of-wedlock is likely to have harmful consequences for the child, the child's parents, and society;

(G) teaches young people how to reject sexual advances and how alcohol and drug use increases vulnerability to sexual advances; and

(H) teaches the importance of attaining self-sufficiency before engaging in sexual activity . . .

Document 3.8: Critiquing "Abstinence-Only" Approaches

- **Document:** Excerpts from the executive summary of a report on federally funded abstinence-only education programs
- **Date:** December 2004
- **Where:** House Committee on Government Oversight and Reform, Washington, DC
- **Significance:** Led by U.S. Representative Henry Waxman of California, the Democratic minority on the committee issued a report critiquing the narrow scope of abstinence-only programs.

Under the Bush Administration, federal support for "abstinence-only" education programs has expanded rapidly. The federal government will spend approximately $170 million on abstinence-only education programs in fiscal year 2005, more than twice the amount spent in fiscal year 2001. As a result, abstinence-only education, which promotes abstinence from sexual activity without teaching basic facts about contraception, now reaches millions of children and adolescents each year.

At the request of Rep. Henry Waxman, this report evaluates the content of the most popular abstinence-only curricula used by grantees of the largest federal abstinence initiative, SPRANS (Special Programs of Regional and National Significance Community-Based Abstinence Education). Through SPRANS, the Department of Health and Human Services provides grants to community organizations that teach abstinence-only curricula to youth. The curricula used in SPRANS and other federally funded programs are not reviewed for accuracy by the federal government.

The report finds that over 80% of the abstinence-only curricula, used by over two thirds of SPRANS grantees in 2003, contain false, misleading, or distorted information about reproductive health. Specifically, the report finds:

"Abstinence-only education, which promotes abstinence from sexual activity without teaching basic facts about contraception, now reaches millions of children and adolescents each year."

- **Abstinence-Only Curricula Contain False Information about the Effectiveness of Contraceptives.** Many of the curricula misrepresent the effectiveness of condoms in preventing sexually transmitted diseases and pregnancy. One curriculum says that "the popular claim that 'condoms help prevent the spread of STDs,' is not supported by the data"; another states that "[i]n heterosexual sex, condoms fail to prevent HIV approximately 31% of the time"; and another teaches that a pregnancy occurs one out of every seven times that couples use condoms. These erroneous statements are presented as proven scientific facts.

- **Abstinence-Only Curricula Contain False Information about the Risks of Abortion.** One curriculum states that 5% to 10% of women who have legal abortions will become sterile; that "[p]remature birth, a major cause of mental retardation, is increased following the abortion of a first pregnancy"; and that "[t]ubal and cervical pregnancies are increased following abortions." In fact, these risks do not rise after the procedure used in most abortions in the United States.

- **Abstinence-Only Curricula Blur Religion and Science.** Many of the curricula present as scientific fact the religious view that life begins at conception. For example, one lesson states: "Conception, also known as fertilization, occurs when one sperm unites with one egg in the upper third of the fallopian tube. This is when life begins." Another curriculum calls a 43-day-old fetus a "thinking person."

- **Abstinence-Only Curricula Treat Stereotypes about Girls and Boys as Scientific Fact.** One curriculum teaches that women need "financial support," while men need "admiration." Another instructs: "Women gauge their happiness and judge their success on their relationships. Men's happiness and success hinge on their accomplishments" . . .

The report finds numerous examples of these errors. Serious and pervasive problems with the accuracy of abstinence-only curricula may help explain why these programs have not been shown to protect adolescents from sexually transmitted diseases and why youth who pledge abstinence are significantly less likely to make informed choices about precautions when they do have sex.

Document 3.9: Critiquing "Comprehensive" Sex Education

- *Document:* Congressional review of comprehensive sex education programs
- *Date:* May 2007
- *Where:* U.S. Department of Health and Human Services, Washington, DC
- *Significance:* Partly in response to criticism of abstinence-only education, U.S. Senators Tom Coburn (R-Oklahoma) and Rick Santorum (R-Pennsylvania) requested a report from the Department of Health and Human Services outlining shortfalls in comprehensive sex education programs. This document represent's the department's reply.

Review of Comprehensive Sex Education Curricula
The Administration for Children and Families (ACF)
Department of Health and Human Services (HHS)

"Comprehensive Sex Education" curricula for adolescents have been endorsed by various governmental agencies, educational organizations, and teenage advocacy groups as the most effective educational method for reducing teenage pregnancy and helping prevent the spread of sexually transmitted diseases (STDs) among America's youth. The National Institutes of Health (NIH) defines Comprehensive Sex Education (CSE) as "teaching both abstinence and the use of protective methods for sexually active youth"; NIH states that CSE curricula have been "shown to delay sexual activity among teens." Non-governmental groups that support CSE have also made statements linking CSE curricula to abstinence as well as reduction of pregnancy and sexually transmitted infections (STIs) . . .

In 2005, Senators Santorum and Coburn requested that the Administration for Children and Families (ACF) review and evaluate comprehensive sex education programs supported with federal dollars. The Senators wrote to the Assistant Secretary for Children and Families, "In particular, we would appreciate a review that explores the effectiveness of these programs in reducing teen pregnancy rates and the transmission of sexually transmitted diseases. In addition, please assess the effectiveness of these programs in advancing the greater goal of

At a January 2006 hearing at the Massachusetts Statehouse in Boston, opponents quietly protest against a proposed bill mandating sex education in Massachusetts public schools. (AP Photo/Chitose Suzuki)

encouraging teens to make the healthy decision to delay sexual activity. Please also include an evaluation of the scientific accuracy of the content of these programs. Finally, we would appreciate an assessment of how the actual content of these programs compares to their stated goals" . . .

The curriculum reviews yielded the following findings:

- **Does the content of the curricula mirror their stated purposes?** While the content of the curricula reviewed adheres to their stated purposes for the most part, these curricula often do not spend as much time discussing abstinence as they do discussing contraception and ways to lessen risks of sexual activity. Of the curricula reviewed, the curriculum with the most balanced discussion of abstinence and safer-sex still discussed condoms and contraception nearly seven times more than abstinence. Three of the nine curricula reviewed did not have a stated purpose of promoting abstinence; however, two of these three curricula still discussed abstinence as an option (although, again, discussion of condoms and safer sex predominated) . . .

- **What is the content of comprehensive sex education curricula?** As mentioned in the previous paragraph, these curricula focus on contraception and ways to lessen risks of sexual activity, although abstinence is at times a non-trivial component. Curriculum approaches to discussing contraception and ways to lessen risks of sexual activity can be grouped in three broad areas: (1) how to obtain protective devices (e.g. condoms), (2) how to broach a discussion on introducing these devices in a relationship, and (3) how to correctly use the devices . . .

- **Do the curricula contain medically inaccurate statements?** Most comprehensive sex education curricula reviewed contain some level of medical inaccuracy . . . Although there were few inaccurate statements regarding condom effectiveness, the curricula do not state the risks of condom failure as extensively as is done in some abstinence-until-marriage curricula, nor do they discuss condom failure rates in context. Indeed, there were misleading statements in every curriculum reviewed . . . For perspective, it may be helpful to compare the error rate reported here with statistics cited in the December 2004 report entitled "The Content of Federally Funded Abstinence Education Programs," which is typically called the Waxman Report.[1] This report found that, of thirteen abstinence-until-marriage curricula reviewed, eleven contained medically inaccurate statements; in all thirteen curricula (nearly 5,000 pages of information), there were 49 instances of questionable information. It could easily be argued that the comprehensive sex education curricula reviewed for this report have a similar rate of error compared with abstinence-until-marriage curricula.

- **Do evaluations of these curricula show them to be effective at (a) delaying sexual debut and (b) reducing sex without condoms?**

"Comprehensive curricula often do not spend as much time discussing abstinence as they do discussing contraception and ways to lessen risks of sexual activity."

Comparative View: Comprehensive Sex Ed in Europe

Sexual health and sex education are closely associated, at least according to the Guttmacher Institute. Their study in 2001 indicated that, in Western Europe, the more educated the population is concerning reproductive health, including contraception use, the fewer instances occur of unwanted pregnancies and sexually transmitted diseases (STDs). Yet, approaches to comprehensive sexual education have been met with reticence in a number of Western nations. The United States, in particular, has in many instances applauded abstinence-only campaigns, even funding faith-based initiatives to promote sexual health under the Social Security Act. The efficacy of U.S. abstinence-only programs is still under review. Yet, approaches worldwide—and in this article, specifically Europe—have begun to cast a broader light upon the contentious topic of the effects of sexual education on the reproductive health of society.

The Netherlands has of late received a good deal of attention regarding its approach to comprehensive sex education. With the highest rate of contraception use among sexually active teenagers in the world, it is no surprise that the "Dutch model" has received such notoriety. It is reported that the Netherlands also experiences the lowest rate of teenage pregnancies in the world, with 8.4 births for every 1,000 girls between 15 and 19. Not only have Dutch schools opened up dialogue among students regarding safer sex practices in a nonjudgmental way, but public education officials have taken strides to revise textbooks to provide for more comprehensive approaches to sexual practices. Educators and parents alike acknowledge that teenagers are going to be engaging in sexual practices. Their pragmatic assumption, it seems, has contributed to a successful campaign.

Switzerland's culture is particularly accepting of sexual health and growth, where sexual intercourse is normally thought to begin at ages 15 or 16. This laissez-faire attitude regarding sexual expression is also codified into law—teens have access to confidential health care, have access to contraception, and begin comprehensive sex education in early adolescence. This does not surprise the Guttmacher Institute, an autonomous wing of the Planned Parenthood Federation of America. Stating that Western Europe avers tolerance of sexual norms, comprehensive approaches to sex education, and clear standards regarding commitments to child rearing, the Institute agrees these all bolster the region's lower levels of teen pregnancy, STDs, and overwhelming support for teenage contraceptive use.

Sweden's compulsory, comprehensive sex education program begins when students are 10 years old in many cases. Students are taught the importance of committed relationships and are informed of the various options at their disposal during their sexual growth. For instance, minors, without parental consent, have access to free medical care, contraception (including condoms and oral contraception), as well as information from clinics about sexual practices. Furthermore, emergency contraception can be obtained without prescription.—*Brandon L. H. Aultman*

SIECUS and Comprehensive Sex Ed

The Sexuality Information and Education Council of the United States (SIECUS) was formed in 1964 to provide Americans with open access to sexual education. According to their Web site (www.siecus.org), "SIECUS provides information and training opportunities for educators, health professionals, parents, and communities across the country to ensure that people of all ages, cultures, and backgrounds receive high quality, *comprehensive education* about sexuality."

SIECUS is spearheading the "No More Money" campaign intending to stem funding to abstinence-only-until-marriage sex education. The campaign is focused on contributing to grassroots organizations in all 50 states in their efforts to supply information concerning the benefits of comprehensive sex education. Specifically, SIECUS feels that the Bush administration's eight-point definition of abstinence-only education was both ineffective and unrealistic; the restrictive federal funding violates basic rights to information; and the conveyance that marriage is a means of sexual health alienates lesbian, gay, or bisexual (LGB) youth, who are forbidden from marrying in a majority of states. Some of their goals have been enacted by the Obama administration.

SIECUS feels that "a vast majority of adults support comprehensive sexuality education and believe young people should be given information about how to protect themselves from unintended pregnancies and sexually transmitted diseases." In their efforts to bolster comprehensive sex-ed in U.S. communities, SIECUS sponsors the National Coalition to Support Sexuality Education (www.ncsse.org).

Project Reality and Abstinence-Only Education

Project Reality (PR), a nonprofit organization, was formed in 1985, blooming from a discussion among a group of parents concerned with their children's sex education. Fearing that comprehensive sex-ed had the propensity to incite sexual activity among America's youth, PR's founders wished to enhance the murky and sometime unpopular theme of abstinence-only education. Its mission: "to give a positive presentation of the benefits of abstinence through curricula, presentations and materials in order to help teens choose abstinence from sexual activity . . . " (www.projectreality.org). PR's influence can be mapped in nearly 23 states across the United States.

"Specifically, in 1995 and 1998, when abstinence education funding was significantly increased, the teen birth rate began its sharpest decline." Although comprehensive sex-ed programs cover abstinence as a part of its curriculum, PR finds it inadequate. For instance, they found the mention of condoms and contraception use nearly 7 times more than abstinence as a part of comprehensive sex-ed programs in 2007. For them, only abstinence education is acceptable for today's youth, as abstinence is the only 100 percent effective way of avoiding STDs and pregnancy. To that end, PR offers a number of curriculum enhancements that are grade-specific. PR's Web site, noted above, offers teachers links to register for seminars and a number of other pedagogical tools for classroom utility.

According to the evaluations reviewed, these curricula show some small positive impacts on (b) reducing sex without condoms, and to a lesser extent (a) delaying sexual debut. Specifically, there were evaluations for eight of the nine curricula reviewed. Of those eight curricula, seven showed at least some positive impacts on condom use; two showed some positive impacts on delay of sexual initiation . . .

Conclusion

Research on the effectiveness of nine commonly used comprehensive sex education curricula demonstrates that, while such curricula show small positive impacts on increasing condom use among youth, only a couple of curricula show impacts on delaying sexual debut; moreover, effects most often disappear over time. The fact that both the stated purposes and the actual content of these curricula emphasize ways to lessen risks associated with sexual activity—and not necessarily avoiding sexual activity—may explain why research shows them to be more effective at increasing condom use than at delaying sexual debut. Lastly, although the medical accuracy of comprehensive sex education curricula is nearly 100%—similar to that of abstinence-until-marriage curricula—efforts could be made to more extensively detail condom failure rates in context.

Document 3.10: Exporting the Abstinence Debate Abroad

- *Document:* Excerpts from a guidance by the U.S. State Department requiring the "ABC" (abstain, be faithful, use condoms) approach to HIV prevention
- *Date:* March 2005
- *Where:* Office of the U.S. Global AIDS Coordinator, Department of State, Washington, DC
- *Significance:* In the 2000s, the United States began to provide increasing funding to developing nations for the prevention of HIV transmission and the medical care of people with AIDS. Such programs, however, became embroiled in domestic politics, with the government requiring approaches to HIV prevention based more on ideology than on epidemiological evidence.

Defining the ABC Approach

The ABC approach employs population-specific interventions that emphasize abstinence for youth and other unmarried persons, including delay of sexual debut; mutual faithfulness and partner reduction for sexually active adults; and correct and consistent use of condoms by those whose behavior places them at risk for transmitting or becoming infected with HIV. It is important to note that ABC is not a program; it is an approach to infuse throughout prevention programs.

Abstinence programs encourage unmarried individuals to abstain from sexual activity as the best and only certain way to protect themselves from exposure to HIV and other sexually transmitted infections. Abstinence until marriage programs are particularly important for young people, as approximately half of all new infections occur in the 15- to 24-year-old age group. Delaying first sexual encounter can have a significant impact on the health and well-being of

A billboard in Kampala, Uganda, promotes abstinence rather than contraceptives, urging young people to delay sexual activity in order to reach their goals. (AP Photo/Riccardo Gangale)

adolescents and on the progress of the epidemic in communities. . . . These programs promote the following:

- Abstaining from sexual activity as the most effective and only certain way to avoid HIV infection;
- The development of skills for practicing abstinence;
- The importance of abstinence in eliminating the risk of HIV transmission among unmarried individuals;
- The decision of unmarried individuals to delay sexual debut until marriage; and
- The adoption of social and community norms that support delaying sex until marriage and that denounce cross-generational sex; transactional sex; and rape, incest, and other forced sexual activity.

Be faithful programs encourage individuals to practice fidelity in marriage and other sexual relationships as a critical way to reduce risk of exposure to HIV. Once a person begins to have sex, the fewer lifetime sexual partners he or she has, the lower the risk of contracting or spreading HIV or another sexually transmitted infection. Some of the most significant gains in Uganda's fight against HIV are a result of specific emphasis on, and funding of, programs to promote changes in behavior related to fidelity in marriage, monogamous relationships, and reducing the number of sexual partners among sexually active unmarried persons . . . Be faithful programs promote the following:

- The elimination of casual sexual partnerships;
- The development of skills for sustaining marital fidelity;
- The importance of mutual faithfulness with an uninfected partner in reducing transmission of HIV among individuals in long-term sexual partnerships;
- HIV counseling and testing with their partner for those couples that do [have] HIV status;
- The endorsement of social and community norms supportive of refraining outside of marriage, partner reduction, and marital fidelity, by using strategies [that] respect and respond to local cultural customs and norms; and
- The adoption of social and community norms that denounce cross-generational transactional sex; and rape, incest, and other forced sexual activity.

Correct and consistent Condom use programs support the provision of full and accurate information about correct and consistent condom use reducing, but not eliminating, the risk of HIV infection; and support access to condoms for those most at risk for transmitting or becoming infected with HIV. Behaviors that increase risk for HIV transmission include engaging in casual sexual encounters, engaging in sex in exchange for money or favors, having sex with an HIV-positive partner or one whose status is unknown, using drugs or abusing alcohol in the context of sexual interactions, and using intravenous drugs. Women, even if faithful themselves, can still be at risk of becoming infected by their spouse, regular male partner, or someone using force against them. Other high-risk persons or groups include men who have sex with men and workers who are employed away from home. Existing research demonstrates that the correct and consistent use of condoms significantly reduces, but does not eliminate, risk of HIV infection ... Condom use programs promote the following:

- The understanding that abstaining from sexual activity is the most effective and only certain way to avoid HIV infection;
- The understanding of how different behaviors increase risk of HIV infections;
- The importance of risk reduction and a consistent risk-reduction strategy when risk elimination is not practiced;
- The importance of correctly and consistently using condoms during every sexual encounter with partners known to be HIV-positive (discordant couples), or partners whose status is unknown;
- The critical role of HIV counseling and testing as a risk-reduction strategy;
- The development of skills for obtaining and correctly and consistently using condoms, including skills for vulnerable persons; and
- The knowledge that condoms do not protect against all STIs.

BIBLIOGRAPHY

Byrd, Cathy, ed. *Potentially Harmful: The Art of American Censorship.* Atlanta: Georgia State University Press, 2006.

Copp, David, and Susan Wendell. *Pornography and Censorship.* Buffalo, NY: Prometheus, 1983.

Deibert, Ronald, ed. *Access Denied: The Practice and Policy of Global Internet Filtering.* Cambridge, MA: MIT Press, 2008.

Foster, Henry H., Jr. "The 'Comstock Load': Obscenity and the Law." *The Journal of Criminal Law, Criminology, and Police Science* 48.3 (September–October 1957): 245–258.

Hagle, Timothy M. "But Do They Have to See It to Know It? The Supreme Court's Obscenity and Pornography Decisions." *The Western Political Quarterly* 44, no. 4 (December 1991): 1039–1054.

Hixson, Richard F. *Pornography and the Justices: The Supreme Court and the Intractable Obscenity Problem.* Carbondale, IL: Southern Illinois University Press, 1996.

Hunt, Lynn. *The Invention of Pornography: Obscenity and the Origins of Modernity, 1500–1800.* New York: Zone, 1993.

Hunter, Ian. *On Pornography: Literature, Sexuality, and Obscenity Law.* New York: St. Martin's Press, 1993.

Irvine, Janice M. *Talk About Sex: The Battles over Sex Education in the United States.* Berkeley: University of California Press, 2004.

Jansen, Sue Curry. *Censorship: The Knot that Binds Power and Knowledge.* New York: Oxford University Press, 1988.

Levine, Judith. *Harmful to Minors: The Perils of Protecting Children from Sex*. New York: Thunder's Mouth Press, 2003.

Lindberg, Laura Duberstein, John S. Santelli, and Susheela Singh. "Changes in Formal Sex Education: 1995–2003." *Perspectives on Sexual and Reproductive Health* 38, no. 4 (December 2006): 182–189.

Luker, Kristin. *When Sex Goes to School: Warring Views on Sex—and Sex Education—Since the Sixties*. New York: W. W. Norton & Co., 2006.

"Married to HIV: Abstinence-Only Programs Are of Little Use in Africa, Where Often It's Husbands Infecting Wives." *Los Angeles Times*, February 22, 2008, Part A, p. 26.

Mayo, Cris. *Disputing the Subject of Sex: Sexuality and Public School Controversies*. Lanham, MD: Rowman & Littlefield, 2007.

McGuire, Kevin T., and Gregory A. Caldeira. "Lawyers, Organized Interests, and the Law of Obscenity: Agenda Setting in the Supreme Court." *The American Political Science Review* 87, no. 3 (September 1993): 715–726.

Ridini, Steven P. *Health and Sexuality Education in Schools: The Process of Social Change*. Westport, CT: Bergin & Garvey, 1998.

Valk, Guus. "The Dutch Model." *The UNESCO Courier*. Available at http://www.unesco.org/courier/2000_07/uk/apprend3.htm.

4

SEXUAL ORIENTATION AND IDENTITY: LESBIAN, GAY, BISEXUAL, AND TRANSGENDER CITIZENS

"Liberty gives substantial protection to adult persons."

SAME-SEX RELATIONS AND THE RIGHT TO PRIVACY

4.1 Criminalizing Sodomy: The Texas Statute (1973)

4.2 Upholding Sodomy Laws: U.S. Supreme Court Ruling in *Bowers v. Hardwick* (1986)

4.3 Overturning Sodomy Laws: U.S. Supreme Court Ruling in *Lawrence v. Texas* (2003)

4.4 Banning "Gays in the Military": The "Don't Ask, Don't Tell" Policy (1993)

"A State cannot deem a class of persons a stranger to its laws."

SEXUAL ORIENTATION AND EQUAL PROTECTION UNDER THE LAW

4.5 Extending Equal Protection: U.S. Supreme Court ruling in *Romer v. Evans* (1996)

4.6 Presidential Proclamation Recognizing "Gay Pride": Presidential Proclamation of Lesbian and Gay Pride Month (1999)

4.7 Outlawing Bias: Oregon State Non-Discrimination Law (2003)

4.8 Federal Anti-Bias Moves: Federal Employment Non-Discrimination Act (ENDA) (2007)

4.9 The Question of Intersexuality: Hearing of the San Francisco Human Rights Commission Hearing (2005)

4.10 Protecting the Transgendered: House Subcommittee Hearing on Transgender Rights (2008)

4.11 The Matthew Shepard and James Byrd, Jr., Hate Crimes Prevention Act (2009)

Introduction

Sexual behavior between members of the same sex is probably as old as the human species itself. Certainly, legends from antiquity include numerous such encounters, whether between the god Zeus and his favorite Ganymede, or between the Roman Emperor Hadrian and his beloved Antinous, or between the poet Sappho and her female lovers on the Greek isle of Lesbos. Such behaviors were also well enough known to be roundly condemned as an "abomination" in even the earliest chapters of the Bible, including the story of the wicked city of Sodom (which provided the word "sodomy").

While homosexual *behavior* is ancient, homosexuality as a stable source of *identity* is quite a new development—particularly in the political sphere. There were a few seeds of political activism early in the twentieth century, notably the work of German sexologist Magnus Hirschfeld who agitated for repeal of anti-sodomy laws in Germany. But real political organization of and by lesbian, gay, and bisexual (LGB) people in the United States did not begin until the 1950s and 1960s when small, largely clandestine groups such as the Mattachine Society and the Daughters of Bilitis quietly advanced the idea of social toleration and political equality for LGB people. The near-universally recognized founding event of the modern LGB rights movement did not come until June 1969, when patrons resisted police harassment at a gay bar called the Stonewall Inn (see the "Historical View" sidebar in this chapter).

For the decade or so after the Stonewall Riots, LGB activism was largely swept up with the other great liberation movements of the day. Indeed, lesbians played a pivotal role in the development of the modern feminist movement, sometimes to the chagrin of heterosexual feminists who termed them a "lavender menace" that might turn public opinion against the women's liberation movement. At the same time, gay men began to pioneer a new model for the organization of social and sexual life in gay enclaves such as New York's Greenwich Village and San Francisco's Castro. Later, in the 1980s and 1990s, the emergence of the AIDS epidemic further politicized LGB communities, who charged that the health crisis was largely met with societal hostility and government indifference. In the 2000s, the "mainstreaming" of LGB people has shifted the focus largely to the issue of same-sex marriage (a topic which is covered in Chapter 3).

Although it has taken many forms and embraced many issues, LGB political activism has clustered around two major themes: personal privacy and equal protection under the law. The concept of personal privacy involves the idea that *individual* LGB people should be able to freely form and openly maintain sexual and romantic relationships with others of the same sex. The concept of privacy rights for LGB people shares much of the same lineage as other privacy rights discussed in Chapter 1 with regard to contraception and abortion. In the first section of this chapter, several documents address this issue, particularly anti-sodomy provisions that criminalized same-sex behavior. Included in this section are a sample anti-sodomy statute from Texas (Document 4.1) and excerpts the Supreme Court rulings that first upheld (Document 4.2) and then overturned (Document 4.3) the constitutionality of anti-sodomy statutes. The final document (4.4) outlines a major exception to generally improving privacy rights, namely the U.S. military's "Don't Ask, Don't Tell" policy.

The other major area of emphasis involves equal protection under the law—the notion that LGB people as a class should be protected from invidious discrimination by the heterosexual majority in such areas as housing, employment, education, and public accommodations. More recently, similar notions of equal protection have begun to be extended to transgender individuals, whose gender appearance, identity, and behavior may be different from what is usually associated with their biological sex. While transgender individuals experience some different forms of discrimination than LGB people do, the two issues have been closely related and intertwined as political issues.

Regarding the question of equal protection, powerful precedents set by Fourteenth Amendment litigation with regard to racial and ethnic minorities, as well as women and other groups, have been largely extended to include LGB people. In this sense, LGB rights can be traced back to *Brown v. Board of Education* and other landmark cases extending equal protection to all. Document 4.5 provides the Supreme Court's rationale—along with dissents—for protecting LGB people as a class. Documents 4.7 and 4.8 provide examples of two anti-discrimination statutes, one actually enacted in Oregon and the other introduced into the U.S. House of Representatives. Both laws include language extending protection from discrimination, notably in employment, on grounds both of sexual orientation and gender identity. During this same period, the Executive Branch of the federal government also expressed its support for LGB citizens, through the issuance of a Presidential Proclamation of Lesbian and Gay Pride Month (Document 4.6).

"Liberty gives substantial protection to adult persons."

Same-Sex Relations and the Right to Privacy

From the 1950s through the 1970s, particularly during the tenures of Chief Justices Earl Warren (1953–1969) and Warren Burger (1969–1986), the Supreme Court championed civil rights for ethnic and racial minorities, expanded the rights of those accused or convicted of crimes, and reinforced freedom of speech and of the press. They also propounded the right of citizens to a zone of privacy in their personal lives. This zone of privacy, inferred particularly from the Fourth and Fourteenth Amendments, led the Court to rule that individuals had a privacy right to practice contraception (see Document 1.1: *Griswold v. Connecticut*, 1965) and that women had the right to terminate a pregnancy (Document 1.3: *Roe v. Wade*, 1973).

However, this expansion of privacy rights was halted by the Supreme Court in 1986. When presented with a challenge to the Georgia state law criminalizing sexual activity between members of the same sex (commonly known as "sodomy"), the Court could have extended the precedents of *Griswold* and *Roe* and ruled that the law unconstitutionally violated the privacy rights of defendant Michael Hardwick, a gay man. However, by 1987, the Court had begun a long-term shift to the political right as a result of two unbroken decades of appointments by Republican presidents. Similarly, the nation was gripped by near hysteria over the then-emerging and poorly understood AIDS epidemic.

And so the Court upheld the law's constitutionality in a ruling that signaled a halt to the expansion of privacy rights and that continued to allow states to criminalize all sexual activity between adults of the same sex. As can be seen in the excerpt below, Document 4.1, the slim 5–4 majority (Justice Lewis Powell later admitted that he wished he had not voted to uphold the statute) ruled that "in constitutional terms there is no such thing as a fundamental right to commit homosexual sodomy." Notably, the ruling was forced to reach back to ancient and medieval precedents, rather than contemporary jurisprudence, for its justification, and used strikingly derisive language.

Although *Bowers v. Hardwick* was a major setback to hopes for equality under the law, individual state supreme courts and legislators continued to decriminalize sodomy. In 2003, the U.S. Supreme Court overturned *Bowers* in the case of *Lawrence v. Texas* (Document 4.3). Although the Supreme Court usually allows existing precedents to stand, they outright repudiated the *Bowers* precedent after just 17 years, reflecting rapidly evolving social attitudes and scientific knowledge about homosexuality as well as about HIV transmission and, perhaps, human sexuality in general. The 6–3 ruling in *Lawrence* was notably broad, stating that "liberty gives substantial protection to adult persons in deciding how to conduct their private lives in matters pertaining to sex" and that the anti-sodomy law in question "furthers no legitimate state interest which can justify its intrusion into the individual's personal and private life." Thus all remaining state and federal anti-sodomy laws were invalidated as they apply to private behavior between consenting adult civilians.

As of this writing, two overt examples of deprivation of privacy rights remain part of official government policy. One is unequal access to the institution of marriage (a topic that is covered in Chapter 5, as it related to larger issues about changing understandings of sexual partnerships). The other is the maintenance of the anti-sodomy provisions of the Uniform Code of Military Justice, and the resulting deprivation of rights to LGB people to serve openly in the U.S. military, although legal challenges to these provisions on the basis of *Lawrence* are pending. Document 4.4 provides the text of the so-called "Don't Ask, Don't Tell" policy, which was enacted as a compromise between the president and Congress. As a presidential candidate, Bill Clinton had promised to overturn the "gays-in-the-military" ban. But influential military leaders and members of Congress who believed that openly gay people living in the close interaction required of the military would undermine discipline, morale, and "unit cohesion." Absent clear evidence of homosexuality or bisexuality, however, military commanders were not authorized to launch investigations, although some still did so.

Under "Don't Ask, Don't Tell," gay and lesbian people are essentially required to lie about their sexual orientation or face discharge—no specific sexual activity is required, a simple statement that one is gay or bisexual is sufficient to trigger separation from the military. Despite the personnel demands caused by the long-running wars in Iraq and Afghanistan, over 10,000 individuals continued to be discharged throughout the 1990s and 2000s. However, evidence from other countries that openly gay people do not necessarily undermine unit cohesion have led even some former military supporters of the ban to call for its elimination.

Document 4.1: Criminalizing Sodomy

- *Document:* Chapter 21 of the Texas State Penal Code defining sexual offenses, including all same-sex "deviate sexual intercourse"
- *Date:* 1973, with various amendments added through 2005
- *When:* Austin, Texas
- *Significance:* This law is a representative sample of the "sexual offenses" laws once found in all states of the United States. In most of its provisions, the law defines sexual offenses in terms of lack of consent or of the ability to consent (as in the case of underaged minors). Section 21.06 is strikingly different in that it is homosexual contact itself which is criminalized, even when between consenting adults. A similar provision from Georgia was upheld by the U.S. Supreme Court in the *Bowers* case in 1986 but was overturned by the court in *Lawrence* in 2005.

PENAL CODE
CHAPTER 21: SEXUAL OFFENSES

§ 21.01. DEFINITIONS. In this chapter:

(1) "Deviate sexual intercourse" means:
(A) any contact between any part of the genitals of one person and the mouth or anus of another person; or
(B) the penetration of the genitals or the anus of another person with an object.

(2) "Sexual contact" means, except as provided by Section 21.11, any touching of the anus, breast, or any part of the genitals of another person with intent to arouse or gratify the sexual desire of any person.

(3) "Sexual intercourse" means any penetration of the female sex organ by the male sex organ.

(4) "Spouse" means a person to whom a person is legally married under Subtitle A, Title 1, Family Code, or a comparable law of another jurisdiction.

§ 21.06. HOMOSEXUAL CONDUCT.

(a) A person commits an offense if he engages in deviate sexual intercourse with another individual of the same sex.

(b) An offense under this section is a Class C misdemeanor.

§ 21.07. PUBLIC LEWDNESS. (a) A person commits an offense if he knowingly engages in any of the following acts in a public place or, if not in a public place, he is reckless about whether another is present who will be offended or alarmed by his:
(1) act of sexual intercourse;
(2) act of deviate sexual intercourse;
(3) act of sexual contact; or
(4) act involving contact between the person's mouth or genitals and the anus or genitals of an animal or fowl.

(b) An offense under this section is a Class A misdemeanor.

§ 21.08. INDECENT EXPOSURE.
(a) A person commits an offense if he exposes his anus or any part of his genitals with intent to arouse or gratify the sexual desire of any person, and he is reckless about whether another is present who will be offended or alarmed by his act.

(b) An offense under this section is a Class B misdemeanor.

§ 21.11. INDECENCY WITH A CHILD.

(a) A person commits an offense if, with a child younger than 17 years and not the person's spouse, whether the child is of the same or opposite sex, the person:
(1) engages in sexual contact with the child or causes the child to engage in sexual contact; or
(2) with intent to arouse or gratify the sexual desire of any person:

    (A) exposes the person's anus or any part of the person's genitals, knowing the child is present; or

    (B) causes the child to expose the child's anus or any part of the child's genitals.

(b) It is an affirmative defense to prosecution under this section that the actor:

    (1) was not more than three years older than the victim and of the opposite sex;

    (2) did not use duress, force, or a threat against the victim at the time of the offense; and

    (3) at the time of the offense:

        (A) was not required under Chapter 62, Code of Criminal Procedure, to register for life as a sex offender; or

(B) was not a person who under Chapter 62 had a reportable conviction or adjudication for an offense under this section.

> "A person commits an offense if he engages in deviate sexual intercourse with another individual of the same sex."

(c) In this section, "sexual contact" means the following acts, if committed with the intent to arouse or gratify the sexual desire of any person:

(1) any touching by a person, including touching through clothing, of the anus, breast, or any part of the genitals of a child; or

(2) any touching of any part of the body of a child, including touching through clothing, with the anus, breast, or any part of the genitals of a person.

(d) An offense under Subsection (a)(1) is a felony of the second degree and an offense under Subsection (a)(2) is a felony of the third degree.

§ 21.12. IMPROPER RELATIONSHIP BETWEEN EDUCATOR AND STUDENT.

(a) An employee of a public or private primary or secondary school commits an offense if the employee engages in sexual contact, sexual intercourse, or deviate sexual intercourse with a person who is enrolled in a public or private primary or secondary school at which the employee works and who is not the employee's spouse.

(b) An offense under this section is a felony of the second degree.

(c) If conduct constituting an offense under this section also constitutes an offense under another section of this code, the actor may be prosecuted under either section or both sections.

§ 21.15. IMPROPER PHOTOGRAPHY OR VISUAL RECORDING.

(a) In this section, "promote" has the meaning assigned by Section 44.21.

Historical View: The Stonewall Riots of 1969

In 1969, official and unofficial harassment of gay people was hardly a novelty, and from time to time bar patrons had even resisted police incursions. But something different happened on the nights of June 27–29, 1969, when customers of the Stonewall Inn in New York's Greenwich Village actively fought back against the plainclothes officers who infiltrated the club and then began making arrests. For three nights, large numbers of gay people congregated near the bar on Christopher Street. Rather than being chased back into the shadows as usual, they heckled and jeered at the police, throwing bricks, bottles, and other objects and ushering in the modern gay and lesbian rights movement.

Ironically, the mocking coverage of the *New York Daily News* perhaps most accurately captured the revolutionary impact of the day. "Queen power reared its bleached-blonde head in revolt. New York City experienced its first homosexual riot . . . The crowd began to get out of hand, eye witnesses said. Then, without warning, a gay atomic bomb. Queens, princesses, and ladies-in-waiting began hurling anything they could lay their polished, manicured fingernails on . . . The war was on. The lilies of the valley had become carnivorous jungle plants."

It is unclear why that particular night should have become the breakthrough event in LGB history. Such a movement by LGB people may simply have been inevitable against the backdrop of the contemporaneous African American, women's, youth, anti-war, and other movements of the day. But the watershed nature of the event is clear: The riots led to a new brand of stridently confrontational gay rights activism. Within a month, a radical new group called the Gay Liberation Front had been formed, with new chapters rapidly proliferating in North America and Europe. Openly gay contingents began to join demonstrations against the Vietnam War. When another New York gay bar was raided nine months later, 500 activists immediately organized a protest. On the first anniversary of Stonewall, a mass march was called through the streets of New York—a tradition which continues to the current day in the form of LGB Pride Parades that involve millions of people around the world each year in the month of June.

(b) A person commits an offense if the person:

(1) photographs or by videotape or other electronic means visually records another:

(A) without the other person's consent; and

(B) with intent to arouse or gratify the sexual desire of any person; or

(2) knowing the character and content of the photograph or recording, promotes a photograph or visual recording described by Subdivision (1).

(c) An offense under this section is a state jail felony.

(d) If conduct that constitutes an offense under this section also constitutes an offense under any other law, the actor may be prosecuted under this section or the other law.

Document 4.2: Upholding Sodomy Laws

- **Document:** Excerpts from the ruling of the U.S. Supreme Court upholding the Georgia state anti-sodomy law, including portions of the syllabus (summary), the majority opinion, and concurring and dissenting opinions
- **Date:** June 30, 1986
- **Where:** Washington, DC
- **Significance:** For two decades following *Griswold v. Connecticut* in 1965, the U.S. Supreme Court established and expanded the right to privacy with regard to sexual and reproductive issues. That trend was strikingly reversed in 1986 in *Bowers v. Hardwick*, in which a Georgia State anti-sodomy law was upheld as constitutional. Bowers was overturned by the U.S. Supreme Court in the case of *Lawrence v. Texas* in 2004.

U.S. SUPREME COURT

478 U.S. 186 (1986)

BOWERS v. HARDWICK,

BOWERS, ATTORNEY GENERAL OF GEORGIA v. HARDWICK ET AL.
CERTIORARI TO THE UNITED STATES COURT OF APPEALS FOR THE ELEVENTH
CIRCUIT

No. 85-140.

Argued: March 31, 1986—Decided June 30, 1986

Syllabus

After being charged with violating the Georgia statute criminalizing sodomy by committing that act with another adult male in the bedroom of his home, respondent Hardwick (respondent) brought suit in Federal District Court, challenging the constitutionality of the statute insofar as it criminalized consensual sodomy. The court granted the defendants' motion to dismiss for failure to state a claim. The Court of Appeals reversed and remanded, holding that the Georgia statute violated respondent's fundamental rights.

Held:
The Georgia statute is constitutional.

(a) The Constitution does not confer a fundamental right upon homosexuals to engage in sodomy. None of the fundamental rights announced in this Court's prior cases involving family relationships, marriage, or procreation bear any resemblance to the right asserted in this case. And any claim that those cases stand for the proposition that any kind of private sexual conduct between consenting adults is constitutionally insulated from state proscription is unsupportable.

(b) Against a background in which many States have criminalized sodomy and still do, to claim that a right to engage in such conduct is "deeply rooted in this Nation's history and tradition" or "implicit in the concept of ordered liberty" is, at best, facetious.

(c) There should be great resistance to expand the reach of the Due Process Clauses to cover new fundamental rights. Otherwise, the Judiciary necessarily would take upon itself further authority to govern the country without constitutional authority. The claimed right in this case falls far short of overcoming this resistance.

(d) The fact that homosexual conduct occurs in the privacy of the home does not affect the result.

(e) Sodomy laws should not be invalidated on the asserted basis that majority belief that sodomy is immoral is an inadequate rationale to support the laws.

WHITE, J., delivered the opinion of the Court.

This case does not require a judgment on whether laws against sodomy between consenting adults in general, or between homosexuals in particular, are wise or desirable. It raises no question about the right or propriety of state legislative decisions to repeal their laws that criminalize homosexual sodomy, or of state-court decisions invalidating those laws on state constitutional grounds. The issue presented is whether the Federal Constitution confers a fundamental right upon homosexuals to engage in sodomy and hence invalidates the laws of the many States that still make such conduct illegal and have done so for a very long time. The case also calls for some judgment about the limits of the Court's role in carrying out its constitutional mandate . . .

We first register our disagreement with the Court of Appeals and with respondent that the Court's prior cases have construed the Constitution to confer a right of privacy that extends to homosexual sodomy and for all intents and purposes have decided this case . . . Accepting the decisions in these cases and the above description of them, we think it evident that none of the rights announced in those cases bears any resemblance to the claimed constitutional right of homosexuals to engage in acts of sodomy that is asserted in this case. No connection between family, marriage, or procreation on the one hand and homosexual activity on the other has been demonstrated, either by the Court of Appeals or by respondent. Moreover, any claim that these cases nevertheless stand for the proposition that any kind of private sexual conduct between consenting adults is constitutionally insulated from state proscription is unsupportable . . .

Precedent aside, however, respondent would have us announce, as the Court of Appeals did, a fundamental right to engage in homosexual sodomy. This we are quite unwilling to do . . .

It is obvious to us that neither of these formulations would extend a fundamental right to homosexuals to engage in acts of consensual sodomy. Proscriptions against that conduct have ancient roots. Sodomy was a criminal offense at common law and was forbidden by the laws of the original 13 States when they ratified the Bill of Rights. In 1868, when the Fourteenth Amendment was ratified, all but 5 of the 37 States in the Union had criminal sodomy laws. In fact, until 1961, all 50 States outlawed sodomy, and today, 24 States and the District of Columbia continue to provide criminal penalties for sodomy performed in private and between consenting adults. Against this background, to claim that a right to engage in such conduct is "deeply rooted in this Nation's history and tradition" or "implicit in the concept of ordered liberty" is, at best, facetious . . .

Even if the conduct at issue here is not a fundamental right, respondent asserts that there must be a rational basis for the law and that there is none in this case other than the presumed belief of a majority of the electorate in Georgia that homosexual sodomy is immoral and unacceptable. This is said to be an inadequate rationale to support the law. The law, however, is constantly based on notions of morality, and if all laws representing essentially moral choices are to be invalidated under the Due Process Clause, the courts will be very busy indeed. Even respondent makes no such claim, but insists that majority sentiments about the morality of homosexuality should be declared inadequate. We do not agree, and are unpersuaded that the sodomy laws of some 25 States should be invalidated on this basis.

CHIEF JUSTICE BURGER, concurring.
I join the Court's opinion, but I write separately to underscore my view that in constitutional terms there is no such thing as a fundamental right to commit homosexual sodomy.
As the Court notes, the proscriptions against sodomy have very "ancient roots." Decisions of individuals relating to homosexual conduct have been subject to state intervention throughout the history of Western civilization. Condemnation of those practices is firmly rooted in Judeao-Christian moral and ethical standards. Homosexual sodomy was a capital crime under Roman law. During the English Reformation when powers of the ecclesiastical courts were transferred to the King's Courts, the first English statute criminalizing sodomy was passed. Blackstone described "the infamous crime against nature" as an offense of "deeper malignity" than rape, a heinous act "the very mention of which is a disgrace to human nature," and "a crime not fit to be named." The common law of England, including its prohibition of sodomy, became the received law of Georgia and the other Colonies. In 1816 the Georgia Legislature passed the statute at issue here, and that statute has been continuously in force in one form or another since that time. To hold that the act of homosexual sodomy is somehow protected as a fundamental right would be to cast aside millennia of moral teaching.

> "To hold that the act of homosexual sodomy is somehow protected as a fundamental right would be to cast aside millennia of moral teaching."

This is essentially not a question of personal "preferences" but rather of the legislative authority of the State. I find nothing in the Constitution depriving a State of the power to enact the statute challenged here.

JUSTICE BLACKMUN, with whom JUSTICE BRENNAN, JUSTICE MARSHALL, and JUSTICE STEVENS join, dissenting.

. . . [T]his case is about "the most comprehensive of rights and the right most valued by civilized men," namely, "the right to be let alone." The statute at issue, Ga. Code Ann. 16-6-2 (1984), denies individuals the right to decide for themselves whether to engage in particular forms of private, consensual sexual activity. The Court concludes that 16-6-2 is valid essentially because "the laws of . . . many States . . . still make such conduct illegal and have done so for a very long time." But the fact that the moral judgments expressed by statutes like 16-6-2 may be "natural and familiar . . . ought not to conclude our judgment upon the question whether statutes embodying them conflict with the Constitution of the United States." (Roe v. Wade)

Like Justice Holmes, I believe that "[i]t is revolting to have no better reason for a rule of law than that so it was laid down in the time of Henry IV. It is still more revolting if the grounds upon which it was laid down have vanished long since, and the rule simply persists from blind imitation of the past." I believe we must analyze respondent Hardwick's claim in the light of the values that underlie the constitutional right to privacy. If that right means anything, it means that, before Georgia can prosecute its citizens for making choices about the most intimate aspects of their lives, it must do more than assert that the choice they have made is an "abominable crime not fit to be named among Christians."

Document 4.3: Overturning Sodomy Laws

- **Document**: Excerpts from U.S. Supreme Court ruling in *Lawrence v. Texas*, including portions of the majority opinion and concurring and dissenting opinions
- **Date**: June 26, 2003
- **Where:** U.S. Supreme Court, Washington, DC
- **Significance:** This ruling overturned *Bowers v. Hardwick* and also invalidated all anti-sodomy laws throughout the country, including not only those directed at same-sex activity but also the regulation of oral and anal intercourse between members of the opposite sex.

SUPREME COURT OF THE UNITED STATES

539 U.S. 558 (2003)

LAWRENCE V. TEXAS

No. 02-102

Argued: March 26, 2003—Decided: June 26, 2003

Syllabus

Responding to a reported weapons disturbance in a private residence, Houston police entered petitioner Lawrence's apartment and saw him and another adult man, petitioner Garner, engaging in a private, consensual sexual act. Petitioners were arrested and convicted of deviate sexual intercourse in violation of a Texas statute forbidding two persons of the same sex to

A lawyer for John Lawrence, left, and Tyron Garner, right, speaks to reporters in December 1998 after her clients were found guilty in Harris County, Texas, criminal court for engaging in homosexual activity. Their eventual appeal to the U.S. Supreme Court in *Lawrence v. Texas* (2003) decisively overturned the Court's decision in *Bowers v. Hardwick* (1986) and struck down state sodomy laws. (AP Photo/Michael Stravato)

engage in certain intimate sexual conduct. In affirming, the State Court of Appeals held, *inter alia*, that the statute was not unconstitutional under the Due Process Clause of the Fourteenth Amendment. The court considered *Bowers v. Hardwick* controlling on that point.

Held: The Texas statute making it a crime for two persons of the same sex to engage in certain intimate sexual conduct violates the Due Process Clause.

(a) Resolution of this case depends on whether petitioners were free as adults to engage in private conduct in the exercise of their liberty under the Due Process Clause. For this inquiry the Court deems it necessary to reconsider its *Bowers* holding. The *Bowers* Court's initial substantive statement—"The issue presented is whether the Federal Constitution confers a fundamental right upon homosexuals to engage in sodomy . . . ,"—discloses the Court's failure to appreciate the extent of the liberty at stake. To say that the issue in *Bowers* was simply the right to engage in certain sexual conduct demeans the claim the individual put forward, just as it would demean a married couple were it said that marriage is just about the right to have sexual intercourse. Although the laws involved in *Bowers* and here purport to do no more than prohibit a particular sexual act, their penalties and purposes have more far-reaching consequences, touching upon the most private human conduct, sexual behavior, and in the most private of places, the home. They seek to control a personal relationship that, whether or not entitled to formal recognition in the law, is within the liberty of persons to choose without being punished as criminals. The liberty protected by the Constitution allows homosexual persons the right to choose to enter upon relationships in the confines of their homes and their own private lives and still retain their dignity as free persons.

(b) Having misapprehended the liberty claim presented to it, the *Bowers* Court stated that proscriptions against sodomy have ancient roots. It should be noted, however, that there is no longstanding history in this country of laws directed at homosexual conduct as a distinct matter. Early American sodomy laws were not directed at homosexuals as such but instead sought to prohibit nonprocreative sexual activity more generally, whether between men and women or men and men. Moreover, early sodomy laws seem not to have been enforced against consenting adults acting in private. Instead, sodomy prosecutions often involved predatory acts against those who could not or did not consent: relations between men and minor girls or boys, between adults involving force, between adults implicating disparity in status, or between men and animals. The longstanding criminal prohibition of homosexual sodomy upon which *Bowers* placed such reliance is as consistent with a general condemnation of nonprocreative sex as it is with an established tradition of prosecuting acts because of their homosexual character. Far from possessing "ancient roots," American laws targeting same-sex couples did not develop until the last third of the 20th century. Even now, only nine States have singled out same-sex relations for criminal prosecution. Thus, the historical grounds relied upon in *Bowers* are more complex than the majority opinion and the concurring opinion by Chief Justice Burger there indicated. They are not without doubt and, at the very least, are overstated. The *Bowers* Court was, of course, making the broader point that for centuries there have been powerful voices to condemn homosexual conduct as immoral, but this Court's obligation is to define the liberty of all, not to mandate its own moral code, *Planned Parenthood of Southeastern Pa. v. Casey*. The Nation's laws and traditions in the past half century are most relevant here. They show an emerging awareness that liberty gives substantial protection to adult persons in deciding how to conduct their private lives in matters pertaining to sex.

(c) *Bowers'* deficiencies became even more apparent in the years following its announcement. The 25 States with laws prohibiting the conduct referenced in *Bowers* are reduced now to 13, of which 4 enforce their laws only against homosexual conduct. In those States, including Texas, that still proscribe sodomy (whether for same-sex or heterosexual conduct), there is a pattern of nonenforcement with respect to consenting adults acting in private—which confirmed that the Due Process Clause protects personal decisions relating to marriage, procreation, contraception, family relationships, child rearing, and education—and *Romer* v. *Evans*, which struck down class-based legislation directed at homosexuals—cast *Bowers'* holding into even more doubt. The stigma the Texas criminal statute imposes, moreover, is not trivial. Although the offense is but a minor misdemeanor, it remains a criminal offense with all that imports for the dignity of the persons charged, including notation of convictions on their records and on job application forms, and registration as sex offenders under state law. Where a case's foundations have sustained serious erosion, criticism from other sources is of greater significance. In the United States, criticism of *Bowers* has been substantial and continuing, disapproving of its reasoning in all respects, not just as to its historical assumptions. And, to the extent *Bowers* relied on values shared with a wider civilization, the case's reasoning and holding have been rejected by the European Court of Human Rights, and that other nations have taken action consistent with an affirmation of the protected right of homosexual adults to engage in intimate, consensual conduct. There has been no showing that in this country the governmental interest in circumscribing personal choice is somehow more legitimate or urgent. . . .

JUSTICE KENNEDY delivered the opinion of the Court.

Liberty protects the person from unwarranted government intrusions into a dwelling or other private places. In our tradition the State is not omnipresent in the home. And there are other spheres of our lives and existence, outside the home, where the State should not be a dominant presence. Freedom extends beyond spatial bounds. Liberty presumes an autonomy of self that includes freedom of thought, belief, expression, and certain intimate conduct. The instant case involves liberty of the person both in its spatial and more transcendent dimensions . . .

Bowers was not correct when it was decided, and it is not correct today. It ought not to remain binding precedent. Bowers v. Hardwick should be and now is overruled.

The present case does not involve minors. It does not involve persons who might be injured or coerced or who are situated in relationships where consent might not easily be refused. It does not involve public conduct or prostitution. It does not involve whether the government must give formal recognition to any relationship that homosexual persons seek to enter. The case does involve two adults who, with full and mutual consent from each other, engaged in sexual practices common to a homosexual lifestyle. The petitioners are entitled to respect for their private lives. The State cannot demean their existence or control their destiny by making their private sexual conduct a crime. Their right to liberty under the Due Process Clause gives them the full right to engage in their conduct without intervention of the government. "It is a promise of the Constitution that there is a realm of personal liberty which the government may not enter." The Texas statute furthers no legitimate state interest which can justify its intrusion into the personal and private life of the individual.

> "Freedom extends beyond spatial bounds. Liberty presumes an autonomy of self that includes freedom of thought, belief, expression, and certain intimate conduct. The instant case involves liberty of the person both in its spatial and more transcendent dimensions . . ."

Had those who drew and ratified the Due Process Clauses of the Fifth Amendment or the Fourteenth Amendment known the components of liberty in its manifold possibilities, they might have been more specific. They did not presume to have this insight. They knew times can blind us to certain truths and later generations can see that laws once thought necessary and proper in fact serve only to oppress. As the Constitution endures, persons in every generation can invoke its principles in their own search for greater freedom.

The judgment of the Court of Appeals for the Texas Fourteenth District is reversed, and the case is remanded for further proceedings not inconsistent with this opinion.

JUSTICE SCALIA, with whom THE CHIEF JUSTICE and JUSTICE THOMAS join, dissenting . . .

State laws against bigamy, same-sex marriage, adult incest, prostitution, masturbation, adultery, fornication, bestiality, and obscenity are . . . sustainable only in light of *Bowers'* validation of laws based on moral choices. Every single one of these laws is called into question by today's decision; the Court makes no effort to cabin the scope of its decision to exclude them from its holding. The impossibility of distinguishing homosexuality from other traditional "morals" offenses is precisely why *Bowers* rejected the rational-basis challenge. "The law," it said, "is constantly based on notions of morality, and if all laws representing essentially moral choices are to be invalidated under the Due Process Clause, the courts will be very busy indeed." What a massive disruption of the current social order, therefore, the overruling of *Bowers* entails. . . .

I turn now to the ground on which the Court squarely rests its holding: the contention that there is no rational basis for the law here under attack. This proposition is so out of accord with our jurisprudence—indeed, with the jurisprudence of *any* society we know—that it requires little discussion.

The Texas statute undeniably seeks to further the belief of its citizens that certain forms of sexual behavior are "immoral and unacceptable," *Bowers*, *supra*, at 196—the same interest furthered by criminal laws against fornication, bigamy, adultery, adult incest, bestiality, and obscenity. *Bowers* held that this *was* a legitimate state interest. The Court today reaches the opposite conclusion. The Texas statute, it says, "furthers *no legitimate state interest* which can justify its intrusion into the personal and private life of the individual," *ante*, at 18 (emphasis added). The Court embraces instead Justice Stevens' declaration in his *Bowers* dissent, that "the fact that the governing majority in a State has traditionally viewed a particular practice as immoral is not a sufficient reason for upholding a law prohibiting the practice," *ante*, at 17. This effectively decrees the end of all morals legislation. If, as the Court asserts, the promotion of majoritarian sexual morality is not even a *legitimate* state interest, none of the above-mentioned laws can survive rational-basis review.

Today's opinion is the product of a Court, which is the product of a law-profession culture, that has largely signed on to the so-called homosexual agenda, by which I mean the agenda promoted by some homosexual activists directed at eliminating the moral opprobrium that has traditionally attached to homosexual conduct. I noted in an earlier opinion the fact that the American Association of Law Schools (to which any reputable law school *must* seek to belong) excludes from membership any school that refuses to ban from its job-interview facilities a law firm (no matter how small) that does not wish to hire as a prospective partner a person who openly engages in homosexual conduct. . . .

Document 4.4: Banning Gays in the Military

- *Document:* The "Don't Ask, Don't Tell" policy concerning homosexuality in the U.S. armed forces
- *Date:* September 16, 1993
- *Where:* U.S. Congress, Washington, DC
- *Significance:* President Bill Clinton had made a campaign promise to allow members of the armed forces to be open about their sexual orientation, but later faced massive resistance from within the military and Congress. He struck a compromise position that came to be called "don't ask, don't tell," which encouraged military officials not to pry into the private lives of members of the armed forces while requiring gay, lesbian, and bisexual service members to remain deeply closeted.

CHAPTER 37 OF TITLE 10, UNITED STATES CODE, IS AMENDED BY ADDING AT THE END THE FOLLOWING NEW SECTION:

654. Policy concerning homosexuality in the armed forces

(a) Findings.—Congress makes the following findings:

(1) Section 8 of article I of the Constitution of the United States commits exclusively to the Congress the powers to raise and support armies, provide and maintain a Navy, and make rules for the government and regulation of the land and naval forces. . . .

(5) The conduct of military operations requires members of the armed forces to make extraordinary sacrifices, including the ultimate sacrifice, in order to provide for the common defense . . .

Plaintiffs challenging the U.S. Department of Defense's "don't ask, don't tell" policy leave Brooklyn Federal Court with a Lambda Legal Defense and Education Fund attorney following closing arguments in the case on March 16, 1995. Litigation in the case, *Able v. United States*, continued until 1998. (AP Photo/Ed Bailey)

(6) Success in combat requires military units that are characterized by high morale, good order and discipline, and unit cohesion.

(7) One of the most critical elements in combat capability is unit cohesion, that is, the bonds of trust among individual service members that make the combat effectiveness of a military unit greater than the sum of the combat effectiveness of the individual unit members.

(8) Military life is fundamentally different from civilian life in that—

(A) the extraordinary responsibilities of the armed forces, the unique conditions of military service, and the critical role of unit cohesion, require that the military community, while subject to civilian control, exist as a specialized society; and

(B) the military society is characterized by its own laws, rules, customs, and traditions, including numerous restrictions on personal behavior, that would not be acceptable in civilian society.

(9) The standards of conduct for members of the armed forces regulate a member's life for 24 hours each day beginning at the moment the member enters military status and not ending until that person is discharged or otherwise separated from the armed forces.

(10) Those standards of conduct, including the Uniform Code of Military Justice, apply to a member of the armed forces at all times that the member has a military status, whether the member is on base or off base, and whether the member is on duty or off duty.

(11) The pervasive application of the standards of conduct is necessary because members of the armed forces must be ready at all times for worldwide deployment to a combat environment.

(12) The worldwide deployment of United States military forces, the international responsibilities of the United States, and the potential for involvement of the armed forces in actual combat routinely make it necessary for members of the armed forces involuntarily to accept living conditions and working conditions that are often spartan, primitive, and characterized by forced intimacy with little or no privacy.

(13) The prohibition against homosexual conduct is a longstanding element of military law that continues to be necessary in the unique circumstances of military service.

(14) The armed forces must maintain personnel policies that exclude persons whose presence in the armed forces would create an unacceptable risk to the armed forces' high standards of morale, good order and discipline, and unit cohesion that are the essence of military capability.

(15) The presence in the armed forces of persons who demonstrate a propensity or intent to engage in homosexual acts would create an unacceptable risk to the high standards of morale, good order and discipline, and unit cohesion that are the essence of military capability.

Policy.

A member of the armed forces shall be separated from the armed forces under regulations prescribed by the Secretary of Defense if one or more of the following findings is made and approved in accordance with procedures set forth in such regulations:

(1) That the member has engaged in, attempted to engage in, or solicited another to engage in, a homosexual act or acts . . .

(2) That the member has stated that he or she is a homosexual or bisexual, or words to that effect, unless there is a further finding, made and approved in accordance with procedures set forth in the regulations, that the member has demonstrated that he or she is not a person who engages in, attempts to engage in, has a propensity to engage in, or intends to engage in homosexual acts.

(3) That the member has married or attempted to marry a person known to be of the same biological sex . . .

Definitions.—In this section:

(1) The term "homosexual" means a person, regardless of sex, who engages in, attempts to engage in, has a propensity to engage in, or intends to engage in homosexual acts, and includes the terms "gay" and "lesbian".

"The presence in the armed forces of persons who demonstrate a propensity or intent to engage in homosexual acts would create an unacceptable risk to the high standards of morale, good order and discipline, and unit cohesion that are the essence of military capability."

(2) The term "bisexual" means a person who engages in, attempts to engage in, has a propensity to engage in, or intends to engage in homosexual and heterosexual acts.

(3) The term "homosexual act" means—

(A) any bodily contact, actively undertaken or passively permitted, between members of the same sex for the purpose of satisfying sexual desires; and
(B) any bodily contact which a reasonable person would understand to demonstrate a propensity or intent to engage in an act described in subparagraph (A).

"A State cannot deem a class of persons a stranger to its laws."

Sexual Orientation and Equal Protection Under the Law

Privacy rights, of the type first denied in *Bowers* and then protected in *Lawrence* (above), are perhaps the paramount concern for *individual* lesbian, gay, and bisexual (LGB) people, ensuring their ability to enter into the intimate relationships of their choice. Equally compelling for LGB people as a *group*, however, are equal protection rights.

The Supreme Court has long recognized that the Constitution offers heightened protection to "discrete and insular" minorities whose rights might otherwise be trammeled by electoral majorities. Thus, the essence of the struggle over LGB equal protection has been the question of whether sexual orientation is a characteristic that creates a distinctive political minority. Opponents of this view have employed a wide variety of political strategies to roll back LGB advances or to forestall further advances, but have had only mixed success in the courts or through legislatures. For this reason, conservative organizations in the 1990s and 2000s have turned to one of the more blunt instruments of majority rule: the initiative, referendum, and state constitutional amendment process whereby citizens can vote directly to establish state-level public policy.

This process began in the fall of 1992, amidst a call for a "Culture War" at the Republican National Convention, when voters in Oregon and Colorado were presented with anti-LGB ballot measures. The harsh, condemnatory Proposition 9 in Oregon failed narrowly, but Amendment 2 in Colorado passed narrowly. As an amendment to the state constitution, Amendment 2 would have overridden any legislative attempts to protect individuals on the basis of their sexual orientation. The immediate effect of the amendment would have been to reverse ordinances in Denver and other cities prohibiting discrimination on the basis of sexual orientation. A more far-reaching effect, however, might have been to create a permanent "second class citizenship" for LGB people by cutting off their ability to petition the government. The text of Amendment 2 was the following:

> Neither the state of Colorado, through any of its branches or departments, nor any of its agencies, political subdivisions, municipalities or school districts, shall enact, adopt or enforce any statute, regulation, ordinance or policy whereby homosexual, lesbian or bisexual orientation, conduct, practices or relationships shall constitute or otherwise be the basis of, or entitle any person or class of persons to have or claim any minority status, quota preferences, protected status or claim of discrimination. This Section of the Constitution shall be in all respects self-executing.

Lower courts immediately issued injunctions preventing the implementation of the Amendment on the grounds that it violated the Fourteenth Amendment's guarantees of equal rights to all citizens. In 1996, the U.S. Supreme Court struck down Amendment 2 in the case of *Romer v. Evans*, stating that "Amendment 2 classifies homosexuals not to further a proper legislative end but to make them unequal to everyone else. This Colorado cannot do. A State cannot so deem a class of persons a stranger to its laws. Amendment 2 violates the Equal Protection Clause." The Supreme Court opinion and dissent in *Romer* is the subject of Document 4.5. Further symbolic support for LGB people was provided by the Executive Branch in the form of a presidential proclamation of June 1999—the 30th anniversary of the landmark Stonewall Riots of 1969—as Gay and Lesbian Pride Month (Document 4.6).

The *Romer* precedent makes clear that LGB people cannot be outright relegated to second-class citizenship by being excluded from the public policy making process. However, more than half of the states, as well as the federal government, have declined to enact legislation to proactively protect LGB people from discrimination in employment, housing, and related areas, in the same way that they outlaw discrimination on the basis of race, ethnicity, disability, age, gender, or religion. At the national level, the Employment Non-Discrimination Act (ENDA) passed the U.S. House of Representatives in 2007, but was not taken up by the U.S. Senate. A heated controversy surrounded the legislation, because the version of the bill that was advanced in Congress removed protections that included gender identity, since it was thought those might damage support for the bill. For this reason, many of the nation's premier LGB political organizations ironically ended up *opposing* the most progressive piece of legislation regarding LGB rights ever to pass a house of Congress. The more inclusive version of the bill can be found in Document 4.8.

As of 2010, however, 21 states plus the District of Columbia did offer some measure of civil rights protections on the basis of sexual orientation. Of these, 13 further extend protections to those who are "transgender" or "gender variant," i.e., whose appearance, expression or behavior are those traditionally associated with the opposite gender. An example of one such law, enacted in Oregon, is the subject of Document 4.7. Gender identity has been an issue of growing attention in recent years, such as in the form of the first-ever Congressional hearing about transgender rights, held in 2008 (Document 4.9). A related area concerns intersexuals (once called "hermaphrodites"), people whose genitalia and/or other characteristics are sexually ambiguous, rendering them neither clearly male nor female. A hearing into the "medical normalization" of intersexuality via surgery was the subject of a first-ever hearing by the San Francisco Human Rights Commission (Document 4.9). While transgendered and intersexual individuals face many concerns quite different from those impacting gay and lesbian people, these issues are politically linked as expressions of sexism, homophobia, and heterosexism.

Document 4.5: Extending Equal Protection

- **Document:** Excerpts from ruling of the U.S. Supreme Court in the case of *Romer v. Evans*, including portions of the syllabus (summary), majority opinion, and dissenting opinion
- **Date:** May 20, 2006
- **Where:** U.S. Supreme Court, Washington, DC
- **Significance:** This ruling, striking down an anti-LGB constitutional amendment in Colorado, was the first major Supreme Court ruling identifying homosexuals as a "class of persons" with distinct civil rights.

U.S. SUPREME COURT
517 U.S. 620 (1996)

ROMER v. EVANS

ROY ROMER, GOVERNOR OF COLORADO, ET AL. PETITIONERS v.
RICHARD G. EVANS
ET AL.

CERTIORARI TO THE SUPREME COURT OF COLORADO

No. 94-1039

Argued: October 10, 1995—Decided: May 20, 1996

Syllabus

At an October 1995 demonstration at the U.S. Supreme Court building in Washington, DC, a gay couple reacts to speakers opposing a Colorado state constitutional amendment banning legislation protecting gays from discrimination. (AP Photo/Tyler Mallory)

After various Colorado municipalities passed ordinances banning discrimination based on sexual orientation in housing, employment, education, public accommodations, health and welfare services, and other transactions and activities, Colorado voters adopted by statewide referendum "Amendment 2" to the State Constitution, which precludes all legislative, executive, or judicial action at any level of state or local government designed to protect the status of persons based on their "homosexual, lesbian or bisexual orientation, conduct, practices or relationships." Respondents, who include aggrieved homosexuals and municipalities, commenced this litigation in state court against petitioner state parties to declare Amendment 2 invalid and enjoin its enforcement. The trial court's grant of a preliminary injunction was sustained by the Colorado Supreme Court, which held that Amendment 2 was subject to strict scrutiny under the Equal Protection Clause of the Fourteenth Amendment because it infringed the fundamental right of gays and lesbians to participate in the political process. On remand, the trial court found that the Amendment failed to satisfy strict scrutiny. It enjoined Amendment 2's enforcement, and the State Supreme Court affirmed.

Held:

Amendment 2 violates the Equal Protection Clause.

(a) The State's principal argument that Amendment 2 puts gays and lesbians in the same position as all other persons by denying them special rights is rejected as implausible. The extent of the change in legal status effected by this law is evident from the authoritative construction of Colorado's Supreme Court—which establishes that the amendment's immediate effect is to repeal all existing statutes, regulations, ordinances, and policies of state and local entities barring discrimination based on sexual orientation, and that its ultimate effect is to prohibit any governmental entity from adopting similar, or more protective, measures in the future absent state constitutional amendment—and from a review of the terms, structure, and operation of the ordinances that would be repealed and prohibited by Amendment 2. Even if, as the State contends, homosexuals can find protection in laws and policies of general application, Amendment 2 goes well beyond merely depriving them of special rights. It imposes a broad disability upon those persons alone, forbidding them, but no others, to seek specific legal protection from injuries caused by discrimination in a wide range of public and private transactions.

(b) In order to reconcile the Fourteenth Amendment's promise that no person shall be denied equal protection with the practical reality that most legislation classifies for one purpose or another, the Court has stated that it will uphold a law that neither burdens a fundamental right nor targets a suspect class so long as the legislative classification bears a rational relation to some independent and legitimate legislative end. Amendment 2 fails, indeed defies, even this conventional inquiry. First, the amendment is at once too narrow and too broad, identifying persons by a single trait and then denying them the possibility of protection across the board. This disqualification of a class of persons from the right to obtain specific protection from the law is unprecedented and is itself a denial of equal protection in the most literal sense. Second, the sheer breadth of Amendment 2, which makes a general announcement that gays and lesbians shall not have any particular protections from the law, is so far removed from the reasons offered for it, i.e., respect for other citizens' freedom of association, particularly landlords or employers who have personal or religious objections to homosexuality, and the State's interest in conserving resources to fight discrimination against other groups, that the amendment cannot be explained by reference to those reasons; the Amendment raises the inevitable inference that it is born of animosity toward the class that it affects. Amendment 2 cannot be said to be directed to an identifiable legitimate purpose or discrete objective. It is a status-based classification of persons undertaken for its own sake, something the Equal Protection Clause does not permit.

JUSTICE KENNEDY delivered the opinion of the Court.

One century ago, the first Justice Harlan admonished this Court that the Constitution "neither knows nor tolerates classes among citizens." Plessy v. Ferguson (1896) (dissenting opinion). Unheeded then, those words now are understood to state a commitment to the law's neutrality where the rights of persons are at stake. The Equal Protection Clause enforces this principle and today requires us to hold invalid a provision of Colorado's Constitution. . . .

Amendment 2 . . . is at once too narrow and too broad. It identifies persons by a single trait and then denies them protection across the board. The resulting disqualification of a class of persons from the right to seek specific protection from the law is unprecedented in our jurisprudence. The absence of precedent for Amendment 2 is itself instructive; "[d]iscriminations of an unusual character especially suggest careful consideration to determine whether they are obnoxious to the constitutional provision." Louisville Gas & Elec. Co. v. Coleman, 277 U.S. 32, 37-38 (1928).

It is not within our constitutional tradition to enact laws of this sort. Central both to the idea of the rule of law and to our own Constitution's guarantee of equal protection is the principle that government and each of its parts remain open on impartial terms to all who seek its assistance. "Equal protection of the laws is not achieved through indiscriminate imposition of inequalities." Respect for this principle explains why laws singling out a certain class of citizens for disfavored legal status or general hardships are rare. A law declaring that in general it shall be more difficult for one group of citizens than for all others to seek aid from the government is itself a denial of equal protection of the laws in the most literal sense . . .

A second and related point is that laws of the kind now before us raise the inevitable inference that the disadvantage imposed is born of animosity toward the class of persons affected. "[I]f the constitutional conception of 'equal protection of the laws' means anything, it must at the very least mean that a bare . . . desire to harm a politically unpopular group cannot constitute a legitimate governmental interest." Even laws enacted for broad and ambitious purposes often can be explained by reference to legitimate public policies which justify the incidental disadvantages they impose on certain persons. Amendment 2, however, in making a general announcement that gays and lesbians shall not have any particular protections from the law, inflicts on them immediate, continuing, and real injuries that outrun and belie any legitimate justifications that may be claimed for it. We conclude that, in addition to the far-reaching deficiencies of Amendment 2 that we have noted, the principles it offends, in another sense, are conventional and venerable; a law must bear a rational relationship to a legitimate governmental purpose, and Amendment 2 does not.

The primary rationale the State offers for Amendment 2 is respect for other citizens' freedom of association, and in particular the liberties of landlords or employers who have personal or religious objections to homosexuality. Colorado also cites its interest in conserving resources to fight discrimination against other groups. The breadth of the Amendment is so far removed from these particular justifications that we find it impossible to credit them. We cannot say that Amendment 2 is directed to any identifiable legitimate purpose or discrete objective. It is a status-based enactment divorced from any factual context from which we could discern a relationship to legitimate state interests; it is a classification of persons undertaken for its own sake, something the Equal Protection Clause does not permit. "[C]lass legislation . . . [is] obnoxious to the prohibitions of the Fourteenth Amendment. . . ."

We must conclude that Amendment 2 classifies homosexuals not to further a proper legislative end but to make them unequal to everyone else. This Colorado cannot do. A State cannot so deem a class of persons a stranger to its laws. Amendment 2 violates the Equal Protection Clause, and the judgment of the Supreme Court of Colorado is affirmed.

It is so ordered.

JUSTICE SCALIA, with whom THE CHIEF JUSTICE and JUSTICE THOMAS join, dissenting.

The Court has mistaken a Kulturkampf for a fit of spite. The constitutional amendment before us here is not the manifestation of a "bare . . . desire to harm" homosexuals, ante, at 13, but is rather a modest attempt by seemingly tolerant Coloradans to preserve traditional sexual mores against the efforts of a politically powerful minority to revise those mores through use of the laws. That objective, and the means chosen to achieve it, are not only unimpeachable under any constitutional doctrine hitherto pronounced (hence the opinion's heavy reliance upon principles of righteousness rather than judicial holdings); they have been specifically approved by the Congress of the United States and by this Court.

In holding that homosexuality cannot be singled out for disfavorable treatment, the Court contradicts a decision, unchallenged here, pronounced only 10 years ago, see Bowers v. Hardwick, (1986), and places the prestige of this institution behind the proposition that opposition to homosexuality is as reprehensible as racial or religious bias. Whether it is or not is precisely the cultural debate that gave rise to the Colorado constitutional amendment (and to the preferential laws against which the amendment was directed). Since the Constitution of the United States says nothing about this subject, it is left to be resolved

> "We must conclude that Amendment 2 classifies homosexuals not to further a proper legislative end but to make them unequal to everyone else. This Colorado cannot do. A State cannot so deem a class of persons a stranger to its laws."

Comparative View: "International LGBT Proliferation"

Prior to the 1970s, most early lesbian, gay, and bisexual communities maintained a low profile and rarely confronted political issues. Following the cathartic Stonewall Riots of 1969 in New York City, however, LGB groups in democracies worldwide created the "gay liberation" movement, participating in the political process in Europe, Latin America, Canada, Africa, and beyond. During this era, the International Lesbian and Gay Association formed in an attempt to establish the basic outlines of a global LGB liberation movement.

Gay groups in Italy, for example, did not form for political purposes until 1972. Combating the Italian government's adoption of religious tenets that disparaged homosexuality, these LGB groups fought alongside other civil rights movements such as the women's liberation movement. The Italian LGB platform would later be incorporated into the larger political system by means of left-wing political parties. Still, the powerful presence of The Vatican in Italy has limited the development of LGB politics when compared to many other European countries.

During its military dictatorship, Argentina heavily suppressed social organization of all kinds, including the development of LGB communities. Indeed, many gays and lesbians were arrested for crimes of immorality. After many years of hostility at the hand of dic-

The Gay Pride parade held in Lima, Peru, in July 2002 was the first parade to be held in Peru's capital for LGBT civil rights. (AP Photo/Martin Mejia)

tatorial rule, however, LGB life began to thrive after democratic elections in the 1980s. Gay clubs and other establishments were still routinely raided, but activists sought political reforms more emphatically. By the early 1990s, a number of LGB interest groups emerged that were formally recognized by the Argentine government, most importantly La Comunidad Homosexual Argentina.

The first Canadian LGB political activists formed interest groups in a number of provinces by the mid-1970s, especially the pan-Canadian National Gay Rights Coalition formed in 1975. By the close of that decade, regional LGB interests had taken part in a number of court cases challenging anti-homosexual policies. It was the first time in Canadian history that open challenges to heterosexual norms had taken place through the country's political process.

South Africa's foundational LGB political group, the Gay Association of South Africa (GASA), was formed in 1982. By the close of the 1990s, with the demise of Apartheid, hostility toward discriminatory policies of all kinds catapulted GASA's agenda of equal protections to the fore. The new South African Constitution was the only one in the world to explicitly outlaw discrimination based on sexual orientation, a provision that was interpreted to require same-sex marriage, which was legalized in 2006.—*Brandon L. H. Aultman*

by normal democratic means, including the democratic adoption of provisions in state constitutions. This Court has no business imposing upon all Americans the resolution favored by the elite class from which the Members of this institution are selected, pronouncing that "animosity" toward homosexuality is evil. I vigorously dissent . . .

Today's opinion has no foundation in American constitutional law, and barely pretends to. The people of Colorado have adopted an entirely reasonable provision which does not even disfavor homosexuals in any substantive sense, but merely denies them preferential treatment.

Amendment 2 is designed to prevent piecemeal deterioration of the sexual morality favored by a majority of Coloradans, and is not only an appropriate means to that legitimate end, but a means that Americans have employed before. Striking it down is an act, not of judicial judgment, but of political will. I dissent.

Document 4.6: Presidential Proclamation Recognizing "Gay Pride"

- **Document:** Proclamations by President Bill Clinton marking June 1999 as National Gay and Lesbian Pride Month
- **Date:** June 11, 1999
- **Where:** The White House, Washington, DC
- **Significance:** On the 30th anniversary of the Stonewall Riots, a U.S. president for the first time issued a proclamation acknowledging the LGB pride events annually held each June throughout the United States.

THE WHITE HOUSE
Office of the Press Secretary

For Immediate Release June 11, 1999
GAY AND LESBIAN PRIDE MONTH, 1999

BY THE PRESIDENT OF THE UNITED STATES OF AMERICA
A PROCLAMATION

Thirty years ago this month, at the Stonewall Inn in New York City, a courageous group of citizens resisted harassment and mistreatment, setting in motion a chain of events that would become known as the Stonewall Uprising and the birth of the modern gay and lesbian civil rights movement. Gays and lesbians, their families and friends, celebrate the anniversary of Stonewall every June in America as Gay and Lesbian Pride Month; and, earlier this month, the National Park Service added the Stonewall Inn, as well as the nearby park and neighborhood streets surrounding it, to the National Register of Historic Places.

I am proud of the measures my Administration has taken to end discrimination against gays and lesbians and ensure that they have the same rights guaranteed to their fellow Americans. Last year, I signed an Executive order that amends Federal equal employment opportunity policy to prohibit

"I encourage all Americans to observe this month with appropriate programs, ceremonies, and activities that celebrate our diversity, and to remember throughout the year the gay and lesbian Americans whose many and varied contributions have enriched our national life."

discrimination in the Federal civilian work force based on sexual orientation. We have also banned discrimination based on sexual orientation in the granting of security clearances. As a result of these and other policies, gay and lesbian Americans serve openly and proudly throughout the Federal Government. My Administration is also working with congressional leaders to pass the Employment Non-Discrimination Act, which would prohibit most private employers from firing workers solely because of their sexual orientation.

America's diversity is our greatest strength. But, while we have come a long way on our journey toward tolerance, understanding, and mutual respect, we still have a long way to go in our efforts to end discrimination. During the past year, people across our country have been shaken by violent acts that struck at the heart of what it means to be an American and at the values that have always defined us as a Nation. In 1997, the most recent year for which we have statistics, there were more than 8,000 reported hate crimes in our country—almost one an hour. Now is the time for us to take strong and decisive action to end all hate crimes, and I reaffirm my pledge to work with the Congress to pass the Hate Crimes Prevention Act.

But we cannot achieve true tolerance merely through legislation; we must change hearts and minds as well. Our greatest hope for a just society is to teach our children to respect one another, to appreciate our differences, and to recognize the fundamental values that we hold in common. As part of our efforts to achieve this goal, earlier this spring, I announced that the Departments of Justice and Education will work in partnership with educational and other private sector organizations to reach out to students and teach them that our diversity is a gift. In addition, the Department of Education has issued landmark guidance that explains Federal standards against sexual harassment and prohibits sexual harassment of all students regardless of their sexual orientation; and I have ordered the Education Department's civil rights office to step up its enforcement of anti-discrimination and harassment rules. That effort has resulted in a groundbreaking guide that provides practical guidance to school administrators and teachers for developing a comprehensive approach to protecting all students, including gays and lesbians, from harassment and violence.

Since our earliest days as a Nation, Americans have strived to make real the ideals of equality and freedom so eloquently expressed in our Declaration of Independence and Constitution. We now have a rare opportunity to enter a new century and a new millennium as one country, living those principles, recognizing our common values, and building on our shared strengths.

NOW, THEREFORE, I, WILLIAM J. CLINTON, President of the United States of America, by virtue of the authority vested in me by the Constitution and laws of the United States, do hereby proclaim June 1999 as Gay and Lesbian Pride Month. I encourage all Americans to observe this month with appropriate programs, ceremonies, and activities that celebrate our diversity, and to remember throughout the year the gay and lesbian Americans whose many and varied contributions have enriched our national life.

IN WITNESS WHEREOF, I have hereunto set my hand this eleventh day of June, in the year of our Lord nineteen hundred and ninety-nine, and of the Independence of the United States of America the two hundred and twenty-third.

WILLIAM J. CLINTON

Document 4.7: Outlawing Bias

- **Document:** Oregon State law prohibiting discrimination on multiple grounds, including sexual orientation and gender identity
- **Date:** August 2, 2003
- **Where:** State Capitol, Salem, Oregon
- **Significance:** Most states have anti-discrimination statutes covering such characteristics as race, ethnicity, religion, and gender; however, many do not offer protections on that basis to LGB or transgender people. Oregon's statute is an example of one that includes both characteristics.

74th OREGON LEGISLATIVE ASSEMBLY—2007 Regular Session

Enrolled, Senate Bill 2 Sponsored by COMMITTEE ON JUDICIARY (at the request of Governor's Task Force on Equality in Oregon)

Be It Enacted by the People of the State of Oregon:

"Sexual orientation" means an individual's actual or perceived heterosexuality, homosexuality, bisexuality or gender identity, regardless of whether the individual's gender identity, appearance, expression or behavior differs from that traditionally associated with the individual's sex at birth . . .

The purpose of this chapter is to encourage the fullest utilization of the available workforce by removing arbitrary standards of race, religion, sex, marital status, sexual orientation, national origin, age or disability as a barrier to employment of the inhabitants of this state, and to ensure the human dignity of all people within this state and protect their health, safety and morals from the consequences of intergroup hostility, tensions and practices of discrimination of any

"The purpose of this chapter is . . . to ensure the human dignity of all people within this state and protect their health, safety and morals from the consequences of intergroup hostility, tensions and practices of discrimination of any kind."

kind based on race, religion, sex, marital status, sexual orientation, national origin, age or disability.

To accomplish this purpose, the Legislative Assembly intends by this chapter to provide:

(1) A program of public education calculated to eliminate attitudes upon which practices of discrimination because of race, religion, sex, marital status, sexual orientation, national origin, age or disability are based.

(2) An adequate remedy for persons aggrieved by certain acts of discrimination because of race, religion, sex, marital status, sexual orientation, national origin, or disability or unreasonable acts of discrimination in employment based upon age . . .

(1) It is declared to be the public policy of Oregon that practices of discrimination against any of its inhabitants because of race, religion, sex, marital status, sexual orientation, national origin, age or disability are a matter of state concern and that discrimination not only threatens the rights and privileges of its inhabitants but menaces the institutions and foundation of a free democratic state.

(2) The opportunity to obtain employment or housing or to use and enjoy places of public accommodation without race, religion, sex, marital status, sexual orientation, national origin, age or disability hereby is recognized as and declared to be a civil right. . . .

(3) It is not an unlawful practice for a bona fide church or other religious institution to take any action with respect to housing or the use of facilities based on a bona fide religious belief about sexual orientation as long as the housing or the use of facilities is closely connected with or related to the primary purposes of the church or institution and is not connected with a commercial or business activity that has no necessary relationship to the church or institution . . .

(1) It is an unlawful employment practice:
   (a) For an employer, because of an individual's race, color, religion, sex, sexual orientation, national origin, marital status or age if the individual is 18 years of age or older, or because of the race, color, religion, sex, sexual orientation, national origin, marital status or age of any other person with whom the individual associates . . .
A person may not, because of the race, color, religion, sex, sexual orientation, national origin, marital status, religion, national origin, familial status or source of income of any person:

   (a) Refuse to sell, lease or rent any real property to a purchaser.
   (b) Expel a purchaser from any real property.
   (c) Make any distinction, discrimination or restriction against a purchaser in the price, terms, conditions or privileges relating to the sale, rental, lease or occupancy of real property or in the furnishing of any facilities or services in connection therewith.
   (d) Attempt to discourage the sale, rental or lease of any real property to a purchaser. . . .

Recruiting, selecting and promoting employees shall be on the basis of their relative ability, knowledge, experience and skills, determined by open competition and consideration of qualified applicants, without regard to an individual's race, color, religion, sex, sexual orientation, national origin, political affiliation, marital status, age, disability, political affiliation or other nonjob related factors, with proper regard for an individual's privacy . . .

Document 4.8: Federal Anti-Bias Moves

- *Document:* A bill introduced in the U.S. House of Representatives to prohibit discrimination throughout the country in employment on the basis of sexual orientation and gender identity.
- *Date:* April 24, 2007
- *Where:* Washington, DC
- *Significance:* This bill was amended to remove protections on the basis of gender identity and then passed the U.S. House of Representatives in 2007. This was the first time that any law had been passed by even one chamber of Congress to prohibit discrimination on the basis of sexual orientation at the federal level. This version, which includes both gender identity and sexual orientation, is preferred by most activists as the basis for future legislation.

ENDA

IN THE HOUSE OF REPRESENTATIVES
APRIL 24, 2007

110TH CONGRESS, 1ST SESSION H. R. 2015

To prohibit employment discrimination on the basis of sexual orientation or gender identity.

A BILL
To prohibit employment discrimination on the basis of sexual orientation or gender identity.

Be it enacted by the Senate and House of Representatives of the United States of America in Congress assembled:

This Act may be cited as the "Employment Non-Discrimination Act of 2007."

The purposes of this Act are—

(1) to provide a comprehensive Federal prohibition of employment discrimination on the basis of sexual orientation or gender identity;
(2) to provide meaningful and effective remedies for employment discrimination on the basis of sexual orientation or gender identity; and
(3) to invoke congressional powers, including the powers to enforce the 14th amendment to the Constitution, and to regulate interstate commerce and provide for the general welfare pursuant to Section 8 of article I of the Constitution, in order to prohibit employment discrimination on the basis of sexual orientation or gender identity.

. . .

The term "gender identity" means the gender-related identity, appearance, or mannerisms or other gender-related characteristics of an individual, with or without regard to the individual's designated sex at birth . . .

The term "sexual orientation" means homosexuality, heterosexuality, or bisexuality . . .

It shall be an unlawful employment practice for an employer—
(1) to fail or refuse to hire or to discharge any individual, or otherwise discriminate against any individual with respect to the compensation, terms, conditions, or privileges of employment of the individual, because of such individual's actual or perceived sexual orientation or gender identity; or

(2) to limit, segregate, or classify the employees or applicants for employment of the employer in any way that would deprive or tend to deprive any individual of employment or otherwise adversely affect the status of the individual as an employee, because of such individual's actual or perceived sexual orientation or gender identity . . .

Nothing in this Act shall be construed or interpreted to require or permit—
(1) any covered entity to grant preferential treatment to any individual or to any group because of the actual or perceived sexual orientation or gender identity of such individual or group . . .

This Act shall not apply to any of the employment practices of a religious corporation, association, educational institution, or society which has as its primary purpose religious ritual or worship or the teaching or spreading of religious doctrine or belief. . . .

In this Act, the term "employment" does not apply to the relationship between the United States and members of the Armed Forces. . . .

Nothing in this Act shall be construed to establish an unlawful employment practice based on actual or perceived gender identity due to the denial of access to shared shower or dressing facilities in which being seen fully unclothed is unavoidable, provided that the employer provides reasonable access to adequate facilities . . .

"It shall be an unlawful employment practice for an employer to . . . discriminate against any individual . . . because of such individual's actual or perceived sexual orientation or gender identity . . . "

The Democratic Party Platform, 2008: Sexual Orientation

"We will also put national security above divisive politics. More than 12,500 service men and women have been discharged on the basis of sexual orientation since the 'Don't Ask, Don't Tell' policy was implemented, at a cost of over $360 million. Many of those forced out had special skills in high demand, such as translators, engineers, and pilots. At a time when the military is having a tough time recruiting and retaining troops, it is wrong to deny our country the service of brave, qualified people. We support the repeal of 'Don't Ask Don't Tell' and the implementation of policies . . . "

"It is not enough to look back in wonder at how far we have come; those who came before us did not strike a blow against injustice only so that we would allow injustice to fester in our time. That means removing the barriers of prejudice and misunderstanding that still exist in America. We support the full inclusion of all families, including same-sex couples, in the life of our nation, and support equal responsibility, benefits, and protections. We will enact a comprehensive bipartisan employment non-discrimination act. We oppose the Defense of Marriage Act and all attempts to use this issue to divide us."

Nothing in this Act shall prohibit an employer from requiring an employee, during the employee's hours at work, to adhere to reasonable dress or grooming standards not prohibited by other provisions of Federal, State, or local law, provided that the employer permits any employee who has undergone gender transition prior to the time of employment, and any employee who has notified the employer that the employee has undergone or is undergoing gender transition after the time of employment, to adhere to the same dress or grooming standards for the gender to which the employee has transitioned or is transitioning. . . .

The Commission shall not collect statistics on actual or perceived sexual orientation or gender identity from covered entities, or compel the collection of such statistics by covered entities.

Document 4.9: The Question of Intersexuality

- *Document:* Excerpts from "A Human Rights Investigation into the Medical 'Normalization' of Intersex People," a report of a hearing of the San Francisco Human Rights Commission
- *Date:* April 28, 2005
- *Where:* City Hall, San Francisco, California
- *Significance:* The rights of intersexuals—people who have genital and/or other characteristics that are both male and female—have traditionally been overlooked, in favor of surgical intervention to establish a clear anatomical gender. This document was the first major government investigation into the potential for such surgery to violate human rights, particularly if the result does not correlate to an individual's underlying gender identity.

A Human Rights Investigation into the Medical "Normalization" of Intersex People

A Report of a Public Hearing by the Human Rights Commission of the City & County of San Francisco

On May 27, 2004, the San Francisco Human Rights Commission held a public hearing to investigate the issue of "normalizing" medical interventions being performed on intersex infants and children. The public hearing and this report resulted from requests from people with intersex anatomies for the Commission to explore the question of unwanted, "normalizing" interventions performed on children born with "ambiguous genitalia." Specifically, the Commission became concerned that homophobia, transphobia, and heterosexism were strong social forces that contributed to the decision-making process for assigning sex and gender to intersex children through "normalizing" genital surgeries and sex hormone treatment . . .

Because, to the Commission's knowledge, no governmental entity in the United States had ever before addressed these concerns as human rights issues, the Task Force worked diligently to ensure comprehensive inclusion of information from as many different sources as would respond to the call for participation. The Commission had specifically asked to hear from doctors, parents, and people with intersex anatomies and to have various medical, academic, legal, and ethical perspectives represented. To this end, the ITF and Commission staff and interns invited people with intersex anatomies, parents, local doctors and medical providers, academicians, legal experts, and ethicists to testify at the hearing and/or to submit written testimony . . .

Findings

The Human Rights Commission, having conducted a public hearing on May 27, 2004 on the question of the medical "normalization" of intersex people and the social, legal, and ethical aspects of intersex issues, and having considered verbal and written testimony, hereby finds that:

1. Infant genital surgeries and sex hormone treatments that are not performed for the treatment of physical illness, such as improving urinary tract or metabolic functioning, and have not been shown to alleviate pain or illness (hereafter referred to as "normalizing" interventions) are unnecessary and are not medical or social emergencies.

2. "Normalizing" interventions done without the patient's informed consent are inherent human rights abuses.

4. "Normalizing" interventions deprive intersex people of the opportunity to express their own identity and to experience their own intact physiology.

4. It is unethical to disregard a child's intrinsic human rights to privacy, dignity, autonomy, and physical integrity by altering genitals through irreversible surgeries for purely psychosocial and aesthetic rationales. It is wrong to deprive a person of the right to determine their sexual experience and identity . . .

50. Most intersex children can live happy and healthy lives without surgical intervention.

51. Rationales for "normalizing" medical interventions are based upon social mores and norms and are not evidence-based.

52. Current treatment protocols are homophobic in that they use heterosexuality as the measure of a successful gender assignment. Homosexuality is considered an undesired or unsuccessful outcome.

53. Parents often are made to believe that their intersex children will be homosexual and/or suicidal if they do not undergo "normalizing" genital surgery.

54. Prejudice against people with nonstandard genitals is culturally determined, and this negative bias does not exist in every culture.

55. Intersex people are subjected to "normalizing" medical interventions that are intended to reinforce gender assignment.

56. "Normalizing" interventions cannot create or change a person's sex, gender, sex identity, or gender identity.

57. Gender identity is not intrinsically tied to physiology in a predictable way. The most accurate way to identify a child's gender is to allow them to assert it . . .

62. Approximately 1 in 2000 children is born with so-called ambiguous genitals. Additionally, some people are discovered to have some type of intersex condition later in life.

RECOMMENDATIONS

In response to the issues and needs of individuals affected by the medical normalization of intersex people and the social, legal, and ethical aspects of intersex issues, and found upon consideration of verbal and written testimony of the May 27, 2004 public hearing, the Human Rights Commission hereby recommends that:

1. "Normalizing" interventions should not occur in infancy or childhood. Any procedures that are not medically necessary should not be performed unless the patient gives their legal consent.

2. A patient-centered treatment model should be implemented which emphasizes peer support, access to information, openness, treating the child as the patient, honoring the person's right to make informed choices about their own bodies, and delaying treatment until the patient can make informed consent.

4. Infant genital surgeries that are undertaken to improve the underlying physical health of an intersex child should be performed within that patient-centered model. All recommendations for any genital surgery should be evidence-based . . .

14. The problem of social discrimination should be addressed rather than offer hormonal or surgical intervention.

14. Intersex children should be encouraged to think positively about their bodies even if those bodies are different in some ways from others.

16. Local, state, and federal legislators should investigate the question of necessity for having gender markers as a requirement for legal identification.

17. Local, state, and federal entities should investigate the need to include intersex as a protected category in anti-discrimination laws.

18. Medical and mental health providers should be educated on various intersex concerns, e.g., how to create safer medical settings for intersex people, on Lesbian Gay Bisexual Transgender ("LGBT") cultural competency so that being LGBT is not seen as a negative outcome, and how to responsibly talk to parents about intersex.

19. School staff and administrators should be educated on intersex issues in order to increase safety in schools for intersex students.

20. Adequate funding should be provided for services that support and protect intersex people, particularly youth, in suicide prevention, peer support, coming out, counseling, and housing services.

"It is unethical to disregard a child's intrinsic human rights to privacy, dignity, autonomy, and physical integrity by altering genitals through irreversible surgeries for purely psychosocial and aesthetic rationales."

21. Public health educators should help end shame, secrecy, and isolation imposed on intersex people by providing factual and affirming information to the public, including children, that variations in anatomy are normal, natural, acceptable, and not necessarily a medical problem.

22. The City and County of San Francisco should sponsor annual public education events on Intersex Awareness Day (October 26th) by collaborating with intersex groups, public health administrators, and human rights groups to raise public awareness of intersex issues. The City and County of San Francisco should urge other governmental entities to do the same.

24. The City and County of San Francisco should dedicate appropriate funds to support the work of community-based organizations that specifically serve the needs of intersex people.

Document 4.10: Protecting the Transgendered

- *Document:* Statements by U.S. Representatives Robert Andrews (D-New Jersey) and Tammy Baldwin (D-Wisconsin) at a hearing by the House Subcommittee on Health, Employment, Labor, and Pensions regarding workplace discrimination against transgendered people.
- *Date:* June 26, 2008
- *Where:* U.S. House of Representatives, Washington, DC
- *Significance:* In the first hearing of its kind, the House explored the issue of workplace discrimination on the basis of gender identity. Speakers included openly lesbian U.S. Representative Tammy Baldwin. No federal legislation has ever been passed providing protection from discrimination for transgendered people.

Chairman Andrews Statement at Subcommittee Hearing on An Examination of Discrimination Against Trangender Americans in the Workplace

Good morning and welcome to the Health, Employment, Labor, and Pensions Subcommittee Hearing entitled "An Examination of Discrimination Against Transgender Americans in the Workplace." The purpose of today's hearing is to educate Congress and the public about the discrimination transgender Americans face particularly in the workplace absent a comprehensive federal law to protect them.

Workplace discrimination against a particular group of people is morally unacceptable and conflicts with the principles we hold sacred in our society. Furthermore, workplace discrimination, unchecked, harms our economy both domestically and globally. When an employer is permitted to deny someone a job based on their identity without consequence, makes increases on our unemployment rate and diminishes our competitive edge in the global economy, making us less competitive in the global economy.

Testifying before us today are some of the most distinguished and brightest members of our society, who were denied employment or fired because they are transgender. These individuals along with the roughly 700,000 to 3 million transgender individuals living in America today run the risk of being fired, demoted or not even hired because of their gender identity.

There are 12 states, including the District of Columbia with laws in place to protect transgender individuals from workplace discrimination, as well as many reputable companies with anti-discrimination policies. Despite these protections, studies and surveys reveal high rates of unemployment and low-income status among transgender Americans.

Today's hearing is simply a first step in identifying the problem workplace discrimination against transgender Americans. I thank the witnesses for coming forward to the subcommittee today and look forward to hearing your testimony.

Statement by Congresswoman Tammy Baldwin

Thank you Chairman Andrews, Ranking Member Kline, and members of the Committee for allowing me the opportunity to testify today at this historic hearing.

Many of my colleagues have asked about the phrase "gender identity" and why employment protections based on gender identity and expression ought to be included in any employment discrimination legislation Congress takes up. I'll do my best to answer any lingering questions and clarify what drives many in the LGBT community to demand an inclusive approach to eliminating discrimination in the workplace—one that does not leave the smallest and most vulnerable part of our community behind.

As you may know, gender identity is a person's internal sense of his or her gender. In the vast majority of the population, an individual's gender identity and his or her birth sex "match." But for a small minority of people, gender identity and anatomical sex conflict. A common way for many transgender people to describe this feeling is to say something to the effect of being "trapped in the wrong body." Gender identity and sexual orientation are not the same and transgender people may be heterosexual, lesbian, gay or bisexual.

There are thousands of transgender Americans who lead incredibly successful, stable lives, are dedicated parents, contribute immeasurably to their communities, their country. I personally know transgender people who work in fields as diverse as defense contracting, broadcasting, community organizing, the legal profession—I could go on. They have transitioned successfully, many with the full support of their employers.

Despite these successes, because an individual was born one sex and presents themselves to the world as another—or in a way that other people may think is inconsistent with how a man or a woman should present themselves—he or she can face many forms of discrimination.

Hate crimes against transgender Americans are tragically common. Transgender people also face discrimination in the mundane tasks of the everyday—trying to find housing, apply for credit, or even see a doctor . . . and, of course, in the focus of today's hearing: trying to provide for themselves and their families.

Some of you know that I practiced law for a few years in a small general practice firm before I was elected to the Wisconsin Assembly. On occasion, I represented clients who were fired in violation of Wisconsin's 1982 non-discrimination law that added sexual orientation to our state's anti-discrimination statutes.

During that time, I met a transgender woman who left a lasting impression, though she was never a client. This woman had been fired from a management position at a large local employer when she announced to her boss that she intended to transition. And because Wisconsin law gave her no legal recourse, she faced an impossible situation—and ended up moving to a different state.

I remember a time in my own life, when I thought I had to choose between living my life with truth and integrity about who I am, as a lesbian, or pursuing the career of my dreams in public service. Among the things that made me change my mind was Wisconsin's Non-Discrimination law that passed four years before I first ran for local office . . . as an out lesbian.

The importance of nondiscrimination laws cannot be overstated. Substantively, they provide real remedies and a chance to seek justice. Symbolically, they say to America, judge your fellow citizens by their integrity, character, and talents, not their sexual orientation, or gender identity, or their race or religion, for that matter. Symbolically, these laws also say that irrational hate or fear have no place in our work place.

Today, 39% of Americans live in areas explicitly banning discrimination based on gender identity and expression and at least 300 major U.S. businesses now ban discrimination based on gender identity and expression. Corporate America and the American people are way ahead of the Congress in acknowledging the basic truth we hold to be self-evident . . . that all of us are created equal . . . and the laws of the land should reflect that equality. It is high time that America declare discrimination based on gender identity and expression unlawful.

Mr. Chairman, I wholeheartedly support your Committee's efforts to do just this. For the record, I support an inclusive bill which ensures that hard-working Americans cannot be denied job opportunities, fired or otherwise be discriminated against just because of their sexual orientation, gender identity, and gender expression.

Human Rights Campaign

Founded in 1980 with the intent of making campaign contributions to Congressional candidates, the Human Rights Campaign (HRC) was the political foil of such conservative groups as the Moral Majority and the National Conservative Political Action Committee. HRC soon found itself among a growing epicenter of gay, lesbian, and bisexual (LGB) political activity. For the HRC, homosexuality is not a matter of choice and should be protected from political discrimination.

According to HRC's Web site (www.hrc.org), "HRC works to secure equal rights for GLBT individuals and families at the federal and state levels by lobbying elected officials, mobilizing grassroots supporters, educating Americans, investing strategically to elect fair-minded officials and partnering with other GLBT organizations." And it has hitherto done just that. HRC has engaged in an extensive list of equality crusades, including securing bans on workplace discrimination, securing key national hate crime legislation, and supporting an interfaith initiative to redirect religious discussion of LGB rights.

HRC has been an influential proponent in the ongoing debates concerning the Employment Non-Discrimination Act (ENDA) that would provide federal legislation ending discrimination on the basis of sexual orientation. Combating many of the extreme right's morally conservative political ideologues, HRC has currently mobilized voters to elect nearly 200 LGB-friendly representatives.—*Brandon L. H. Aultman*

All of us who have had the honor of working in this institution know that one of the greatest things about America is that it is both a nation and an idea. Our American Dream promises that no matter where we start, no matter who we are, if we work hard, we will have the opportunity to advance. This Committee can help fulfill that promise.

Thank you.

Document 4.11: The Matthew Shepard and James Byrd, Jr., Hate Crimes Prevention Act

- **Document:** Excerpts from the National Defense Authorization Act for Fiscal Year 2010
- **Date:** October 28, 2009
- **Where:** U.S. Capitol, Washington, DC
- **Significance:** Passed as an amendment to a broader National Defense bill for the 2010 fiscal year, the Matthew Shepard Act included provisions for sexual orientation, gender, gender identity, and disability in definitions of federal hate crimes. It was introduced in former sessions of Congress but consistently failed to garner enough votes in either chamber.

SECTION 1. SHORT TITLE.

This Act may be cited as the "Matthew Shepard Local Law Enforcement Hate Crimes Prevention Act of 2007."

SEC. 2. FINDINGS.

Congress makes the following findings:

(1) The incidence of violence motivated by the actual or perceived race, color, religion, national origin, **gender, sexual orientation, gender identity, or disability** of the victim poses a serious national problem.

(2) Such violence disrupts the tranquility and safety of communities and is deeply divisive.

(3) State and local authorities are now and will continue to be responsible for prosecuting the overwhelming majority of violent crimes in the United States, including violent crimes motivated by bias. These authorities can carry out their responsibilities more effectively with greater Federal assistance.

(4) Existing Federal law is inadequate to address this problem.

(5) A prominent characteristic of a violent crime motivated by bias is that it devastates not just the actual victim and the family and friends of the victim, but frequently savages the community sharing the traits that caused the victim to be selected.

> "The incidence of violence motivated by the actual or perceived race, color, religion, national origin, gender, sexual orientation, gender identity, or disability of the victim poses a serious national problem."

(6) Such violence substantially affects interstate commerce in many ways, including the following:

(A) The movement of members of targeted groups is impeded, and members of such groups are forced to move across State lines to escape the incidence or risk of such violence.

(B) Members of targeted groups are prevented from purchasing goods and services, obtaining or sustaining employment, or participating in other commercial activity.

(C) Perpetrators cross State lines to commit such violence.

(D) Channels, facilities, and instrumentalities of interstate commerce are used to facilitate the commission of such violence.

(E) Such violence is committed using articles that have traveled in interstate commerce.

. . .

SEC. 7. PROHIBITION OF CERTAIN HATE CRIME ACTS.

(a) In General—Chapter 13 of title 18, United States Code, is amended by adding at the end the following:

Sec. 249. Hate crime acts

. . .

(2) OFFENSES INVOLVING ACTUAL OR PERCEIVED RELIGION, NATIONAL ORIGIN, **GENDER, SEXUAL ORIENTATION, GENDER IDENTITY**, OR DISABILITY—

(A) IN GENERAL—Whoever, whether or not acting under color of law, in any circumstance described in subparagraph (B), willfully causes bodily injury to any person or, through the use of fire, a firearm, or an explosive or incendiary device,

---

Family Research Council

The Family Research Council (FRC; www.frc.org) is a conservative nonprofit interest group with a deeply held belief in the sanctity of marriage between one man and one woman and in the institution of the family. FRC "champions marriage and family as the foundation of civilization, the seedbed of virtue, and the wellspring of society. FRC shapes public debate and formulates public policy that values human life and upholds the institutions of marriage and the family. Believing that God is the author of life, liberty, and the family, FRC promotes the Judeo-Christian worldview as the basis for a just, free, and stable society."

As LGB political rights became a hot topic in the mid to late 1990s, the FRC represented a population of the belief that "homosexual conduct is harmful to the persons who engage in it and to society at large, and can never be affirmed. It is by definition unnatural, and as such is associated with negative physical and psychological health effects." In 2004, the FRC submitted an *amicus curiae* brief in the Supreme Court case *Lawrence v. Texas*, in which the FRC supported the validity of sodomy laws. It also routinely sponsors the publication of political pamphlets that regard the proliferation of homosexual political rights as detrimental to liberty. The FRC feels same-sex attraction is an unnatural anomaly. "Sympathy must be extended to those who struggle with unwanted same-sex attractions, and every effort should be made to assist such persons to overcome those attractions, as many already have."—*Brandon L. H. Aultman*

attempts to cause bodily injury to any person, because of the actual or perceived religion, national origin, **gender, sexual orientation, gender identity or disability of any person—**

(i) shall be imprisoned not more than 10 years, fined in accordance with this title, or both; and

(ii) shall be imprisoned for any term of years or for life, fined in accordance with this title, or both, if—

(I) death results from the offense; or

(II) the offense includes kidnaping or an attempt to kidnap, aggravated sexual abuse or an attempt to commit aggravated sexual abuse, or an attempt to kill.

. . .

BIBLIOGRAPHY

Caplan, Gary S. "Fourteenth Amendment: The Supreme Court Limits The Right to Privacy." *The Journal of Criminal Law and Criminology* 77.3 (Autumn 1986): 894–930.

Embser-Herbert, Melissa Sheridan. *The U.S. Military's "Don't Ask Don't Tell" Policy: A Reference Handbook.* Westport, CT: Praeger, 2007.

Gallagher, John, and Chris Bull. *Perfect Enemies: The Religious Right, the Gay Movement, and the Politics of the 1990s.* New York: Crown, 1996.

Gilreath, Shannon. "Sexually Speaking: 'Don't Ask Don't Tell' and the First Amendment after *Lawrence v. Texas.*" *Duke Journal of Gender, Law and Policy* 14 (May 2007): 953–977.

Goldberg, Suzanne, and Lisa Keen. *Strangers to the Law: Gay People on Trial.* Ann Arbor: University of Michigan Press, 2000.

Hertzog, Mark. *The Lavender Vote: Lesbians, Gay Men, and Bisexuals in American Electoral Politics.* New York: New York University Press, 1996.

Karst, Kenneth L. "The Liberties of Equal Citizens: Groups and the Due Process Clause." *UCLA Law Review* 55.1 (October 2007): 99–142.

Klarman, Michael J. "Brown and Lawrence (and Goodridge)." *Michigan Law Review* 104.3 (December 2005): 431–490.

Riggle, Ellen D. B., and Barry L. Tadlock, eds. *Gays and Lesbians in the Democratic Process: Public Policy, Public Opinion, and Political Representation.* New York: Columbia University Press, 1999.

Sherrill, Kenneth. "The Political Power of Lesbians, Gays and Bisexuals." *PS: Political Science and Politics* 29.3 (September 1996): 469–474.

Shilts, Randy. *Conduct Unbecoming: Gays and Lesbians in the U.S. Military.* New York: St. Martin's Press, 1994.

5

SEXUAL PARTNERSHIPS: CHANGING NORMS AND DEFINITIONS OF MARRIAGE

"Marriage is one of the 'basic civil rights of man'..."

FREEDOM TO CHOOSE A PARTNER

5.1 Permitting Interracial Marriage: U.S. Supreme Court case of *Loving v. Virginia* (1968)

5.2 Providing a Marriage Alternative: San Francisco domestic partnership ordinance (1992)

5.3 Banning Same-Sex Marriages: The Defense of Marriage Act (DOMA) (1996)

5.4 Creating Civil Unions by Court Action: Vermont Supreme Court case of *Baker v. Vermont* (1999)

5.5 Establishing Marriage Equality for Same-Sex Couples: Massachusetts Supreme Court ruling in *Goodridge v. Massachusetts* (2003)

5.6 Affirming the "Dignity" of Same-Sex Couples: California Supreme Court ruling *In Re: Marriage Cases* (2008)

5.7 Legislating Civil Unions: The Connecticut State Law

THE RULES OF MARRIAGE: EVOLVING NORMS AND STANDARDS

5.8 Regulating Marriage and Sexual Behavior: Virginia criminal code excerpts (1975)

5.9 Recognizing Irreconcilable Differences: California "no-fault" divorce law (1970)

5.10 Outlawing Marital Rape: The Nebraska State Law (1976)

5.11 Eliminating Common-Law Marriage: Ohio law banning common law marriages (1991)

5.12 Promoting Lasting Unions: Arizona "covenant marriage" law (1998)

5.13 Continuing Prohibitions on Polygamy: Utah Supreme Court ruling in *State v. Green* (2004)

Introduction

At first glance, marriage can seem like a timeless and unchanging institution. Yet as anthropologists and historians alike can attest, concepts of marriage vary greatly from culture to culture and era to era. While biological reproduction may always involve one man and one woman (or more precisely one sperm and one ovum, at least thus far . . .), the forms of marriage as a social and personal institution vary greatly.

For example, some marriage norms have endorsed polygamy; others require monogamy. In some cultures, marriage has been less about the individuals involved than about strengthening bonds between families, or about safeguarding or transmitting wealth, or about forming viable economic household units. Some marriages are arranged by families or brokered by "matchmakers"; others are bound by strict social stratifications. Some are even about love and romance. In some legal systems, divorce is difficult or impossible; in others it is relatively easy for one or both partners. Some jurisdictions recognize only official marriages registered with civil authorities; others acknowledge long-term "common law" marriages even without a marriage certificate or ceremony. The variations are so great that it is impossible to speak of a single "institution of marriage."

In the United States, marriage norms have mostly adhered to those prevalent in the Western European Judeo-Christian tradition, which heavily emphasized the role of marriage in procreation and child rearing. Yet even a brief consideration of a few of the most prominent of the American founders reveals many different marital configurations. John and Abigail Adams had a five-decade, lifelong "peer relationship" and raised five children, one of whom became a U.S. president. As a relatively young widower, Thomas Jefferson developed a long-term relationship with the half-sister of his deceased wife—his slave Sally Hemings, with whom he had children who automatically also became his slaves. George Washington married a widow named Martha Custis and helped raise her children, but they had none of their own; he may have been infertile. Alexander Hamilton had an adulterous affair with a married woman that became public, ruined his political career, and indirectly led to the duel that ended his life.

Since the founding, marriage has been a recurrent theme of contention in the United States. Perhaps most famously, the Church of Jesus Christ of Latter-day Saints (the Mormons) were required to renounce their support for polygamy in order for Utah to enter the union. Throughout much of early American history, African American slaves were prohibited from marriage; even after Emancipation, segregation laws continued to prohibit marriage across racial lines. And until relatively recently, women were subordinated to "second-class citizenship" under the laws of marriage (see "Historical View" sidebar in this chapter).

Since 1965, there has been a major evolution in U.S. marriage norms toward greater autonomy in the selection of a partner and also in the conduct of marriage itself. Coming in 1967 at the tail end of the Civil Rights Movement, the Supreme Court case of *Loving v. Virginia* (Document 5.1) set a major modern precedent by its declaration that marriage is so fundamental a right that race and ethnicity cannot be barriers to partner selection. Recognizing that marriage is not the only viable model for a long-term relationship, San Francisco in 1990 enacted a domestic partnership law (Document 5.2), providing limited rights to committed couples—notably, whether of the opposite or the same sex.

More recently, the most polarizing source of contention has been whether to admit individuals of the same sex into the institution of marriage, or into some parallel institution with similar status and rights. The federal government has banned recognition of same-sex marriage through the "Defense of Marriage Act" (Document 5.3), a position taken by most of the individual states through laws or constitutional amendments. However, in 1999, the Vermont supreme court (Document 5.4) required that same-sex couples receive the same benefits of marriage. The court left it to the legislature to determine how to proceed, and they created a new status of "civil unions" with all the benefits of marriage without the name. Under court mandate, New Jersey did the same, while Connecticut created civil unions on its own (Document 5.7). Determining that civil unions were de facto unequal, the supreme courts of Massachusetts (Document 5.5) and California (Document 5.6) required that the institution of marriage itself in those states be opened to members of the same sex. The California ruling was overturned by a controversial referendum called Proposition 8 to amend the California State Constitution. Its ultimate disposition remains undetermined as of this writing.

Alongside the issue of who can marry, political battles have also been waged over what can happen once a marriage is commenced—including if and how it can be dissolved. The legal codes of many states include a variety of prohibitions on sexual behaviors relating to marriage status, including extramarital sex, which was categorized alongside incest and bigamy (Document 5.8 provides an example from Virginia). Over time, however, legal norms on other issues have changed. Women's autonomy has been enhanced by the exclusion of a long-standing "martial exception" to rape laws (see Nebraska's groundbreaking legislation in Document 5.10). Recognition of the long-standing practice of common law marriage has been decreasing (see an example from Ohio in Document 5.11, while the ability to exit a marriage has been simplified through the concept of "no-fault" divorce (see the first statute from California in Document 5.9).

Partly in reaction to these trends, some states have begun to create new forms of "covenant" marriage which, once chosen, make it *more* difficult to end a marriage. (Document 5.11). At the same time, a ban has remained in place on polygamy, one of the most ancient expressions of marriage, most recently affirmed by the Utah Supreme Court (Document 5.12).

"Marriage is one of the 'basic civil rights of man'..."

Freedom to Choose a Partner

Although the Fourteenth Amendment to the U.S. Constitution was ratified in 1870 to ensure "equal protection under the law," it was not until nearly a century later that Congress asserted its proper role in ensuring equal rights on the basis of race and ethnicity. Until then, an odious system of legalized segregation in the South—and de facto segregation in many other places—separated the races, to the acute disadvantage of minorities. However, the Civil Rights Act of 1964 outlawed discrimination in such areas as housing, employment, and education, while the Voting Rights Act of 1965 prohibited mechanisms such as literacy tests designed to block the ability of African Americans to vote.

It was in the context of these and other major breakthroughs that the Supreme Court was presented with the opportunity to dismantle segregation within the most intimate of human relationships: marriage. During the era of segregation, "racial integrity" laws in many states, mainly but not only in the South, prohibited "miscegenation" or the marriage of a white person to a nonwhite person. Applying the peculiar logic of racial discrimination then prevalent, the law in Virginia specified that:

[A]ll marriages between a white person and a colored person shall be absolutely void without any decree of divorce or other legal process . . . It shall hereafter be unlawful for any white person in this State to marry any save a white person, or a person with no other admixture of blood than white and American Indian. For the purpose of this chapter, the term "white person" shall apply only to such person as has no trace whatever of any blood other than Caucasian; but persons who have one-sixteenth or less of the blood of the

American Indian and have no other non-Caucasic blood shall be deemed to be white persons . . .

Violators of the law—including Richard and Mildred Loving in 1959—could be convicted of a felony and sentenced to prison, in addition to having their marriage declared void within Virginia. In the case of *Loving v. Virginia*, the 1967 landmark (Document 5.1), the Supreme Court unanimously invalidated all remaining anti-miscegenation laws. "These statutes," stated the Supreme Court, "deprive the Lovings of liberty without due process of law in violation of the Due Process Clause of the Fourteenth Amendment. The freedom to marry has long been recognized as one of the vital personal rights essential to the orderly pursuit of happiness by free men."

A similar logic has animated the debate over whether marriage should be limited only to people of the opposite sex. Although there is some evidence that same-sex unions have in various forms been recognized in different times and places historically, the logic of procreation (and the legacy of deeply entrenched homophobia) has mostly limited marriage to members of the opposite sex. On the other hand, marriage as an institution has been to a great extent delinked from procreation in modern society via hormonal and barrier forms of contraception and surgical sterilization and abortion. Similarly, marriages involving people known to be infertile or women who are postmenopausal are common and uncontroversial.

In this new social reality, then, marriage is largely a vehicle for personal commitment between two people—a situation in which homosexuals and bisexuals may find themselves as frequently as heterosexuals. To a great extent, then, the debate over same-sex marriage has been as much about the nature of marriage itself as about gay and lesbian rights (which is the reason it is covered in this chapter). Proponents of opening marriage to members of the same sex thus prefer the term "marriage equality."

Some of the earliest legal steps in acknowledging the changing nature of sexual partnerships began in major urban centers with large gay and lesbian populations. While falling well short of full marriage, "domestic partnerships" began to be offered by some cities guaranteeing such rights as hospital visitation and succession in apartments. Most of these apply only to members of the same sex (because they are ineligible to marry), although one of the earliest—enacted by Washington, DC, in 1992—includes opposite-sex couples as well (see Document 5.2). Since then, numerous cities and several states have enacted domestic partnership laws, varying widely in the rights they provide.

Much as it had played a crucial role in ending racial segregation, litigation in the courts has been central to the question of same-sex marriage. A crucial early case took place in 1993 when the Hawaii Supreme Court ruled that excluding same-sex couples from marriage constituted sex discrimination. The court did not, however, immediately order the issuance of marriage licenses, and in 1998, the people of Hawaii voted to amend their constitution to allow the legislature to limit marriage to people of the opposite sex. Underscoring the ambiguity of the debate, the Hawaii state legislature took advantage of their new power—but then also created statewide domestic partnership rights as well, a route later also followed by California, Maine, Washington State, and Oregon.

Recognizing that another court might some day mandate same-sex matrimony, social conservatives mobilized in the mid-1990s to preserve traditional marriage. They were concerned in particular that the "full faith and credit" clause of Article IV of the Constitution might require a same-sex marriage recognized in one state to be recognized by the other 49 and by the federal government as well. Their preferred vehicle was an amendment to the U.S. Constitution, but since this is so difficult to accomplish, they settled instead for the "Defense of Marriage Act" (DOMA), the text of which is presented in Document 5.3.

Subsequently, enactment began of state-level DOMAs as well as Hawaii-style constitutional amendments, until most of the states had prohibited same-sex marriage of one type or another. The major exceptions occurred, perhaps not surprisingly, in the nation's most liberal region, the Northeast. In the case of *Baker v. Vermont* (Document 5.4) the Vermont Supreme Court demanded equality for same-sex couples, although it allowed that such unions need not necessarily be termed "marriages," and the state legislature then created a parallel institution of "civil unions." A similar trajectory occurred in New Jersey, and then the Connecticut legislature created civil unions on its own, without a court order. (The Connecticut legislation is provided in Document 5.7.) The use of the term "civil union" is more political than legal, since the actual rights conferred to same-sex couples are in theory identical to those of opposite-sex couples. Thus, the term is intended to defer to the sensibilities of traditionalists who think of "marriage" in religious terms. Early evidence from New Jersey, however, has suggested that "civil unions" are, in fact, not only separate but also unequal in that in practice they are not recognized or accepted as truly equal in practice.

The boldest move, however, came from the Massachusetts Supreme Court (Document 5.5), which ruled in 2003 not only that same-sex couples had to be treated in identical fashion as opposite-sex couples but that their unions also had to be termed "marriages." The Court found that

> [t]he marriage ban works a deep and scarring hardship on a very real segment of the community for no rational reason. The absence of any reasonable relationship between, on the one hand, an absolute disqualification of same-sex couples who wish to enter into civil marriage and, on the other, protection of public health, safety, or general welfare, suggests that the marriage restriction is rooted in persistent prejudices against persons who are (or who are believed to be) homosexual.

In 2008, the California state supreme court (Document 5.6) expanded upon and confirmed the Massachusetts precedent, and the nation's largest state began issuing marriage licenses to same-sex couples that June. This halted in November, however, after the California State Constitution was amended via a controversial referendum known as Proposition 8.

As of this writing, the issue of same-sex marriage remains highly fluid and volatile. On the one hand, Massachusetts, Vermont, and New Hampshire are but three jurisdictions among several internationally that have begun offering marriage equality, including several entire countries (see "Comparative View" sidebar in this chapter). On the other hand, opposition to same-sex marriage remains solid, even vehement, in many areas of the United States. Opposition is decidedly stronger among older than among younger people, however. Similarly, the example of same-sex marriage in states where it is legal (as well as, to a lesser extent, throughout neighboring Canada) has tended to defuse arguments that admission of same-sex marriages somehow fundamentally alters the nature of marriage as an institution. In the near term, the relatively murky institutions of "domestic partnerships" and "civil unions" may continue to expand as a point of compromise over conflicting views of the nature and function of marriage.

Document 5.1: Permitting Interracial Marriage

- **Document:** Supreme Court opinion in the case of *Loving v. Virginia*
- **Date:** June 12, 1967
- **Where:** U.S. Supreme Court, Washington, DC
- **Significance:** Coming on the heels of the Civil Rights Movement and desegregation, this ruling struck down all existing "anti-miscegenation" laws designed to prevent interracial marriage.

SUPREME COURT OF THE UNITED STATES

388 U.S. 1

Loving v. Virginia

APPEAL FROM THE SUPREME COURT OF APPEALS OF VIRGINIA

No. 395

Argued: April 10, 1967—Decided: June 12, 1967

MR. CHIEF JUSTICE WARREN delivered the opinion of the Court.

This case presents a constitutional question never addressed by this Court: whether a statutory scheme adopted by the State of Virginia to prevent marriages between persons solely on the basis of racial classifications violates the Equal Protection and Due Process Clauses of the Fourteenth

Amendment. For reasons which seem to us to reflect the central meaning of those constitutional commands, we conclude that these statutes cannot stand consistently with the Fourteenth Amendment.

In June, 1958, two residents of Virginia, Mildred Jeter, a Negro woman, and Richard Loving, a white man, were married in the District of Columbia pursuant to its laws. Shortly after their marriage, the Lovings returned to Virginia and established their marital abode in Caroline County. At the October Term, 1958, of the Circuit Court of Caroline County, a grand jury issued an indictment charging the Lovings with violating Virginia's ban on interracial marriages. On January 6, 1959, the Lovings pleaded guilty to the charge, and were sentenced to one year in jail; however, the trial judge suspended the sentence for a period of 25 years on the condition that the Lovings leave the State and not return to Virginia together for 25 years. He stated in an opinion that:

Richard and Mildred Loving were convicted in 1961 of violating a Virginia law prohibiting racially "mixed" marriages. In June 1967 the U.S. Supreme Court's decision in *Loving v. Virginia* overturned the Virginia statute, invalidating such laws in more than a dozen states. (AP Photo)

Almighty God created the races white, black, yellow, malay and red, and he placed them on separate continents. And, but for the interference with his arrangement, there would be no cause for such marriage. The fact that he separated the races shows that he did not intend for the races to mix . . .

The two statutes under which appellants were convicted and sentenced are part of a comprehensive statutory scheme aimed at prohibiting and punishing interracial marriages. The Lovings were convicted of violating § 258 of the Virginia Code:

Leaving State to evade law.—If any white person and colored person shall go out of this State, for the purpose of being married, and with the intention of returning, and be married out of it, and afterwards return to and reside in it, cohabiting as man and wife, they shall be punished as provided in § 20-59, and the marriage shall be governed by the same law as if it had been solemnized in this State. The fact of their cohabitation here as man and wife shall be evidence of their marriage.

Section 259, which defines the penalty for miscegenation, provides:

Punishment for marriage.—If any white person intermarry with a colored person, or any colored person intermarry with a white person, he shall be guilty of a felony and shall be punished by confinement in the penitentiary for not less than one nor more than five years.

Other central provisions in the Virginia statutory scheme are § 20-57, which automatically voids all marriages between "a white person and a colored person" without any judicial proceeding, and §§ 20-54 and 1-14 which, [p5] respectively, define "white persons" and "colored

> "The Fourteenth Amendment requires that the freedom of choice to marry not be restricted by invidious racial discriminations. Under our Constitution, the freedom to marry, or not marry, a person of another race resides with the individual, and cannot be infringed by the State."

persons and Indians" for purposes of the statutory prohibitions. The Lovings have never disputed in the course of this litigation that Mrs. Loving is a "colored person" or that Mr. Loving is a "white person" within the meanings given those terms by the Virginia statutes.

Virginia is now one of 16 States which prohibit and punish marriages on the basis of racial classifications. Penalties for miscegenation arose as an incident to slavery, and have been common in Virginia since the colonial period. The present statutory scheme dates from the adoption of the Racial Integrity Act of 1924, passed during the period of extreme nativism which followed the end of the First World War. The central features of this Act, and current Virginia law, are the absolute prohibition of a "white person" marrying other than another "white person," a prohibition against issuing marriage licenses until the issuing official is satisfied that the applicants' statements as to their race are correct, certificates of "racial composition" to be kept by both local and state registrars, and the carrying forward of earlier prohibitions against racial intermarriage.

In upholding the constitutionality of these provisions in the decision below, the Supreme Court of Appeals of Virginia referred to its 1965 decision in Naim v. Naim, as stating the reasons supporting the validity of these laws. In Naim, the state court concluded that the State's legitimate purposes were "to preserve the racial integrity of its citizens," and to prevent "the corruption of blood," "a mongrel breed of citizens," and "the obliteration of racial pride," obviously an endorsement of the doctrine of White Supremacy. The court also reasoned that marriage has traditionally been subject to state regulation without federal intervention, and, consequently, the regulation of marriage should be left to exclusive state control by the Tenth Amendment . . .

There is patently no legitimate overriding purpose independent of invidious racial discrimination which justifies this classification. The fact that Virginia prohibits only interracial marriages involving white persons demonstrates that the racial classifications must stand on their own justification, as measures designed to maintain White Supremacy. We have consistently denied the constitutionality of measures which restrict the rights of citizens on account of race. There can be no doubt that restricting the freedom to marry solely because of racial classifications violates the central meaning of the Equal Protection Clause.

II

These statutes also deprive the Lovings of liberty without due process of law in violation of the Due Process Clause of the Fourteenth Amendment. The freedom to marry has long been recognized as one of the vital personal rights essential to the orderly pursuit of happiness by free men.

Marriage is one of the "basic civil rights of man," fundamental to our very existence and survival. To deny this fundamental freedom on so unsupportable a basis as the racial classifications embodied in these statutes, classifications so directly subversive of the principle of equality at the heart of the Fourteenth Amendment, is surely to deprive all the State's citizens of liberty without due process of law. The Fourteenth Amendment requires that the freedom of choice to marry not be restricted by invidious racial discriminations. Under our Constitution, the freedom to marry, or not marry, a person of another race resides with the individual, and cannot be infringed by the State.

These convictions must be reversed.

Document 5.2: Providing a Marriage Alternative

- **Document:** Proposition K, enacted by the voters of San Francisco, creating domestic partnerships in the city
- **Date:** November 6, 1990
- **Where:** City Hall, San Francisco, California
- **Significance:** This domestic partnership law recognizes relationships between members both of the opposite and of the same sex, outside of the traditional definition of marriage. Since it is only a municipal ordinance, however, it can confer only limited rights, such as retirement benefits for the surviving partner of a city employee.

San Francisco Administrative Code

CHAPTER 62

DOMESTIC PARTNERSHIPS

SEC. 62.1. PURPOSE.

The purpose of this ordinance is to create a way to recognize intimate committed relationships, including those of same-sex couples who otherwise may be denied the right to marry under California law, and to afford to domestic partners, to the fullest extent legally possible, the same rights, benefits, responsibilities, obligations, and duties as spouses. All costs of registration must be covered by fees to be established by ordinance.

SEC. 62.2. DEFINITIONS.

> "Domestic Partners are two adults who have chosen to share one another's lives in an intimate and committed relationship of mutual caring, who live together, and who have agreed to be jointly responsible for basic living expenses."

(a) Domestic Partnership. Domestic Partners are two adults who have chosen to share one another's lives in an intimate and committed relationship of mutual caring, who live together, and who have agreed to be jointly responsible for basic living expenses incurred during the Domestic Partnership. They must sign a Declaration of Domestic Partnership, and establish the partnership under Section 62.3 of this chapter.

(b) "Live Together." "Live together" means that two people share the same living quarters. It is not necessary that the legal right to possess the quarters be in both of their names. Two people may live together even if one or both have additional living quarters. Domestic Partners do not cease to live together if one leaves the shared quarters but intends to return.

(c) "Basic Living Expenses." "Basic living expenses" means the cost of basic food and shelter. It also includes the expenses which are paid at least in part by a program or benefit for which the partner qualified because of the domestic partnership. The individuals need not contribute equally or jointly to the cost of these expenses as long as they agree that both are responsible for the costs.

(d) "Declaration of Domestic Partnership." A "Declaration of Domestic Partnership" is a form provided by the County Clerk. By signing it, two people agree to be jointly responsible for basic living expenses which they incur during the domestic partnership and that this agreement can be enforced by anyone to whom those expenses are owed. They also state under penalty of perjury that they met the definition of domestic partnership when they signed the statement, that neither is married, and that they are not related to each other in a way which would bar marriage in California . . .

SEC. 62.4. ENDING DOMESTIC PARTNERSHIPS.

(a) When the Partnership Ends. A Domestic Partnership ends when:

(1) One partner sends the other a written notice that he or she has ended the partnership; or
(2) One of the partners dies; or
(3) One of the partners marries or the partners no longer live together . . .

Document 5.3: Banning Same-Sex Marriages

- *Document:* The Defense of Marriage Act (DOMA) of 1996
- *Date:* January 3, 1996
- *Where:* U.S. Capitol, Washington, DC
- *Significance:* Lawmakers were concerned that the recognition of same-sex marriages by one state would require recognition by all the other states, and the federal government. This Act is intended to preclude that possibility.

Defense of Marriage Act
(Enrolled as Agreed to or Passed by Both House and Senate)

H.R.3396

One Hundred Fourth Congress of the United States of America

AT THE SECOND SESSION

Begun and held at the City of Washington on Wednesday, the third day of January, one thousand nine hundred and ninety-six

An Act to define and protect the institution of marriage.
Be it enacted by the Senate and House of Representatives of the United States of America in Congress assembled,
This Act may be cited as the "Defense of Marriage Act"...

"No State, territory, or possession of the United States, or Indian tribe, shall be required to give

"The word 'marriage' means only a legal union between one man and one woman as husband and wife, and the word 'spouse' refers only to a person of the opposite sex who is a husband or a wife ..."

Comparative View: Same-Sex Marriage around the World

For the first time, lesbian, gay, and bisexual (LGB) people in a number of countries have begun to be provided with full equality in the area of marriage rights. On the whole, however, the right to marry a person of the same gender exists for only a tiny percentage of the world's population.

Unsurprisingly, the most progressive region of the world with regard to same-sex marriage has been Western Europe. The Netherlands began the trend in 2001, with Belgium, Spain, Sweden, and Norway following. Parallel institutions, such as civil unions, have also been introduced in 12 other countries, including such Central European states as Hungary, Slovenia, and the Czech Republic.

In North America, Canada has led the way. When the Canadian Charter of Rights and Freedoms was written into its constitution in 1982, sexual orientation was not explicitly stipulated as a protected characteristic. Indeed, a decade elapsed before the Supreme Court of Canada found that sexual orientation amounted to a protected class under the charter. The decision was met with some controversy; however, it set the framework for later LGB plaintiffs. Although the federal government extended many of the financial benefits of marriage to same-sex couples in 1999, provincial jurisdictions varied on the issue. Throughout the provinces, same-sex couples challenged marital statutes in the respective court systems at the turn of the twenty-first century. In 2003, Ontario became the first province to offer full marriage benefits to same-sex couples; Quebec, British Columbia, and other Canadian provinces soon followed. By 2005, the federal parliament had legalized same-sex marriage throughout the entire country, with relatively little controversy. In the rest of the Americas, only a few U.S. states, Washington, D.C., and Mexico City offer full marriage equality.

Perhaps the most surprising foothold for same-sex marriage has been the Republic of South Africa. Under its Apartheid government, South Africa was no stranger to discriminatory policies. LGB activists found mobilizing difficult in such an unfriendly atmosphere. It was not until the late 1980s that a hard-and-fast LGB agenda across racial lines stood much chance of being adopted by political actors. By the 1990s, with the ban on the African National Congress lifted and Apartheid in its death throes, the LGB message developed political teeth. Adopting a zero-tolerance policy against discrimination,

A South African lesbian couple display their engagement rings after the South African Parliament approved legislation recognizing gay marriage in November 2006. (AP Photo/Denis Farrell)

the new South African government drafted a constitution that included provisions for the protection of sexual orientation against discrimination. Following a court ruling that interpreted these rights expansively, same-sex marriage was established in 2006.—*Brandon L. H. Aultman*

effect to any public act, record, or judicial proceeding of any other State, territory, possession, or tribe respecting a relationship between persons of the same sex that is treated as a marriage under the laws of such other State, territory, possession, or tribe, or a right or claim arising from such relationship."...

In determining the meaning of any Act of Congress, or of any ruling, regulation, or interpretation of the various administrative bureaus and agencies of the United States, the word "marriage" means only a legal union between one man and one woman as husband and wife, and the word "spouse" refers only to a person of the opposite sex who is a husband or a wife...

Speaker of the House of Representatives.

Vice President of the United States and President of the Senate.

Document 5.4: Creating Civil Unions by Court Action

- **Document:** Excerpts from the Vermont Supreme Court ruling in *Baker v. Vermont*
- **Date:** December 20, 1999
- **Where:** Vermont Supreme Court, Montpelier, Vermont
- **Significance:** This landmark ruling established that, under the "common benefits" provision of the Vermont State Constitution, members of the same sex could not be denied equal access to the benefits of the institution of marriage, though not necessarily the word "marriage."

ENTRY ORDER
SUPREME COURT DOCKET NO. 98 -032
NOVEMBER TERM, 1998

APPEALED FROM:
Stan Baker, et al. v. Chittenden Superior Court

State of Vermont, et al.

DOCKET NO. 1009-97CnC

May the State of Vermont exclude same-sex couples from the benefits and protections that its laws provide to opposite-sex married couples? That is the fundamental question we address in this appeal, a question that the Court well knows arouses deeply-felt religious, moral, and political beliefs. Our constitutional responsibility to consider the legal merits of issues properly before us provides no exception for the controversial case. The issue before the Court, moreover, does not turn on the religious or moral debate over intimate same-sex relationships, but rather on the statutory and constitutional basis for the exclusion of same-sex couples from the secular benefits and protections offered married couples.

In 2009, having recognized civil unions between people of the same sex since 2000, Vermont legalized gay marriage after the state's legislature overrode the governor's veto. Supporters had held that civil unions did not represent full equality for same-sex couples. (AP Photo/Toby Talbot)

We conclude that under the Common Benefits Clause of the Vermont Constitution, which, in pertinent part, reads, That government is, or ought to be, instituted for the common benefit, protection, and security of the people, nation, or community, and not for the particular emolument or advantage of any single person, family, or set of persons, who are a part only of that community, Vt. Const., ch. I, art 7., plaintiffs may not be deprived of the statutory benefits and protections afforded persons of the opposite sex who choose to marry. We hold that the State is constitutionally required to extend to same-sex couples the common benefits and protections that flow from marriage under Vermont law. Whether this ultimately takes the form of inclusion within the marriage laws themselves or a parallel "domestic partnership" system or some equivalent statutory alternative, rests with the Legislature. Whatever system is chosen, however, must conform with the constitutional imperative to afford all Vermonters the common benefit, protection, and security of the law.

Plaintiffs are three same-sex couples who have lived together in committed relationships for periods ranging from four to twenty-five years. Two of the couples have raised children together. Each couple applied for a marriage license from their respective town clerk, and each

> "The State is constitutionally required to extend to same-sex couples the common benefits and protections that flow from marriage under Vermont law."

was refused a license as ineligible under the applicable state marriage laws. Plaintiffs thereupon filed this lawsuit against defendants—the State of Vermont, the Towns of Milton and Shelburne, and the City of South Burlington—seeking a declaratory judgment that the refusal to issue them a license violated the marriage statutes and the Vermont Constitution . . .

III. Conclusion

While many have noted the symbolic or spiritual significance of the marital relation, it is plaintiffs' claim to the secular benefits and protections of a singularly human relationship that, in our view, characterizes this case. The State's interest in extending official recognition and legal protection to the professed commitment of two individuals to a lasting relationship of mutual affection is predicated on the belief that legal support of a couple's commitment provides stability for the individuals, their family, and the broader community. Although plaintiffs' interest in seeking state recognition and protection of their mutual commitment may—in view of divorce statistics—represent "the triumph of hope over experience" the essential aspect of their claim is simply and fundamentally for inclusion in the family of State-sanctioned human relations. The past provides many instances where the law refused to see a human being when it should have. The future may provide instances where the law will be asked to see a human when it should not.

The challenge for future generations will be to define what is most essentially human. The extension of the Common Benefits Clause to acknowledge plaintiffs as Vermonters who seek nothing more, nor less, than legal protection and security for their avowed commitment to an intimate and lasting human relationship is simply, when all is said and done, a recognition of our common humanity. The judgment of the superior court upholding the constitutionality of the Vermont marriage statutes under Chapter I, Article 7 of the Vermont Constitution is reversed. The effect of the Court's decision is suspended, and jurisdiction is retained in this Court, to permit the Legislature to consider and enact legislation consistent with the constitutional mandate described herein . . .

Document 5.5: Establishing Marriage Equality for Same-Sex Couples

- **Document:** Massachusetts State Supreme Judicial Court ruling in the case of *Goodridge v. Department of Health and Commissioner of Health*, including portions of the majority opinion and dissenting opinions
- **Date:** November 18, 2003
- **Where:** State Supreme Judicial Court Building, Boston, Massachusetts
- **Significance:** Although various courts had previously found grounds for the constitutional recognition of same-sex unions, this case was a breakthrough in that it required the state of Massachusetts to open marriage itself, not a parallel (and lesser) status.

Massachusetts Supreme Judicial Court

Hillary Goodridge, et al. v. Department of Public Health and Commissioner of Public Health, 440 Mass. 309 (2003)

SJC-08860

Argued March 4, 2003

Decided November 18, 2003

JUSTICE MARSHALL delivered the opinion of the court.

Marriage is a vital social institution. The exclusive commitment of two individuals to each other nurtures love and mutual support; it brings stability to our society. For those who choose to marry, and for their children, marriage provides an abundance of legal, financial, and social benefits. In return it imposes weighty legal, financial, and social obligations. The question before us is whether, consistent with the Massachusetts Constitution, the Commonwealth may deny the protections, benefits, and obligations conferred by civil marriage to two individuals of the same sex who wish to marry. We conclude that it may not. The Massachusetts Constitution affirms the dignity and equality of all individuals. It forbids the creation of second-class citizens. In reaching our conclusion we have given full deference to the arguments made by the Commonwealth. But it has failed to identify any constitutionally adequate reason for denying civil marriage to same-sex couples . . .

The plaintiffs' claim that the marriage restriction violates the Massachusetts Constitution can be analyzed in two ways. Does it offend the Constitution's guarantees of equality before the law? Or do the liberty and due process provisions of the Massachusetts Constitution secure the plaintiffs' right to marry their chosen partner? . . . Without the right to marry—or more properly, the right to choose to marry—one is excluded from the full range of human experience and denied full protection of the laws. . . . Because civil marriage is central to the lives of individuals and the welfare of the community, our laws assiduously protect the individual's right to marry against undue government incursion. Laws may not "interfere directly and substantially with the right to marry."

. . . The individual liberty and equality safeguards of the Massachusetts Constitution protect both "freedom from" unwarranted government intrusion into protected spheres of life and "freedom to" partake in benefits created by the State for the common good. Both freedoms are involved here. Whether and whom to marry, how to express sexual intimacy, and whether and how to establish a family—these are among the most basic of every individual's liberty and due process rights.

. . . The marriage ban works a deep and scarring hardship on a very real segment of the community for no rational reason. The absence of any reasonable relationship between, on the one hand, an absolute disqualification of same-sex couples who wish to enter into civil marriage and, on the other, protection of public health, safety, or general welfare, suggests that the marriage restriction is rooted in persistent prejudices against persons who are (or who are believed to be) homosexual. Limiting the protections, benefits, and obligations of civil marriage to opposite-sex couples violates the basic premises of individual liberty and equality under law protected by the Massachusetts Constitution . . .

We construe civil marriage to mean the voluntary union of two persons as spouses, to the exclusion of all others. This reformulation redresses the plaintiffs' constitutional injury and furthers the aim of marriage to promote stable, exclusive relationships. It advances the two legitimate State interests the department has identified: providing a stable setting for child rearing and conserving State resources. It leaves intact the Legislature's broad discretion to regulate marriage.

. . . We declare that barring an individual from the protections, benefits, and obligations of civil marriage solely because that person would marry a person of the same sex violates the Massachusetts Constitution. We vacate the summary judgment for the department. We remand this case to the Superior Court for entry of judgment consistent with this opinion. Entry of judgment shall be stayed for 180 days to permit the Legislature to take such action as it may deem appropriate in light of this opinion.

JUSTICE SPINA, with whom JUSTICE SOSMAN and JUSTICE CORDY join, dissenting.

What is at stake in this case is not the unequal treatment of individuals or whether individual rights have been impermissibly burdened, but the power of the Legislature to effectuate social change without interference from the courts. . . . The power to regulate marriage lies with the Legislature, not with the judiciary. Today, the court has transformed its role as protector of individual rights into the role of creator of rights, and I respectfully dissent.

. . . The marriage statutes do not disqualify individuals on the basis of sexual orientation from entering into marriage. All individuals, with certain exceptions not relevant here, are free to marry. Whether an individual chooses not to marry because of sexual orientation or any other reason should be of no concern to the court.

. . . Same-sex marriage, or the "right to marry the person of one's choice" as the court today defines that right, does not fall within the fundamental right to marry. Same-sex marriage is not "deeply rooted in this Nation's history," and the court does not suggest that it is. . . . Same-sex marriage is not a right, fundamental or otherwise, recognized in this country. . . . In this Commonwealth and in this country, the roots of the institution of marriage are deeply set in history as a civil union between a single man and a single woman. There is no basis for the court to recognize same-sex marriage as a constitutionally protected right.

JUSTICE SOSMAN, with whom JUSTICE SPINA and JUSTICE CORDY join, dissenting.
. . . Conspicuously absent from the court's opinion today is any acknowledgment that the attempts at scientific study of the ramifications of raising children in same-sex couple households are themselves in their infancy and have so far produced inconclusive and conflicting results. Notwithstanding our belief that gender and sexual orientation of parents should not matter to the success of the child rearing venture, studies to date reveal that there are still some observable differences between children raised by opposite-sex couples and children raised by same-sex couples. Interpretation of the data gathered by those studies then becomes clouded by the personal and political beliefs of the investigators, both as to whether the differences identified are positive or negative, and as to the untested explanations of what might account for those differences. . . . The Legislature can rationally view the state of the scientific evidence as unsettled on the critical question it now faces: Are families headed by same-sex parents equally successful in rearing children from infancy to adulthood as families headed by parents of opposite sexes? Our belief that children raised by same-sex couples should fare the same as children raised in traditional families is just that: a passionately held but utterly untested belief. The Legislature is not required to share that belief but may, as the creator of the institution of civil marriage, wish to see the proof before making a fundamental alteration to that institution.

. . . As a matter of social history, today's opinion may represent a great turning point that many will hail as a tremendous step toward a more just society. As a matter of constitutional jurisprudence, however, the case stands as an aberration. . . . The exclusion of gay and lesbian couples from the institution of civil marriage passes constitutional muster. I respectfully dissent.

JUSTICE CORDY, with whom JUSTICE SPINA and JUSTICE SOSMAN join, dissenting.

The court's opinion concludes that the Department of Public Health has failed to identify any "constitutionally adequate reason" for limiting civil marriage to opposite-sex unions, and that there is no "reasonable relationship" between a disqualification of same-sex couples who wish to enter into a civil marriage and the protection of public health, safety, or general welfare. Consequently, it holds that the marriage statute cannot withstand scrutiny under the Massachusetts Constitution. Because I find these conclusions to be unsupportable in light of

"Without the right to marry—or more properly, the right to choose to marry—one is excluded from the full range of human experience and denied full protection of the laws. . . ."

the nature of the rights and regulations at issue, the presumption of constitutional validity and significant deference afforded to legislative enactments, and the "undesirability of the judiciary substituting its notions of correct policy for that of a popularly elected Legislature" responsible for making such policy, I respectfully dissent. Although it may be desirable for many reasons to extend to same-sex couples the benefits and burdens of civil marriage (and the plaintiffs have made a powerfully reasoned case for that extension), that decision must be made by the Legislature, not the court.

Document 5.6: Affirming the "Dignity" of Same-Sex Couples

- *Document:* Excerpts from the California Supreme Court ruling of *In Re: Marriage Cases*
- *Date:* May 15, 2008
- *Where:* California Supreme Court, Sacramento, California
- *Significance:* With this ruling, the California State Supreme Court eliminated legal distinctions between same-sex couples and opposite-sex couples, excluding the former from "marriage." The Court reasoned that by denying same-sex couples the respect and dignity afforded the opposite-sex partners via "marriage," the statutes infringed on the Equal Protections guarantees of the California Constitution. The ruling was overturned by a state constitutional amendment on November 5, 2008, via a referendum called Proposition 8. The outcome of legal challenges in this case remain unresolved as of this writing.

In re MARRIAGE CASES.

City and County of San Francisco v. State of California (A110449 [Super. Ct. S.F. City & County, No. CGC-04-429539]); Tyler v. State of California (A110450 [Super. Ct. L.A. County, No. BS-088506]); Woo v. Lockyer (A110451 [Super. Ct. S.F. City & County, No. CPF-04-504038]); Clinton v. State of California (A110463 [Super. Ct. S.F. City & County, No. CGC-04-429548]); Proposition 22 Legal Defense and Education Fund v. City and County of San Francisco (A110651 [Super. Ct. S.F. City & County, No. CPF-04-503943]); Campaign for California Families v. Newsom (A110652 [Super. Ct. S.F. City & County, No. CGC-04-428794]).

S147999

SUPREME COURT OF CALIFORNIA

43 Cal. 4th 757; 76 Cal. Rptr. 3d 683; 2008 Cal. LEXIS 5247

May 15, 2008, Filed

JUDGES: Opinion by George, C. J., with Kennard, Werdegar, and Moreno, JJ., concurring. Concurring opinion by Kennard, J.

Concurring and dissenting opinion by Baxter, J., with Chin, J., concurring. Concurring and dissenting opinion by Corrigan, J.

CHIEF JUSTICE GEORGE delivered the opinion of the court,

In *Lockyer v. City and County of San Francisco* (2004), this court concluded that public officials of the City and County of San Francisco acted unlawfully by issuing marriage licenses to same-sex couples in the absence of a judicial determination that the California statutes limiting marriage to a union between a man and a woman are unconstitutional. Our decision in Lockyer emphasized, however, that the substantive question of the constitutional validity of the California marriage statutes was not before this court in that proceeding, and that our decision was not intended to reflect any view on that issue. The present proceeding, involving the consolidated appeal of six cases that were litigated in the superior court and the Court of Appeal in the wake of this court's decision in Lockyer, squarely presents the substantive constitutional question that was not addressed in Lockyer.

In considering this question, we note at the outset that the constitutional issue before us differs in a significant respect from the constitutional issue that has been addressed by a number of other state supreme courts and intermediate appellate courts that recently have had occasion, in interpreting the applicable provisions of their respective state constitutions, to determine the validity of statutory provisions or common law rules limiting marriage to a union of a man and a woman. These courts, often by a one-vote margin, have ruled upon the validity of statutory schemes that contrast with that of California, which in recent years has enacted comprehensive domestic partnership legislation under which a same-sex couple may enter into a legal relationship that affords the couple virtually all of the same legal benefits and privileges, and imposes upon the couple virtually all of the same legal obligations and duties, that California law affords to and imposes upon a married couple . . .

Accordingly, the legal issue we must resolve is not whether it would be constitutionally permissible under the California Constitution for the state to limit marriage only to opposite-sex couples while denying same-sex couples any opportunity to enter into an official relationship with all or virtually all of the same substantive attributes, but rather whether our state Constitution prohibits the state from establishing a statutory scheme in which both opposite-sex and same-sex couples are granted the right to enter into an officially recognized family relationship that affords all of the significant legal rights and obligations traditionally associated under state law with the institution of marriage, but under which the union of an opposite-sex couple is officially designated a "marriage" whereas the union of a same-sex couple is officially designated a "domestic partnership." The question we must address is whether, under these circumstances, the failure to designate the official relationship of same-sex couples as marriage violates the California Constitution.

First, we must determine the nature and scope of the "right to marry"—a right that past cases establish as one of the fundamental constitutional rights embodied in the California Constitution. . . . We conclude that, under this state's Constitution, the constitutionally based right to marry properly must be understood to encompass the core set of basic substantive legal rights and attributes traditionally associated with marriage that are so integral to an individual's liberty and personal autonomy that they may not be eliminated or abrogated by the Legislature or by the electorate through the statutory initiative process. These core substantive rights include, most fundamentally, the opportunity of an individual to establish—with the person with whom the individual has chosen to share his or her life—an officially recognized and protected family possessing mutual rights and responsibilities and entitled to the same respect and dignity accorded a union traditionally designated as marriage. As past cases establish, the substantive right of two adults who share a loving relationship to join together to establish an officially recognized family of their own—and, if the couple chooses, to raise children within that family—constitutes a vitally important attribute of the fundamental interest in liberty and personal autonomy that the California Constitution secures to all persons for the benefit of both the individual and society . . .

Under the current statutes, the state has not revised the name of the official family relationship for all couples, but rather has drawn a distinction between the name for the official family relationship of opposite-sex couples (marriage) and that for same-sex couples (domestic partnership). One of the core elements of the right to establish an officially recognized family that is embodied in the California constitutional right to marry is a couple's right to have their family relationship accorded dignity and respect equal to that accorded other officially recognized families, and assigning a different designation for the family relationship of same-sex couples while reserving the historic designation of "marriage" exclusively for opposite-sex couples poses at least a serious risk of denying the family relationship of same-sex couples such equal dignity and respect. We therefore conclude that although the provisions of the current domestic partnership legislation afford same-sex couples most of the substantive elements embodied in the constitutional right to marry, the current California statutes nonetheless must be viewed as potentially impinging upon a same-sex couple's constitutional right to marry under the California Constitution . . .

In the present case, it is readily apparent that extending the designation of marriage to same-sex couples clearly is more consistent with the probable legislative intent than withholding that designation from both opposite-sex couples and same-sex couples in favor of some other, uniform designation. In view of the lengthy history of the use of the term "marriage" to describe the family relationship here at issue, and the importance that both the supporters of the 1977 amendment to the marriage statutes and the electors who voted in favor of Proposition 22 unquestionably attached to the designation of marriage, there can be no doubt that extending the designation of marriage to same-sex couples, rather than denying it to all couples, is the equal protection remedy that is most consistent with our state's general legislative policy and preference.

Accordingly, in light of the conclusions we reach concerning the constitutional questions brought to us for resolution, we determine that the language of section 300 limiting the designation of marriage to a union "between a man and a woman" is unconstitutional and must be stricken from the statute, and that the remaining statutory language must be understood as making the designation of marriage available both to opposite-sex and same-sex couples. In addition, because the limitation of marriage to opposite-sex couples imposed by section 308.5 can have no constitutionally permissible effect in light of the constitutional conclusions set forth in this opinion, that provision cannot stand.

JUSTICE KENNARD, with whom JUSTICES BAXTER (in part) and CORRIGAN (in part) join, concurring.

The court's opinion, authored by the Chief Justice, carefully and fully explains why the constitutionality of the marriage laws' exclusion of same-sex couples is an issue particularly appropriate for decision by this court, rather than a social or political issue inappropriate for judicial consideration. Because of its importance, this point deserves special emphasis.

In holding today that the right to marry guaranteed by the state Constitution may not be withheld from anyone on the ground of sexual orientation, this court discharges its gravest and most important responsibility under our constitutional form of government. There is a reason why the words "Equal Justice Under Law" are inscribed above the entrance to the courthouse of the United States Supreme Court. Both the federal and the state Constitutions guarantee to all the "equal protection of the laws", and it is the particular responsibility of the judiciary to enforce those guarantees. The architects of our federal and state Constitutions understood that widespread and deeply rooted prejudices may lead majoritarian institutions to deny fundamental freedoms to unpopular minority groups, and that the most effective remedy for this form of oppression is an independent judiciary charged with the solemn responsibility to interpret and enforce the constitutional provisions guaranteeing fundamental freedoms and equal protection.

Here, we decide only the scope of the equal protection guarantee under the state Constitution, which operates independently of the federal Constitution. Absent a compelling justification, our state government may not deny a right as fundamental as marriage to any segment of society. Whether an unconstitutional denial of a fundamental right has occurred is not a matter to be decided by the executive or legislative branch, or by popular vote, but is instead an issue of constitutional law for resolution by the judicial branch of state government. Indeed, this court's decision in Lockyer made it clear that the courts alone must decide whether excluding individuals from marriage because of sexual orientation can be reconciled with our state Constitution's equal protection guarantee. The court today discharges its constitutional obligation by resolving that issue.

With these observations, I concur fully in the court's opinion authored by the Chief Justice.

JUSTICE BAXTER, with whom JUSTICE CORRIGAN (in part) joins, dissenting.

The majority opinion reflects considerable research, thought, and effort on a significant and sensitive case, and I actually agree with several of the majority's conclusions. However, I cannot join the majority's holding that the California Constitution gives same-sex couples a right to marry. In reaching this decision, I believe, the majority violates the separation of powers, and thereby commits profound error.

The question presented by this case is simple and stark. It comes down to this: Even though California's progressive laws, recently adopted through the democratic process, have pioneered the rights of same-sex partners to enter legal unions with all the substantive benefits of opposite-sex legal unions, do those laws nonetheless violate the California Constitution because at present, in deference to long and universal tradition, by a convincing popular vote, and in accord with express national policy, they reserve the label "marriage" for opposite-sex legal unions? I must conclude that the answer is no. . . . Left to its own devices, the ordinary democratic process might well produce, ere long, a consensus among most Californians that the term "marriage" should, in civil parlance, include the legal unions of same-sex partners. . . . But a bare majority of this court, not satisfied with the pace of democratic change, now abruptly forestalls that process and substitutes, by judicial fiat, its own social policy views for those expressed by the People themselves. Undeterred by the strong weight of state and federal law

---

Historical View: Marriage Controversies: Nothing New in the United States

While same-sex marriage may be the most controversial issue with regard to marriage today, historically the issue of polygamy has been at least as polarizing. Polygamists, especially those of the Mormon faith, have often faced the brunt of prohibitive marriage laws. When George Reynolds, a member of the Church of Jesus Christ of Latter-day Saints (the Mormons), took a second wife, he informed a Utah state court that his bigamous marriage was an aspect of his faith and thus protected by the First Amendment. The lower court disagreed and found him guilty, fining him. His appeal to the Supreme Court yielded similar results. In defining marriage, the Court in 1878 found that tradition limited the number of spouses to two, one man and one woman. Furthermore, the legislature may circumscribe actions, not opinion, without infringing on First Amendment protections. To permit bigamy would permit every citizen to be "a law unto himself."

Marriage has also been heavily regulated, and at times forbidden, among African Americans. Slaves were forbidden from marrying without the express consent of their masters. Although the ceremonies would be solemnized by a preacher, the slaves would participate in other ceremonies more derivative of their African heritage. Literally jumping the broom would sometimes solidify the marriage outside the aegis of the slaveholder. Although this traditional ceremony would replace the exchange of marriage vows outside the purview of the master, slaves would oftentimes wait to have a solemnized marriage; to this day, the practice of "jumping the broom" has come to symbolize the strength of African American culture in the face of cruelty of coerced servitude in the old American South.

A number of other aspects of state marriage laws should share in the controversy. The property rights of married women were often ignored in the states during the nineteenth century; New York became the first state to protect the rights of married women to own property in 1848. In a number of American states until the early twentieth century, it was legal for boys as young as 14 and girls as young as 12 to marry. Marital rape was not banned via statute until 1978 in New York. It was not until 1993 that all 50 states of the United States revised their laws to include marital rape stipulations.—*Brandon L. H. Aultman*

---

and authority, the majority invents a new constitutional right, immune from the ordinary process of legislative consideration. The majority finds that our Constitution suddenly demands no less than a permanent redefinition of marriage, regardless of the popular will . . .

History confirms the importance of the judiciary's constitutional role as a check against majoritarian abuse. Still, courts must use caution when exercising the potentially transformative authority to articulate constitutional rights. Otherwise, judges with limited accountability risk infringing upon our society's most basic shared premise—the People's general right, directly or through their chosen legislators, to decide fundamental issues of public policy for themselves. Judicial restraint is particularly appropriate where, as here, the claimed constitutional entitlement is of recent conception and challenges the most fundamental assumption about a basic social institution.

The majority has violated these principles. It simply does not have the right to erase, then recast, the age-old definition of marriage, as virtually all societies have understood it, in order to satisfy its own contemporary notions of equality and justice. . . . The process of reform and familiarization should go forward in the legislative sphere and in society at large. We are in the midst of a major social change. Societies seldom make such changes smoothly. For some the process is frustratingly slow. For others it is jarringly fast. In a democracy, the people should be given a fair chance to set the pace of change without judicial interference. That is the way democracies work. Ideas are proposed, debated, tested. Often new ideas are initially resisted, only to be ultimately embraced. But when ideas are imposed, opposition hardens and progress may be hampered.

Document 5.7: Legislating Civil Unions

- **Document:** Connecticut State law creating civil unions for same-sex couples
- **Date:** October 1, 2005
- **Where:** State House, Hartford, Connecticut
- **Significance:** Interested in providing equal rights to gay and lesbian citizens, but aware that the term "marriage" carries significant religious and social connotations, the Connecticut state legislature enacted "marriage in all but name" for same-sex couples. Connecticut was the first state to provide such rights without a prior court order forcing it to act. In 2007, the legislature enacted full marriage rights.

AN ACT CONCERNING CIVIL UNIONS.

Be it enacted by the Senate and House of Representatives in General Assembly convened . . .

Sec. 2. A person is eligible to enter into a civil union if such person is:

(1) Not a party to another civil union or a marriage;
(2) Of the same sex as the other party to the civil union;
(3) Except as provided in section 10 of this act, at least eighteen years of age . . .

Sec. 14. Parties to a civil union shall have all the same benefits, protections and responsibilities under law, whether derived from the general statutes, administrative regulations or court rules, policy, common law or any other source of civil law, as are granted to spouses in a marriage, which is defined as the union of one man and one woman . . .

Sec. 15. Wherever in the general statutes the terms "spouse", "family", "immediate family", "dependent", "next of kin" or any other term that denotes the spousal relationship are used or defined, a party to a civil union shall be included in such use or definition, and wherever in the general statutes . . . the term "marriage" is used or defined, a civil union shall be included in such use or definition.

> "Parties to a civil union shall have all the same benefits, protections and responsibilities under law . . . as are granted to spouses in a marriage."

The Rules of Marriage: Evolving Norms and Standards

While the most acrimonious battles over marriage have involved the freedom to choose one's partner, there have also been political debates over the degree to which the government should regulate behavior once a marriage has commenced, including the decision to terminate a marriage. Traditionally, states have claimed a great deal of authority in prohibiting sexual behavior. As discussed in Chapter 4, in the context of anti-sodomy laws, until 2003 states were able to prohibit certain types of sexual behavior both within and outside a marriage; for instance, oral and anal sex could be rendered illegal under all circumstances. This is no longer the case, since the Supreme Court's ruling in *Lawrence v. Texas* (see Document 4.3). However, the implications of *Lawrence* have not yet fully been determined with regard to whether one's marital status can influence the legality of sexual behaviors.

Earlier in this chapter, the Virginia ban on interracial marriage was discussed, including its invalidation in the case of *Loving v. Virginia*. Document 5.8 includes additional elements of the Virginia criminal code, including such offenses as "fornication" (sex outside of marriage), "lascivious cohabitation" (being "live-in" but unmarried sexual partners), and "adultery" (sex in which one or more partner is married to someone else). Also banned is bigamy or polygamy (illicit marriage to more than one person).

Bigamy and polygamy remain firmly illegal across the country, although the issue does have some continuing legal and political resonance. From the traditionalist/conservative side, groups

---

Freedom to Marry Coalition

Founded in 2003, the Freedom to Marry Coalition is a nonprofit, nonpartisan interest group dedicated to the procurement of equal marriage rights for lesbians, gays, and bisexual (LGB) people. The Coalition works through litigation, legislation, and public education to promote this cause. Central to its same-sex marriage belief has been its opposition to federal efforts in 2004 and 2006 to introduce a heterosexual-only marriage amendment to the U.S. Constitution.

The Coalition also "targeted state and local efforts, and promotes fairness for all families, including same-sex couples and the children raised by gay parents. . . . By ending sex discrimination in marriage, much as we ended race discrimination in marriage a generation ago, we are building a better America, protecting and supporting families, children, and the freedom of choice for all" (www.freedomtomarry.org).

The Coalition works closely with a number of other LGB and non-LGB interest groups in their fight for marriage equality. Groups like the American Civil Liberties Union, Soulforce, and Lambda Legal promote the Coalition as it makes state-by-state attempts to influence marriage policy. They applaud states like Vermont that recognize civil unions. However, "marriage" is held as an indispensable indication of America's acceptance of LGB political equality.—*Brandon L. H. Aultman*

such as the Fundamentalist Church of Jesus Christ of Latter-day Saints, an offshoot of the mainstream Mormon Church, maintain "plural marriages" more or less openly. The constitutionality of such polygamy bans was upheld as recently as 2004 by the Utah Supreme Court in the case of *State v. Green* (Document 5.13). Absent accusations of child abuse and/or the forcing of young women to be unwilling brides, however, many such groups have often been left undisturbed as long as they do not flout the law too openly. From the radical/leftist side, some have argued for governmental recognition of "polyamorous" relationships, which are arrangements in which three, four, five, or more people, of various genders, should be able to legally marry one another.

On the one hand, the right of individuals to choose their partners, and precedents relating to interracial and same-sex marriages, would seem to argue in favor of such a right of self-determination for practitioners of polygamous/polyamorous relationships. On the other hand, the ability to choose a partner of a different race or of the same gender can be achieved with the legislative "stroke of a pen," whereas multiple partners would raise complex new legal issues such as which one out of a group of multiple partners would have medical decision-making authority or inheritance rights.

Rather more surprising than the continued prohibition of bigamy/polygamy is the fact that laws technically criminalizing fornication and adultery remain "on the books" in many jurisdictions. Like anti-sodomy laws, they are rarely enforced, but exceptions do occur. The Virginia example (Document 5.8) remains particularly relevant here because a man was convicted of adultery in that state as recently as 2004, upon complaint to the police by his former lover after he rejected her and returned to his wife. While the penalty was only a $250 fine, the man nonetheless then had a criminal record, and the power of the state in this area of sexuality was clearly reasserted.

Remarkably, until the 1970s, the concept was not widely accepted that a woman could be "raped" by her husband. Indeed, because wedlock was seen as conferring a right to intercourse, "marital rape" was deemed a contradiction in terms. As it came to be understood that a marriage license was not also a license for sexual activity without ongoing consent, states began to remove the "marital rape" exception, beginning with Nebraska in 1976 (Document 5.10).

Another long-standing practice to be changed is the concept of "common law marriage." Before the advent of the modern administrative state, which demands official paperwork and procedures, there was a long-standing practice that a man and a woman who cohabited as husband and wife, and who publicly presented themselves as such for a number of years, would be recognized as being de facto married under the law. In recent years, however, the trend has been toward the abolition of this old practice. Document 5.11 reflects the step taken by the state of Ohio to protect those common law marriages that already existed as of 1991, but to ban the practice further after that time. Today, only about 20 percent of the states still recognize new marriages under common law provisions.

Yet another complex issue has been how and under what circumstances a marriage can be dissolved. For many years, in nearly all states, it was necessary to show that at least one partner has been "at fault," such as by committing adultery, cruelty, or abandonment. Absent convincing proof of such fault, judges would routinely refuse to dissolve a marriage, leaving the unhappily married with little recourse. Complex legal battles, and sometimes contrived stories of adultery, would often ensue. These ensnarled the family courts and resulted in huge legal fees, all to little apparent benefit. In 1970, California led the way in establishing so-called "no-fault divorce" in which a couple simply needed to assert that they had "irreconcilable differences" as a valid ground for divorce (see Document 5.9).

Many conservatives have opposed this as an assault on traditional marriage, even though it was, ironically, signed into law by their champion Ronald Reagan, who was in 1970 the governor of California (and a divorced and remarried man himself). By 2008, all of the states except New York had adopted no-fault divorce, and there was significant movement in New York as well in this direction. To counter this new ease in the dissolution of marriage, several states have created a more binding version of marriage, which a couple can freely choose to enter.

Those who select a "covenant marriage" promise to undergo premarital counseling and to take every possible step to preserve their marriage. Covenant marriage statutes (see the example from Arizona in Document 5.11) also reinstitute the idea of "fault" into divorce proceedings, although ordinary marriages with no-fault divorce policies also generally remain in effect alongside covenant marriage provisions. Critics worry that covenant marriages make it unduly difficult for one spouse, particularly wives, to quickly exit an abusive or otherwise dysfunctional marriage.

Document 5.8: Regulating Marriage and Sexual Behavior

- *Document:* Excerpts from the Virginia criminal code with regards to marriage and sexual behavior
- *Date:* 1975 amendments to 1950 Code of Virginia
- *Where:* State Capitol, Richmond, Virginia
- *Significance:* This document provides a representative example of sections of a state criminal code relating to such areas as marriage to more than one person (bigamy), sexual behavior outside marriage ("fornication"), and extramarital sexual relations ("adultery"). Although rarely enforced, many such laws technically remain in force.

Title 18.2 - CRIMES AND OFFENSES GENERALLY.

Chapter 8 - Crimes Involving Morals and Decency

§ 18.2-344. Fornication.
Any person, not being married, who voluntarily shall have sexual intercourse with any other person, shall be guilty of fornication, punishable as a Class 4 misdemeanor.

§ 18.2-345. Lewd and lascivious cohabitation.
If any persons, not married to each other, lewdly and lasciviously associate and cohabit together, or, whether married or not, be guilty of open and gross lewdness and lasciviousness, each of them shall be guilty of a Class 3 misdemeanor; and upon a repetition of the offense, and conviction thereof, each of them shall be guilty of a Class 1 misdemeanor . . .

§ 18.2-362. Person marrying when husband or wife is living; penalty; venue.

If any person, being married, shall, during the life of the husband or wife, marry another person in this Commonwealth, or if the marriage with such other person take place out of the Commonwealth, shall thereafter cohabit with such other person in this Commonwealth, he or she shall be guilty of a Class 4 felony. Venue for a violation of this section may be in the county or city where the subsequent marriage occurred or where the parties to the subsequent marriage cohabited.

> "Any person, not being married, who voluntarily shall have sexual intercourse with any other person, shall be guilty of fornication . . . Any person, being married, who voluntarily shall have sexual intercourse with any person not his or her spouse shall be guilty of adultery."

§ 18.2-363. Leaving Commonwealth to evade law against bigamy.

If any persons, resident in this Commonwealth, one of whom has a husband or wife living, shall, with the intention of returning to reside in this Commonwealth, go into another state or country and there intermarry and return to and reside in this Commonwealth cohabiting as man and wife, such marriage shall be governed by the same law, in all respects, as if it had been solemnized in this Commonwealth.

§ 18.2-364. Exceptions to preceding sections.

Sections 18.2-362 and 18.2-363 shall not extend to a person whose husband or wife shall have been continuously absent from such person for seven years next before marriage of such person to another, and shall not have been known by such person to be living within that time; nor to a person who can show that the second marriage was contracted in good faith under a reasonable belief that the former consort was dead; nor to a person who shall, at the time of the subsequent marriage, have been divorced from the bond of the former marriage; nor to a person whose former marriage was void.

§ 18.2-365. Adultery defined; penalty.

Any person, being married, who voluntarily shall have sexual intercourse with any person not his or her spouse shall be guilty of adultery, punishable as a Class 4 misdemeanor.

§ 18.2-366. Adultery and fornication by persons forbidden to marry; incest.

A. Any person who commits adultery or fornication with any person whom he or she is forbidden by law to marry shall be guilty of a Class 1 misdemeanor except as provided by subsection B.

Focus on the Family

In June of 1977, Focus on the Family (FoF) formed as a faith-based nonprofit organization promoting a Biblical way of life. To that end, FoF has taken a traditionalist stance on marriage, even in the area of divorce reform. A strong advocate of covenant marriages—providing stricter grounds for divorce—and a staunch opponent of same-sex marriage, FoF has worked to spread its message internationally and has become one of the largest faith-based nonprofits in the United States.

FoF (www.family.org) expresses that "All of the family experimentation over the past 30 years—no fault divorce, the sexual revolution, cohabitation, fatherlessness—have all been documented failures, harming adults and children in far deeper ways, for longer periods of time, than anyone ever imagined." This may, too, hold true for same-sex couples. "Where does it stop?" FoF asks. "That is why we cannot accept the same-sex family. It serves no public purpose."

As for Bush's failed amendment proposals in 2004 and 2006: "Our United States Constitution is going to be changed one way or the other. Either a small handful of unaccountable, activist judges are going to write a radical new definition of marriage into the Constitution, or, the American people can protect marriage constitutionally through the option the founding fathers provided via the amendment process."—*Brandon L. H. Aultman*

B. Any person who commits adultery or fornication with his daughter or granddaughter, or with her son or grandson, or her father or his mother, shall be guilty of a Class 5 felony. However, if a parent or grandparent commits adultery or fornication with his or her child or grandchild, and such child or grandchild is at least thirteen years of age but less than eighteen years of age at the time of the offense, such parent or grandparent shall be guilty of a Class 3 felony.

Document 5.9: Recognizing Irreconcilable Differences

- **Document:** The California Family Law Act of 1970, creating "no-fault" divorce
- **Date:** January 1, 1970
- **Where:** State Capitol, Sacramento, California
- **Significance:** This first-in-the-nation law created the concept of "irreconcilable differences" as the basis for a divorce, rather than some specific action by one or both spouses. This "no-fault" divorce legislation made it much easier to dissolve a marriage at will.

California Family Code Sections 2310-2313

2310. Dissolution of the marriage or legal separation of the parties may be based on either of the following grounds, which shall be pleaded generally:

(a) Irreconcilable differences, which have caused the irremediable breakdown of the marriage.
(b) Incurable insanity.

2311. Irreconcilable differences are those grounds which are determined by the court to be substantial reasons for not continuing the marriage and which make it appear that the marriage should be dissolved.

2312. A marriage may be dissolved on the grounds of incurable insanity only upon proof, including competent medical or psychiatric testimony, that the insane spouse was at the time the petition was filed, and remains, incurably insane.

"Irreconcilable differences are those grounds which are determined by the court to be substantial reasons for not continuing the marriage and which make it appear that the marriage should be dissolved."

2313. No dissolution of marriage granted on the ground of incurable insanity relieves a spouse from any obligation imposed by law as a result of the marriage for the support of the spouse who is incurably insane, and the court may make such order for support, or require a bond therefore, as the circumstances require.

Document 5.10: Outlawing Marital Rape

- *Document:* Text of Nebraska law that invalidated marital rape exemptions
- *Date:* 1976
- *Where:* Lincoln, Nebraska
- *Significance:* With the passage of this general rape provision, Nebraska became the first state of the United States to remove traditional marital exemptions.

Chapter 28, Section 28-319

Sexual assault; first degree; penalty.

(1) **Any** person who subjects another person to sexual penetration (a) without the consent of the victim, (b) who knew or should have known that the victim was mentally or physically incapable of resisting or appraising the nature of his or her conduct, or (c) when the actor is nineteen years of age or older and the victim is at least twelve but less than sixteen years of age is guilty of sexual assault in the first degree.

(2) Sexual assault in the first degree is a Class II felony. The sentencing judge shall consider whether the actor caused serious personal injury to the victim in reaching a decision on the sentence.

(3) Any person who is found guilty of sexual assault in the first degree for a second time when the first conviction was pursuant to this section or any other state or federal law with essentially the same elements as this section shall be sentenced to a mandatory minimum term of twenty-five years in prison.

Document 5.11: Requiring Civil Marriage

- *Document:* Ohio law ending recognition of new common law marriages
- *Date:* October 10, 1991
- *Where:* State Capitol, Columbus, Ohio
- *Significance:* A long-standing tradition, "common law marriage" allowed a man and a woman who lived together as husband and wife to be legally recognized as such without a formal ceremony or certificate. This Ohio law is one of several state laws that have begun putting an end to this version of the institution of marriage.

Ohio Code 3105.12 Proof of marriage

(A) Except as provided in division (B) of this section, proof of cohabitation and reputation of the marriage of a man and woman is competent evidence to prove their marriage, and, in the discretion of the court, that proof may be sufficient to establish their marriage for a particular purpose.

(B)(1) On and after October 10, 1991, except as provided in divisions (B)(2) and (3) of this section, common law marriages are prohibited in this state, and the marriage of a man and woman may occur in this state only if the marriage is solemnized by a person described in section 3101.08 of the Revised Code and only if the marriage otherwise is in compliance with Chapter 3101. of the Revised Code.

(2) Common law marriages that occurred in this state prior to October 10, 1991, and that have not been terminated by death, divorce, dissolution of marriage, or annulment remain valid on and after October 10, 1991.

(3) Common law marriages that satisfy all of the following remain valid on and after October 10, 1991:

(a) They came into existence prior to October 10, 1991, or come into existence on or after that date, in another state or nation that recognizes the validity of common law marriages in accordance with all relevant aspects of the law of that state or nation.

> "Proof of cohabitation and reputation of the marriage of a man and woman is competent evidence to prove their marriage."

(b) They have not been terminated by death, divorce, dissolution of marriage, annulment, or other judicial determination in this or another state or in another nation . . .

Document 5.12: Promoting Lasting Unions

- **Document:** Arizona state law establishing "covenant marriage"
- **Date:** May 21, 1998
- **Where:** State Capital Building, Phoenix, Arizona
- **Significance:** In reaction to loosening standards for "no-fault" divorce in recent years, a number of states have created a special type of "covenant marriage," in which a couple agrees to premarital counseling and to a narrower range of allowable reasons for divorce. The goal is to strengthen the commitment of the couple to the success and perpetuation of their marriage.

Be it enacted by the Legislature of the State of Arizona:

*1 Section 1. Title 25, Arizona Revised Statutes, is amended by adding chapter 7, to read:

Chapter 7 covenant marriage

Article 1. General provisions

25-901. Covenant marriage; declaration of intent; filing requirements

A. Persons who have the legal capacity to marry pursuant to this title may enter into a covenant marriage by declaring their intent to do so on their application for a license obtained pursuant to section 25-121 and by complying with the requirements of this chapter. The marriage license shall be recorded as provided by section 25-123 with an indication that the marriage is a covenant marriage.

B. A declaration of intent to enter into a covenant marriage shall contain all of the following:

1. The following written statement:

We solemnly declare that marriage is a covenant between a man and a woman who agree to live together as husband and wife for as long as they both live. We have chosen each other carefully and have received premarital counseling on the nature, purposes and responsibilities of marriage. We understand that a covenant marriage is for life. If we experience marital difficulties, we commit ourselves to take all reasonable efforts to preserve our marriage, including marital counseling.

With full knowledge of what this commitment means, we do declare that our marriage will be bound by Arizona law on covenant marriages and we promise to love, honor and care for one another as husband and wife for the rest of our lives.

2. An affidavit by the parties that they have received premarital counseling from a member of the clergy or from a marriage counselor. Premarital counseling shall include a discussion of the seriousness of covenant marriage, communication of the fact that a covenant marriage is a commitment for life, a discussion of the obligation to seek marital counseling in times of marital difficulties and a discussion of the exclusive grounds for legally terminating a covenant marriage by dissolution of marriage or legal separation.

3. The signatures of both parties witnessed by a court clerk.

C. A notarized attestation that is signed by the clergy or counselor must be submitted with the application for a license and confirm that the parties were counseled as to the nature and purpose of the marriage and the grounds for its termination and that the counselor provided to the parties the informational pamphlet developed by the supreme court pursuant to this chapter . . .

25-903. Dissolution of a covenant marriage; grounds

Notwithstanding any law to the contrary, if a husband and wife have entered into a covenant marriage pursuant to this chapter the court shall not enter a decree of dissolution of marriage pursuant to chapter 3, article 2 of this title unless it finds any of the following:

1. The respondent spouse has committed adultery.

2. The respondent spouse has committed a felony and has been sentenced to death or imprisonment in any federal, state, county or municipal correctional facility.

3. The respondent spouse has abandoned the matrimonial domicile for at least one year before the petitioner filed for dissolution of marriage and refuses to return . . .

4. The respondent spouse has physically or sexually abused the spouse seeking the dissolution of marriage, a child, a relative of either spouse permanently living in the matrimonial domicile or has committed domestic violence as defined in section 13-3601 or emotional abuse.

5. The spouses have been living separate and apart continuously without reconciliation for at least two years before the petitioner filed for dissolution of marriage . . .

> "We understand that a covenant marriage is for life. If we experience marital difficulties, we commit ourselves to take all reasonable efforts to preserve our marriage, including marital counseling."

6. The spouses have been living separate and apart continuously without reconciliation for at least one year from the date the decree of legal separation was entered.

7. The respondent spouse has habitually abused drugs or alcohol.

8. The husband and wife both agree to a dissolution of marriage.

The Republican Party Platform, 2008: Marriage

Because our children's future is best preserved within the traditional understanding of marriage, we call for a constitutional amendment that fully protects marriage as a union of a man and a woman, so that judges cannot make other arrangements equivalent to it. In the absence of a national amendment, we support the right of the people of the various states to affirm traditional marriage through state initiatives.

Republicans recognize the importance of having in the home a father and a mother who are married. The two-parent family still provides the best environment of stability, discipline, responsibility, and character. Children in homes without fathers are more likely to commit a crime, drop out of school, become violent, become teen parents, use illegal drugs, become mired in poverty, or have emotional or behavioral problems. We support the courageous efforts of single-parent families to provide a stable home for their children. Children are our nation's most precious resource. We also salute and support the efforts of foster and adoptive families.

Republicans have been at the forefront of protecting traditional marriage laws, both in the states and in Congress. A Republican Congress enacted the Defense of Marriage Act, affirming the right of states not to recognize same-sex "marriages" licensed in other states. Unbelievably, the Democratic Party has now pledged to repeal the Defense of Marriage Act, which would subject every state to the redefinition of marriage by a judge without ever allowing the people to vote on the matter.

We also urge Congress to use its Article III, Section 2 power to prevent activist federal judges from imposing upon the rest of the nation the judicial activism in Massachusetts and California. We also encourage states to review their marriage and divorce laws in order to strengthen marriage. As the family is our basic unit of society, we oppose initiatives to erode parental rights.

Document 5.13: Continuing Prohibitions on Polygamy

- **Document:** Utah Supreme Court ruling in *State v. Green* upholding the state's ban on polygamy
- **Date:** September 3, 2004
- **Where:** Supreme Court Building, Salt Lake City, Utah
- **Significance:** Amidst social changes in the understanding of the meaning and purpose of marriage, some have expected century-old prohibitions on polygamy, or "plural marriage," to also be repealed. This state supreme court ruling closes the door on this possibility, at least for now.

IN THE SUPREME COURT OF THE STATE OF UTAH

State of Utah,

Plaintiff and Appellee,

v.

Thomas Arthur Green,

Defendant and Appellant.

No. 20010788

FILED
September 3, 2004

PARRISH, Justice:

Tom Green, an open polygamist, speaks with his five current wives and his children before entering the Utah courtroom where, in May 2001, he became the first person tried on polygamy charges in Utah in nearly 50 years. Green was convicted of bigamy and criminal nonsupport and served six years in prison before being paroled. (AP Photo/Deseret News/Stuart Johnson)

A jury convicted Thomas Green of criminal nonsupport and four counts of bigamy. Green appeals his bigamy convictions. He asserts that they violate the Free Exercise Clause of the First Amendment to the United States Constitution. He also argues that Utah's bigamy statute, Utah Code Ann. § 76-7-101 (1999), is unconstitutionally vague and that the district court erred in applying Utah's unsolemnized marriage statute. We affirm.

BACKGROUND

An avowed polygamist, Green has participated in simultaneous conjugal-type relationships with multiple women. These women all use Green's surname and have borne children who also use the Green surname. Between 1970 and 1996, Green formed relationships with Lynda Penman, Beth Cook, Linda Kunz, Shirley Beagley, June Johnson, LeeAnn Beagley, Cari Bjorkman, Hannah Bjorkman, and Julie Dawn McKinley. Through his relationships with these women, Green has fathered approximately twenty-five children.

Some of the women entered into licensed marriages with Green. The remaining women participated in unlicensed ceremonies, after which they considered themselves married to Green. Green avoided being in more than one licensed marriage at a time by terminating each licensed marriage by divorce prior to obtaining a license for a new marriage. Green then continued his relationships with each of the women he divorced as if no divorce had occurred.

In 1995, Green and his family moved to Juab County, Utah, where they resided together in a collection of shared mobile homes that the family called "Green Haven." Green quartered in one mobile home, while the women and children quartered in others. Some of the mobile home areas were set aside as common dining and laundry areas, and the family shared the bathrooms scattered among the mobile homes. The women spent nights individually with Green in his mobile home on a rotating schedule.

Each of the women shared with Green the duties of raising the children and managing the family by dividing the tasks of cooking for the entire family, doing the family laundry, and home schooling all of the children. In addition, the women assisted with the family business, which consisted of selling magazine subscriptions. All money earned by the family business was pooled into "the Green Family Household account."

Between 1988 and 2001, Green appeared on various television shows with the women, consistently referring to the women as his wives, and the women likewise acknowledged spousal relationships. In these television appearances, Green acknowledged that his conduct was potentially punishable under Utah criminal statutes.

In April 2000, the State filed an information charging Green with, among other things, four counts of bigamy. Prior to a preliminary hearing on the charges, the State filed a motion asking that the court recognize the existence of a valid marriage between Green and Linda Kunz ...

II. FREE EXERCISE OF RELIGION CLAIM

Utah's bigamy statute provides, in relevant part, as follows:

A person is guilty of bigamy when, knowing he has a husband or wife or knowing the other person has a husband or wife, the person purports to marry another person or cohabits with another person.

Green argues that this statute is unconstitutional under the First Amendment to the United States Constitution because it punishes his marital practices in violation of his right to freely exercise his religion. Specifically, Green argues that a law effectively prohibiting religiously motivated bigamy (which we refer to as polygamy) cannot withstand a challenge under the standards articulated by the United States Supreme Court. Green's constitutional challenge to a statute presents questions of law, which we review for correctness ...

The First Amendment states that "Congress shall make no law respecting an establishment of religion, or prohibiting the free exercise thereof." The Free Exercise Clause was made applicable to the states by incorporation into the Fourteenth Amendment. The scope and contours of the Free Exercise Clause have been defined over time by the United States Supreme Court. These cases inform our analysis and mandate the conclusion that Utah's bigamy statute does not violate the First Amendment as interpreted by the United States Supreme Court for the following reasons.

First, Green is not the first polygamist to launch an attack on the constitutionality of a law burdening the practice of polygamy. In 1878, polygamist George Reynolds challenged the constitutionality of the Morrill Antibigamy Act, which prohibited bigamy in all territories of the United States. [In] *Reynolds v. United States*, Reynolds argued that he could not be found guilty under the law inasmuch as he believed that marrying more than one woman was his religious duty.

The Supreme Court held that the law did not violate the Free Exercise Clause of the First Amendment, finding, in part, that "[l]aws are made for the government of actions, and while they cannot interfere with mere religious belief and opinions, they may with practices." Otherwise, reasoned the Court, "professed doctrines of religious belief [would be] superior to the law of the land, and in effect . . . permit every citizen to become a law unto himself." The Supreme Court reviewed the practice of polygamy, found it to be socially undesirable, and upheld Reynolds' bigamy conviction.

We are cognizant of the fact that *Reynolds* was decided over a century ago and may be antiquated in its wording and analysis. We are similarly cognizant of the fact that its reasoning may not necessarily comport with today's understanding of the language and apparent purpose of the Free Exercise Clause. Nevertheless, the Supreme Court has never explicitly overruled the decision. To the contrary, the Court has cited *Reynolds* with approval in subsequent cases, evidencing its continued validity . . . This court is therefore unable to disregard the United States Supreme Court's holding in *Reynolds*.

Second, even if this court were required to extend its analysis beyond *Reynolds*, Utah's bigamy statute would survive a federal free exercise of religion challenge under the most recent standards enunciated by the United States Supreme Court. In *Smith*, the Court held that the state of Oregon did not violate the Free Exercise Clause of the First Amendment to the United States Constitution when it refused unemployment benefits to certain practitioners of the Native American religion who had been fired for illegally using peyote. The Court announced that a neutral law of general applicability need not be justified by a compelling governmental interest even if the law has the incidental effect of burdening a particular religious practice . . .

Utah's bigamy statute does not attempt to target only religiously motivated bigamy. Any individual who violates the statute, whether for religious or secular reasons, is subject to prosecution. Thus, Utah's prohibition on bigamy is not a prohibition that our society is "prepared to impose upon [polygamists] but not upon itself."

It is true that Utah's bigamy statute has an adverse impact on those wishing to practice polygamy as a tenet of their religion. An adverse impact on religion does not by itself, however, prove impermissible targeting because "a social harm may have been a legitimate concern of government for reasons quite apart from [religious] discrimination." Indeed, "[i]n many instances, the Congress or state legislatures conclude that the general welfare of society, wholly apart from any religious considerations," demands "regulation of conduct whose reason or effect merely happens to coincide or harmonize with the tenets of some or all religions."

The Utah legislature has determined that prohibiting bigamy serves this state's best interests. Because Utah's bigamy statute is neutral and of general applicability, the State is not required to show that the interests it serves are compelling or that the statute is narrowly tailored in pursuit of those interests . . .

> "It is true that Utah's bigamy statute has an adverse impact on those wishing to practice polygamy as a tenet of their religion. An adverse impact on religion does not by itself, however, prove impermissible targeting because a social harm may have been a legitimate concern of government."

Having concluded that the State need only show a rational relationship between its bigamy law and a legitimate government interest, we assess whether the State has met its burden in this regard. We conclude that Utah's bigamy statute is rationally related to several legitimate government ends. First, this state has an interest in regulating marriage. As stated in *Reynolds*, marriage may be viewed as a type of "civil contract": "Upon it society may be said to be built, and out of its fruits spring social relations and social obligations and duties, with which government is necessarily required to deal." Moreover, [m]arriage . . . has always been subject to the control of the legislature. That body prescribes the age at which parties may contract to marry, the procedure or form essential to constitute marriage, the duties and obligations it creates, its effects upon the property rights of both, present and prospective, and the acts which may constitute grounds for its dissolution. . . .

BIBLIOGRAPHY

Boele-Woelki, Katharina, and Angelika Fuchs, eds. *Legal Recognition of Same Sex Couples in Europe*. New York: Intersentia, 2003.

Dupuis, Martin. *Same-Sex Marriage, Legal Mobilization and the Politics of Rights*. New York: Peter Lang, 2002.

Eskridge, William N., Jr. "A History of Same-Sex Marriage." *Virginia Law Review* 79, no. 7 (October 1993): 1419–1513.

Everett, Craig A. *Divorce and Remarriage: International Studies*. New York: Haworth, 1997.

Feldmeier, John P. "Federalism and Full Faith and Credit: Must States Recognize Out-of-State Same-Sex Marriages?" *Publius* 25, no. 4 (Autumn 1995): 107–126.

Gozemba, Patricia A. *Courting Equality: A Documentary History of America's First Legal Same-Sex Marriages*. Boston: Beacon Press, 2007.

Graff, E. J. *What Is Marriage For?: The Strange Social History of Our Most Intimate Institution*. Boston: Beacon Press, 2004.

Harvard Law Review Association. "Litigating the Defense of Marriage Act: The Next Battle-ground for Same-Sex Marriage." *Harvard Law Review* 117, no. 8 (June 2004): 2684–2707.

Hull, Katherine. *Same-Sex Marriage: The Cultural Politics of Love and Law*. Cambridge, U.K.: Cambridge University Press, 2006.

Larocque, Sylvain. *Gay Marriage: The story of a Canadian Social Revolution*. Toronto: J. Lorimer, 2006.

Marvell, Thomas B. "Divorce Rates and the Fault Requirement." *Law & Society Review* 23, no. 4 (1989): 543–568.

Parkmen, Allen M. *Good Intentions Gone Awry: No-Fault Divorce and The American Family*. Lanham, MD: Rowman and Littlefield, 2000.

Phy-Osen, Allene. *Same-Sex Marriage*. Westport, CT: Greenwood Press, 2006.

Polikoff, Nancy D. *Beyond (Straight and Gay) Marriage: Valuing All Families Under the Law*. Boston: Beacon Press, 2008.

Soule, Sarah A. "Going to the Chapel? Same-Sex Marriage Bans in the United States, 1973–2000." *Social Problems* 51, no. 4 (November 2004): 453–477.

Strasser, Mark. *On Same-Sex Marriage, Civil Unions, and The Rule of Law: Constitutional Interpretation at The Crossroads*. Westport, CT: Praeger, 2002.

Welch, Charles E., III, and Sharon Price-Bonham. "A Decade of No-Fault Divorce Revisited: California, Georgia, and Washington." *Journal of Marriage and the Family* 45, no. 2 (May 1983): 411–418.

Wintemute, Robert, and Mads Andenaes, eds. *Legal Recognition of Same-Sex Partnerships: A Study of National, European and International Law*. Portland, OR: Hart, 2001.

Witte, John, Jr. "The Future of Marriage: State Laws and Religious Laws Cannot Co-Exist, Can They?" *The Atlanta Journal-Constitution*, February 24, 2008, p. 1B.

—— and Eliza Ellison, eds. *Covenant Marriage in Comparative Perspective (Religion, Marriage, and Family Series)*. Grand Rapids, MI: Eerdmans, 2005.

6

SEXUAL SCANDAL: THE PRIVATE CONDUCT OF PUBLIC FIGURES

"I will not provide rope for my own lynching ..."

THE CONFIRMATION HEARINGS FOR SUPREME COURT JUSTICE CLARENCE THOMAS

6.1: Testimony of Anita Hill before the Senate Judiciary Committee
6.2: Response by Judge Clarence Thomas

"I did not have sexual relations with that woman ..."

THE IMPEACHMENT OF PRESIDENT BILL CLINTON

6.3 The Starr Commission Report
6.4 Statement to the Nation by President Bill Clinton
6.5 The Articles of Impeachment
6.6 Speech by Senator Joseph Lieberman

"I am a gay American."

THE RESIGNATION OF NEW JERSEY GOVERNOR JIM MCGREEVEY

6.7 Press Conference Transcript

"I am not gay and have never been gay."

THE ARREST OF U.S. SENATOR LARRY CRAIG OF IDAHO

6.8 Transcript of the Police Interview

"CLIENT 9" AND "KRISTEN": THE FBI INVESTIGATION OF NEW YORK GOVERNOR ELIOT SPITZER

6.9 Affidavit Regarding a Federal Wiretap

Introduction

Sex scandals are nothing new in American politics (see "Historical View" sidebar in this chapter), but until the 1980s, the mass media were often willing to turn a blind eye to allegations of sexual improprieties among public officials. At a time when detailed discussion of sexuality was all but forbidden in the media, politicians were allowed a greater zone of privacy. Perhaps the best example is the now-startling willingness of the mass media not to report the multiple indiscretions of President John F. Kennedy, even with one of the most famous starlets of the day, Marilyn Monroe. Other presidents, from Franklin Roosevelt, to Dwight Eisenhower, to Lyndon Johnson, were also widely rumored to have had affairs, albeit with decidedly less glamorous women.

The modern history of sexual scandal among politicians in the United States is usually traced to the 1988 presidential campaign of Colorado Senator Gary Hart. The front-runner for the Democratic nomination, Hart responded to media allegations of marital infidelity with the challenge to "follow me around. I don't care. I'm serious. If anybody wants to put a tail on me, go ahead. They'll be very bored." Boredom was not the mood, however, when evidence surfaced that Hart had been conducting an extramarital affair with a 29-year-old named Donna Rice. But even then, only the low-end *National Enquirer* newspaper was willing to publish photos of Rice sitting in a suggestive pose in Hart's lap on a yacht; Hart withdrew from the race a week later.

The Hart affair toppled prior taboos within the media at a time when the burgeoning AIDS epidemic was also promoting far more explicit and extensive discussion of sexuality than ever before. Thus the stage was set for the long-running political soap opera of the marriage of Bill and Hillary Clinton. First accused of an affair with a state employee, Gennifer Flowers, during his time as Arkansas governor, Clinton publicly admitted to having "caused pain in my marriage," as his wife stayed stalwartly by his side. Rumors continued to rage about the extent of his infidelity, but Clinton was able to ignore, deny, or explain them away—until his now notorious affair with Monica Lewinsky, which is the subject of Documents 6.3–6.6.

From late 1998 to early 1999, Clinton was first impeached by the House and then acquitted by the Senate on charges of perjury and obstruction of justice in his attempts to cover up his affair with Lewinsky. Republican leaders in Congress repeatedly framed their actions in terms of the need for the president to uphold the rule of law, claiming that it was merely incidental that the subject involved was sexual in nature. At the same time, many attempted to claim the moral high ground as defenders of "family values," but themselves became victims of their own hypocrisy. Most strikingly, House Speaker Newt Gingrich, a driving force behind the impeachment process, stepped down midway through the process; he later acknowledged being in an ongoing extramarital affair with a House aide at the time. The man elected to be his successor as speaker, Robert Livingston of Louisiana, ended up resigning from Congress before he could take over the speakership after revelations of his own extramarital affair. Livingston's seat was filled by a "traditional values" champion named David Vitter, who as a U.S. Senator in 2007 was implicated as being a client of a prostitution ring, but survived the media firestorm without being forced to resign. When another major political sex scandal involving prostitution broke a few months later, however, the perpetrator did not escape the scrutiny. Following news that he had hired at least one, and probably many, prostitutes from a high-priced call-girl ring, New York Governor Eliot Spitzer—once a rising star in the Democratic Party—was abruptly forced from office in March 2008; this is the subject of Document 6.9.

The other great political sex scandal of the 1990s was the allegations of sexual harassment made against Clarence Thomas during the Senate hearings on his nomination to the U.S. Supreme Court, as discussed in Documents 6.1 and 6.2. After a lurid round of charges and rebuttals, Thomas was confirmed, but the concept of sexual harassment became far more clearly established in the public mind. Shortly thereafter, for offenses that might earlier have been overlooked, U.S. Senator Bob Packwood of Oregon was forced to resign after the Senate Ethics Committee unanimously recommended his expulsion from the Senate following sexual harassment charges.

When sexual scandal involves homosexuality, an extra dimension is often added: There is not only the accusation of impropriety but also the news that a high public official is gay or lesbian. Allegations of improper sexual relationships with young male Congressional pages led to the censure of Representative Gary Studds of Massachusetts in 1983, although he went on to be reelected. In 2006, Representative Mark Foley of Florida, who was chair of the House Caucus on Missing and Exploited Children, resigned after sending salacious text messages to other young pages. Representative Barney Frank had been in a relationship with a male prostitute who had secretly used Frank's own residence as a brothel, which provoked a House Ethics Committee reprimand in 1990. Frank survived the storm, however, winning reelection multiple times and rising to be chairman of the powerful House Financial Services Committee.

Quite a different outcome occurred with the sudden and startling resignation of New Jersey Governor Jim McGreevey during a press conference in 2005 in which he confessed his clandestine affair with a male state employee, the subject of Document 6.7. Yet some politicians do manage to avoid being forced from office. In August 2007, news broke that U.S. Senator Larry Craig of Idaho had pled guilty to disorderly conduct charges after being charged with soliciting sex with an undercover police officer in an airport men's room. The details of the incident are provided in the transcript of the subsequent police interrogation in Document 6.8.

"I will not provide rope for my own lynching . . ."

The Confirmation Hearings for Supreme Court Justice Clarence Thomas

The 1991 resignation of Supreme Court Associate Justice Thurgood Marshall created the second of two openings on the Supreme Court during the presidency of George H. W. Bush. As head of the National Association for the Advancement of Colored People (NAACP) Legal and Educational Fund, Marshall had been a leader of the Civil Rights Movement and the first African American on the Supreme Court. Bush was thus faced with the dilemma of maintaining what was seen as the "black seat" on the Court but was hard pressed to find an African American jurist who was both conservative and well qualified, given that most African Americans are Democrats. Bush decided upon Clarence Thomas, whom he had appointed as a federal appeals court judge the prior year after eight years as chairman of a major civil rights office within the federal government, the U.S. Equal Employment Opportunity Commission (EEOC).

The ensuing confirmation battle before the U.S. Senate was extraordinarily strange. Groups ranging from the NAACP to the National Organization for Women came out strongly against Thomas's nomination, questioning his support for affirmative action and abortion rights among other issues. The American Bar Association, which usually rated most Supreme Court appointees as "well-qualified" gave Thomas a lower rating, in part because he had only a single year of experience as a judge. Criticism was particularly fierce within the African American community who saw Thomas, despite his race, as a betrayal rather than a continuation of the work of Thurgood Marshall.

The Thomas confirmation hearings in the Senate are best remembered, however, for incendiary charges of sexual impropriety (see Document 6.1) made by a law professor named Anita Hill, who had previously worked for Thomas at the EEOC, which ironically is the federal agency tasked with enforcing sexual harassment laws! Thomas defended himself (see Document 6.2) by claiming that he was being targeted by liberal Democrats for not sharing their political views, invoking the incendiary imagery of a "lynching." The incident was both electrifying and demoralizing to many, reinforcing the segregation-era cultural stereotype of the "sexually rapacious" black man. The fact that Hill was herself black further complicated the situation. What might have been a tremendous breakthrough moment for African Americans in U.S. politics became instead a sordid media spectacle.

In part because of lack of corroborating evidence about Hill's charges, the Senate went on to narrowly confirm Thomas, underscoring how difficult it is to establish claims of sexual harassment as well as how hard it is to remove the stigma of having been accused. As of 2010, Thomas remains on the Supreme Court where he has been a highly conservative voting record and has drawn the sustained scorn of most African Americans. Still, the extraordinarily high profile of the encounter firmly established the concept of "sexual harassment" among the broader American public. To read about federal laws and regulations regarding sexual harassment, see Document 2.9.

Document 6.1: Testimony of Anita Hill before the Senate Judiciary Committee

- **Document:** Excerpts from the testimony of Anita Hill during confirmation hearings for the nomination of Judge Clarence Thomas to the U.S. Supreme Court
- **Date:** October 11, 1991
- **Where:** The Judiciary Committee, U.S. Senate, Washington, DC
- **Significance:** Anita Hill, a former employee of Clarence Thomas at the Equal Employment Opportunity Commission, accuses him of sexual harassment. The testimony nearly derailed his nomination to the Supreme Court and brought the concept of sexual harassment more widely into the public consciousness.

I thought that by saying no and explaining my reasons my employer would abandon his social suggestions. However, to my regret, in the following few weeks, he continued to ask me out on several occasions. He pressed me to justify my reasons for saying no to him. These incidents took place in his office or mine. They were in the form of private conversations which would not have been overheard by anyone else.

My working relationship became even more strained when Judge Thomas began to use work situations to discuss sex. On these occasions, he would call me into his office for reports on education issues and projects, or he might suggest that, because of the time pressures of his schedule, we go to lunch to a government cafeteria. After a brief discussion of work, he would turn the conversation to a discussion of sexual matters.

His conversations were very vivid. He spoke about acts that he had seen in pornographic films involving such matters as women having sex with animals and films showing group sex or rape scenes. He talked about pornographic materials depicting individuals with large penises or large breasts involved in various sex acts. On several occasions, Thomas told me graphically of his own sexual prowess.

Because I was extremely uncomfortable talking about sex with him at all and particularly in such a graphic way, I told him that I did not want to talk about these subjects. I would also try to change the subject to education matters or to nonsexual personal matters such as his background or his beliefs. My efforts to change the subject were rarely successful . . .

For my first months at the EEOC, where I continued to be an assistant to Judge Thomas, there were no sexual conversations or overtures. However, during the fall and winter of 1982, these began again. The comments were random and ranged from pressing me about why I didn't go out with him to remarks about my personal appearance. I remember his saying that some day I would have to tell him the real reason that I wouldn't go out with him.

He began to show displeasure in his tone and voice and his demeanor and his continued pressure for an explanation. He commented on what I was wearing in terms of whether it made me more or less sexually attractive. The incidents occurred in his inner office at the EEOC.

One of the oddest episodes I remember was an occasion in which Thomas was drinking a Coke in his office. He got up from the table at which we were working, went over to his desk to get the Coke, looked at the can and asked, "Who has pubic hair on my Coke?" On other occasions, he referred to the size of his own penis as being larger than normal, and he also spoke on some occasions of the pleasures he had given to women with oral sex.

At this point, late 1982, I began to feel severe stress on the job. I began to be concerned that Clarence Thomas might take out his anger with me by degrading me or not giving me important assignments. I also thought that he might find an excuse for dismissing me . . .

When I informed him that I was leaving in July, I recall that his response was that now I would no longer have an excuse for not going out with him. I told him that I still preferred not to do so. At some time after that meeting, he asked if he could take me to dinner at the end of the term. When I declined, he assured me that the dinner was a professional courtesy only and not a social invitation. I reluctantly agreed to accept that invitation, but only if it was at the very end of a working day.

On, as I recall, the last day of my employment at the EEOC in the summer of 1983, I did have dinner with Clarence Thomas. We went directly from work to a restaurant near the office. We talked about the work I had done, both at education and at the EEOC. He told me that he was pleased with all of it except for an article and speech that I had done for him while we were at the Office for Civil Rights. Finally, he made a comment that I will vividly remember. He said that if I ever told anyone of his behavior that it would ruin his career. This was not an apology, nor was it an explanation. That was his last remark about the possibility of our going out or reference to his behavior. . . .

It is only after a great deal of agonizing consideration that I am able to talk of these unpleasant matters to anyone except my closest friends. As I've said before these last few days have been very trying and very hard for me and it hasn't just been the last few days this week. It has actually been over a month now that I have been under the strain of this issue.

Telling the world is the most difficult experience of my life, but it is very close to having to live through the experiences that occasion this meeting. I may have used poor judgment early on in my relationship with this issue. I was aware, however, that telling at any point in my career could adversely affect my future career. And I did not want early on to burn all the bridges to the EEOC . . .

It would have been more comfortable to remain silent. I took no initiative to inform anyone. But when I was asked by a representative of this committee to report my experience, I felt that I had to tell the truth. I could not keep silent.

"I thought that by saying no and explaining my reasons my employer would abandon his social suggestions. However, to my regret, in the following few weeks, he continued to ask me out on several occasions. He pressed me to justify my reasons for saying no to him."

Document 6.2: Response by Judge Clarence Thomas

- *Document:* Excerpts from the testimony of Judge Clarence Thomas during confirmation hearings for his nomination to the U.S. Supreme Court
- *Date:* October 11, 1991
- *Where:* The Judiciary Committee, U.S. Senate, Washington, DC
- *Significance*: Judge Clarence Thomas rebuts the accusations of sexual harassment and inappropriate discussion of sexual issues made by his former employee Anita Hill. His thorough denial and tone of indignation help to save his nomination, which is later approved 52–48 by the Senate.

Mr. Chairman, Senator Thurmond, members of the committee. As excruciatingly difficult as the last two weeks have been, I welcome the opportunity to clear my name today. No one other than my wife and Senator Danforth, to whom I read this statement at 6:30 a.m. has seen or heard this statement. No handlers, no advisors.

The first I learned of the allegations by Professor Anita Hill was on September 25, 1991, when the FBI came to my home to investigate her allegations. When informed by the FBI agent of the nature of the allegations and the person making them, I was shocked, surprised, hurt and enormously saddened. I have not been the same since that day.

For almost a decade my responsibilities included enforcing the rights of victims of sexual harassment. As a boss, as a friend, and as a human being I was proud that I had never had such an allegation leveled against me, even as I sought to promote women and minorities into non-traditional jobs.

In addition, several of my friends who are women have confided in me about the horror of harassment on the job or elsewhere. I thought I really understood the anguish, the fears, the doubts, the seriousness of the matter. But since September 25th, I have suffered immensely as these very serious charges were leveled against me. I have been racking my brains and eating my insides out trying to think of what I could have said or done to Anita Hill to lead her to allege that I was interested in her in more than a professional way and that I talked with her about pornographic or X-rated films.

Contrary to some press reports, I categorically denied all of the allegations and denied that I ever attempted to date Anita Hill when first interviewed by the FBI. I strongly reaffirm that denial . . .

At no time did I become aware, either directly or indirectly, that she felt I had said or done anything to change the cordial nature of our relationship. I detected nothing from her or from my staff, or from Gil Hardy, our mutual friend, with whom I maintained regular contact. I am certain that had any statement or conduct on my part been brought to my attention I would remember it clearly because of the nature

U.S. Supreme Court nominee Judge Clarence Thomas testifies before the Senate Judiciary Committee in October 1991. (AP Photo/Dennis Cook)

and seriousness of such conduct, as well as my adamant opposition to sex discrimination and sexual harassment. But there were no such statements . . .

When I stood next to the President in Kennebunkport being nominated to the Supreme Court of the United States, that was a high honor; but as I sit here before you 103 days later, that honor has been crushed. From the very beginning, charges were leveled against me from the shadows, charges of drug abuse, antisemitism, wife beating, drug use by family members, that I was a quota appointment, confirmation conversion, and much, much more. And now, this . . .

I'm not going to allow myself to be further humiliated in order to be confirmed. I am here specifically to respond to allegations of sex harassment in the workplace. I am not here to be further humiliated by this committee or anyone else, or to put my private life on display for prurient interests or other reasons. I will not allow this committee or anyone else to probe into my private life. This is not what America is all about. To ask me to do that would be to ask me to go beyond fundamental fairness.

Yesterday I called my mother. She was confined to her bed, unable to work and unable to stop crying. Enough is enough.

Mr. Chairman, in my 43 years on this earth I have been able with the help of others and with the help of God to defy poverty, avoid prison, overcome segregation, bigotry, racism and obtain one of the finest educations available in this country, but I have not been able to overcome this process. This is worse than any obstacle or anything that I have ever faced. . . .

Mr. Chairman, I am a victim of this process. My name has been harmed. My integrity has been harmed. My character has been harmed. My family has been harmed. My friends have been harmed. There is nothing this committee, this body, or this country can do to give me my good name back. Nothing.

I will not provide the rope for my own lynching or for further humiliation. I am not going to engage in discussions nor will I submit to roving questions of what goes on in the most intimate

> "I have been racking my brains and eating my insides out trying to think of what I could have said or done to Anita Hill to lead her to allege that I was interested in her in more than a professional way and that I talked with her about pornographic or X-rated films."

parts of my private life or the sanctity of my bedroom. These are the most intimate parts of my privacy, and they will remain just that, private.

"I did not have sex with that woman . . ."

The Impeachment of President Bill Clinton

The greatest sex scandal involving a politician in modern times—perhaps in all of American history—is the affair between President Bill Clinton and White House intern Monica Lewinsky. During an impasse with Congress over the federal budget in 1995, many government employees were sent on unpaid furlough, including even employees of the White House itself. Unpaid interns were called on to fill in, and several suddenly had far more direct access to the president than is usually the case. Lewinsky, infatuated with Clinton and aware of his reputation as a womanizer, flirted with the president when they were briefly alone one evening.

Clinton subsequently arranged a series of clandestine meetings with Lewinsky in and near the Oval Office over the next two years. Clinton also called Lewinsky on a few occasions and, in her telling, began a romantic relationship. The two engage in a variety of fleeting sexual encounters, up to and including oral sex performed by Lewinsky on Clinton. The lurid details of these encounters, as related by Lewinsky, were later recounted in graphic detail by Independent Counsel Kenneth Starr in a report to Congress (see Document 6.3).

During the same time period, Clinton had been sued for monetary damages by Paula Jones, a former Arkansas state employee who said that he sexually harassed her when he was that state's governor in the 1980s. Clinton gave a deposition under oath in the case, during which he

---

Historical View: 18th and 19th Century Political Sex Scandals in America

The sexual behavior of American political figures has long been subject to public scrutiny, if not perhaps in as much lurid detail as today. Early colonists in New York, for example, wrote to London complaining that their newly appointed governor was a transvestite; he was reported to have—unconvincingly—countered that as the representative of the Queen, he needed to dress as she would.

Of more enduring significance was the 1797 press coverage of an extramarital affair between founding father Alexander Hamilton and Maria Reynolds, both of whom were married to other people. Hamilton was blackmailed, and then later exposed, by Reynolds's husband. The news stories forced Hamilton to produce a detailed confession and to step down as secretary of the treasury, derailing his presidential aspirations. The scandal also helped to set in motion events that would lead to the infamous duel in which Hamilton was killed by U.S. Vice President Aaron Burr.

America's only bachelor president, James Buchanan, was reputed to have had a longtime relationship with William Rufus King, who was a senator and then vice president under Buchanan's predecessor, Franklin Pierce. Buchanan and King lived together and wrote strikingly affectionate letters to one another, provoking rumors at the time that the two were lovers. Similar letters to a friend have also led some to speculate that Buchanan's successor, Abraham Lincoln, was homosexual as well. However, others have noted that such sentimental language was quite common between close male friends in the nineteenth century.

In 1884, political opponents taunted presidential candidate Grover Cleveland with the ditty "Ma, ma, where's my pa? Gone to the White House, ha, ha, ha!" to circulate the claim that he had fathered a child out of wedlock when he was a lawyer in Buffalo. Although not sure about the child's paternity, the then-unmarried Cleveland agreed to pay child support and told his campaign to tell the truth about the matter. He went on to win the presidency twice, in nonconsecutive terms.

denied ever having had "sexual relations" with a variety of women, including Lewinsky. Throughout the affair with the president, however, Lewinsky had been confiding in her supposed friend Linda Tripp, who was surreptitiously recording their phone conversations. Tripp turned the tapes over to Starr, who was conducting a wide-ranging investigation of Clinton's possible activities before and during his time as president. Under pressure and the threat of prosecution for having herself lied about the affair while under oath, Lewinsky provided a now-infamous blue dress stained with semen that subsequent DNA testing determined to be Clinton's. For Starr, this provided irrefutable physical evidence of their affair—and thus that Clinton had committed the criminal offense of perjury.

The Starr Commission Report listed eight potential violations committed by Clinton in the context of the Lewinsky scandal, terming them potential grounds for the impeachment and removal of the president. Clinton eventually made a nationally televised address (see Document 6.4) admitting to having had "an inappropriate relationship" with Lewinsky. Using tortured logic and fine semantic parsing, however, he argued that he had technically been truthful since the term "sexual relations" connoted full sexual intercourse, which they did not have.

To the amazement of much of the world—and no small part of the American public itself—the most powerful man in the world soon found himself besieged over whether he had tried to cover up an extramarital liaison. Unlike during the Watergate scandal of two decades prior, no allegations were made that Clinton has abused the powers of his office, nor that the affair had affected the way in which he used those powers. Nonetheless, the Republican leadership claimed that Clinton's actions met the standard for "high crimes and misdemeanors" identified in the Constitution as necessary for impeachment (Document 6.5). Disingenuously, they argued that the scandal was "not about sex" but about the need to prove that even the president was subject to the rule of law.

Most Democrats—most notably First Lady Hillary Rodham Clinton and Vice President Al Gore—continued to support Clinton even while criticizing his behavior. Amid a torrent of words, the speech that captured the prevailing sentiment in the country was best captured by Democratic Senator Joseph Lieberman, a longtime friend and ally of the president (see Document 6.6). From the Senate floor, Lieberman condemned Clinton's behavior as reckless and disgraceful, but argued that impeachment was far too severe a punishment. Several proposals were advanced, including one by former Republican President Gerald Ford and former Democratic President Jimmy Carter, for a formal censure of the president that would fall short of an attempt to remove him from office. Nevertheless, the House of Representatives, almost entirely along party lines, approved two articles of impeachment (see Document 6.6). This was only the second presidential impeachment in U.S. history. The first had been against Andrew Johnson in 1868, with Richard Nixon's resignation in 1974 coming just before he was about to be formally impeached.

The first article of impeachment, claiming that Clinton had committed perjury about Lewinsky during the Jones case, passed the House by a vote of 228–206. The second article, accusing Clinton obstruction of justice by keeping his personal secretary from providing legal testimony, passed 221–212. The articles were then sent to the Senate, which held a trial presided over by the chief justice. Removal of the president from office required the support of two-thirds of the Senate (67 votes), but the first article received just 45 votes and the second 50.

Clinton to some degree recovered from the impeachment and served out the remainder of his term, but his reputation remains indelibly marred by the Lewinsky affair. Clinton eventually all but admitted that he had committed perjury, and he agreed to give up his Arkansas state law license for five years. In the minds of many, the affair and the media barrage surrounding it led to a "new low" in American culture. To some, it represented reprehensible behavior at even the highest levels of government that diminished the office of the presidency and posed an acutely embarrassing subject for discussion, especially among children. To others, it appeared to be the latest manifestation of sexual Puritanism in American society and the viciousness of partisan conflict in Washington.

Document 6.3: The Starr Commission Report

- **Document:** Referral to the United States House of Representatives by the Office of Independent Counsel Kenneth Starr
- **Date:** September 9, 1998
- **Where:** Office of the Independent Counsel, Washington, DC
- **Significance:** The Starr Report provides an extraordinarily detailed and graphic recounting of the affair between President Bill Clinton and former White House intern Monica Lewinsky. Because the report's accusations of perjury involved the term "sexual relations," it revolves around painstakingly close scrutiny of specific sexual acts. The report led directly to the impeachment of the president.

Introduction

As required by Section 595(c) of Title 28 of the United States Code, the Office of the Independent Counsel ("OIC" or "Office") hereby submits substantial and credible information that President William Jefferson Clinton committed acts that may constitute grounds for an impeachment.[1]

The information reveals that President Clinton:

lied under oath at a civil deposition while he was a defendant in a sexual harassment lawsuit;

lied under oath to a grand jury;

attempted to influence the testimony of a potential witness who had direct knowledge of facts that would reveal the falsity of his deposition testimony;

---

[1]http://icreport.access.gpo.gov/report/5intro.htm#N_1_

attempted to obstruct justice by facilitating a witness's plan to refuse to comply with a subpoena;

attempted to obstruct justice by encouraging a witness to file an affidavit that the President knew would be false, and then by making use of that false affidavit at his own deposition;

lied to potential grand jury witnesses, knowing that they would repeat those lies before the grand jury; and

engaged in a pattern of conduct that was inconsistent with his constitutional duty to faithfully execute the laws.

The evidence shows that these acts, and others, were part of a pattern that began as an effort to prevent the disclosure of information about the President's relationship with a former White House intern and employee, Monica S. Lewinsky, and continued as an effort to prevent the information from being disclosed in an ongoing criminal investigation. . . .

A still from a video taken at a White House lawn reception in November 1996 shows President Clinton greeting intern Monica Lewinsky. The president's "improper" relationship with Lewinsky led to his impeachment in 1998. (AP Photo/APTV)

The Contents of the Referral

The Referral consists of several parts. Part One is a Narrative. It begins with an overview of the information relevant to this investigation, then sets forth that information in chronological sequence. A large part of the Narrative is devoted to a description of the President's relationship with Monica Lewinsky. The nature of the relationship was the subject of many of the President's false statements, and his desire to keep the relationship secret provides a motive for many of his actions that apparently were designed to obstruct justice.

The Narrative is lengthy and detailed. It is the view of this Office that the details are crucial to an informed evaluation of the testimony, the credibility of witnesses, and the reliability of other evidence. Many of the details reveal highly personal information; many are sexually explicit. This is unfortunate, but it is essential. The President's defense to many of the allegations is based on a close parsing of the definitions that were used to describe his conduct. We have, after careful review, identified no manner of providing the information that reveals the falsity of the President's statements other than to describe his conduct with precision. . . .

First Meetings with the President

In the autumn of 1995, an impasse over the budget forced the federal government to shut down for one week, from Tuesday, November 14, to Monday, November 20. Only essential federal employees were permitted to work during the furlough, and the White House staff of

430 shrank to about 90 people for the week. White House interns could continue working because of their unpaid status, and they took on a wide range of additional duties.

During the shutdown, Ms. Lewinsky worked in Chief of Staff Panetta's West Wing office, where she answered phones and ran errands. The President came to Mr. Panetta's office frequently because of the shutdown, and he sometimes talked with Ms. Lewinsky. She characterized these encounters as "continued flirtation." According to Ms. Lewinsky, a Senior Adviser to the Chief of Staff, Barry Toiv, remarked to her that she was getting a great deal of "face time" with the President.

C. November 15 Sexual Encounter

Ms. Lewinsky testified that Wednesday, November 15, 1995—the second day of the government shutdown—marked the beginning of her sexual relationship with the President. . . . According to Ms. Lewinsky, she and the President made eye contact when he came to the West Wing to see Mr. Panetta and Deputy Chief of Staff Harold Ickes, then again later at an informal birthday party for Jennifer Palmieri, Special Assistant to the Chief of Staff. At one point, Ms. Lewinsky and the President talked alone in the Chief of Staff's office. In the course of flirting with him, she raised her jacket in the back and showed him the straps of her thong underwear, which extended above her pants . . .

According to Ms. Lewinsky, she and the President kissed. She unbuttoned her jacket; either she unhooked her bra or he lifted her bra up; and he touched her breasts with his hands and mouth. Ms. Lewinsky testified: "I believe he took a phone call . . . and so we moved from the hallway into the back office. . . . [H]e put his hand down my pants and stimulated me manually in the genital area." While the President continued talking on the phone (Ms. Lewinsky understood that the caller was a Member of Congress or a Senator), she performed oral sex on him. He finished his call, and, a moment later, told Ms. Lewinsky to stop. In her recollection: "I told him that I wanted . . . to complete that. And he said . . . that he needed to wait until he trusted me more. And then I think he made a joke . . . that he hadn't had that in a long time." . . .

D. November 17 Sexual Encounter

Ms. Lewinsky and the President went into the area of the private study, according to Ms. Lewinsky. There, either in the hallway or the bathroom, she and the President kissed. After a few minutes, in Ms. Lewinsky's recollection, she told him that she needed to get back to her desk. The President suggested that she bring him some slices of pizza. A few minutes later, she returned to the Oval Office area with pizza and told Ms. Currie that the President had requested it. . . .

Ms. Lewinsky testified that she and the President had a sexual encounter during this visit. They kissed, and the President touched Ms. Lewinsky's bare breasts with his hands and mouth. At some point, Ms. Currie approached the door leading to the hallway, which was ajar, and said that the President had a telephone call. Ms. Lewinsky recalled that the caller was a Member of Congress with a nickname. While the President was on the telephone, according to Ms. Lewinsky, "he unzipped his pants and exposed himself," and she performed oral sex. Again, he stopped her before he ejaculated.

During this visit, according to Ms. Lewinsky, the President told her that he liked her smile and her energy. He also said: "I'm usually around on weekends, no one else is around, and you can come and see me." . . .

A. January 7 Sexual Encounter

Ms. Lewinsky testified that during this bathroom encounter, she and the President kissed, and he touched her bare breasts with his hands and his mouth. The President "was talking about performing oral sex on me," according to Ms. Lewinsky. But she stopped him because she was menstruating and he did not. Ms. Lewinsky did perform oral sex on him.

Afterward, she and the President moved to the Oval Office and talked. According to Ms. Lewinsky: "[H]e was chewing on a cigar. And then he had the cigar in his hand and he was kind of looking at the cigar in . . . sort of a naughty way. And so . . . I looked at the cigar and I looked at him and I said, we can do that, too, some time." . . .

I. There is substantial and credible information that President Clinton lied under oath as a defendant in *Jones v. Clinton* regarding his sexual relationship with Monica Lewinsky.

(1) He denied that he had a "sexual relationship" with Monica Lewinsky.
(2) He denied that he had a "sexual affair" with Monica Lewinsky.
(3) He denied that he had "sexual relations" with Monica Lewinsky.
(4) He denied that he engaged in or caused contact with the genitalia of "any person" with an intent to arouse or gratify (oral sex performed on him by Ms. Lewinsky).
(5) He denied that he made contact with Monica Lewinsky's breasts or genitalia with an intent to arouse or gratify.

A. Evidence that President Clinton Lied Under Oath During the Civil Case

1. President Clinton's Statements Under Oath About Monica Lewinsky

At the January 17, 1998, deposition of the President, Ms. Jones's attorneys asked the President specific questions about possible sexual activity with Monica Lewinsky. The attorneys used various terms in their questions, including "sexual affair," "sexual relationship," and "sexual relations." The terms "sexual affair" and "sexual relationship" were not specially defined by Ms. Jones's attorneys. The term "sexual relations" was defined:

For the purposes of this deposition, a person engages in "sexual relations" when the person knowingly engages in or causes . . . contact with the genitalia, anus, groin, breast, inner thigh, or buttocks of any person with an intent to arouse or gratify the sexual desire of any person. . . . "Contact" means intentional touching, either directly or through clothing.

President Clinton answered a series of questions about Ms. Lewinsky, including:

Q: Did you have an extramarital sexual affair with Monica Lewinsky?

WJC: *No.*

Q: If she told someone that she had a sexual affair with you beginning in November of 1995, would that be a lie?

WJC: *It's certainly not the truth. It would not be the truth.*

Q: I think I used the term "sexual affair." And so the record is completely clear, have you ever had sexual relations with Monica Lewinsky, as that term is defined in Deposition Exhibit 1, as modified by the Court?

Mr. Bennett: I object because I don't know that he can remember—

Judge Wright: Well, it's real short. He can—I will permit the question and you may show the witness definition number one.

WJC: *I have never had sexual relations with Monica Lewinsky. I've never had an affair with her . . .*

The ten incidents are recounted here because they are necessary to assess whether the President lied under oath, both in his civil deposition, where he denied any sexual relationship at all, and in his grand jury testimony, where he acknowledged an "inappropriate intimate contact" but denied *any* sexual contact with Ms. Lewinsky's breasts or genitalia. When reading the following descriptions, the President's denials under oath should be kept in mind.

Unfortunately, the nature of the President's denials requires that the contrary evidence be set forth in detail. If the President, in his grand jury appearance, had admitted the sexual activity recounted by Ms. Lewinsky and conceded that he had lied under oath in his civil deposition, these particular descriptions would be superfluous. Indeed, we refrained from questioning Ms. Lewinsky under oath about particular details until after the President's August 17 testimony made that questioning necessary. But in view of (i) the President's denials, (ii) his continued contention that his civil deposition testimony was legally accurate under the terms and definitions employed, and (iii) his refusal to answer related questions, the detail is critical. The detail provides credibility and corroboration to Ms. Lewinsky's testimony. It also demonstrates with clarity that the President lied under oath *both* in his civil deposition *and* to the federal grand jury. There is substantial and credible information that the President's lies about his relationship with Ms. Lewinsky were abundant and calculating . . .

Physical Evidence

Ms. Lewinsky produced to OIC investigators a dress she wore during the encounter on February 28, 1997, which she believed might be stained with the President's semen. At the request of the OIC, the FBI Laboratory examined the dress and found semen stains. At that point, the OIC requested a DNA sample from the President. On August 3, 1998, two weeks before the President's grand jury testimony, a White House physician drew blood from the President in the presence of a senior OIC attorney and a FBI special agent. Through the most sensitive DNA testing, RFLP testing, the FBI Laboratory determined conclusively that the semen on Ms. Lewinsky's dress was, in fact, the President's. The chance that the semen is not the President's is one in 7.87 trillion.

Summary

The detailed testimony of Ms. Lewinsky, her corroborating prior consistent statements to her friends, family members, and counselors, and the evidence of the President's semen on Ms. Lewinsky's dress establish that Ms. Lewinsky and the President engaged in substantial sexual activity between November 15, 1995, and December 28, 1997.

The President, however, testified under oath in the civil case—both in his deposition and in a written answer to an interrogatory—that he did *not* have a "sexual relationship" or a "sexual affair" or "sexual relations" with Ms. Lewinsky. In addition, he denied engaging in activity covered by a more specific definition of "sexual relations" used at the deposition.

In his civil case, the President made five different false statements related to the sexual relationship. For four of the five statements, the President asserts a semantic defense: The President argues that the terms used in the *Jones* deposition to cover sexual activity did not cover the sexual activity in which he engaged with Ms. Lewinsky. For his other false statements, the President's response is factual—namely, he disputes Ms. Lewinsky's account that he ever touched her breasts or genitalia during sexual activity.

The President's denials—semantic and factual—do not withstand scrutiny.

First, in his civil deposition, the President denied a "sexual affair" with Ms. Lewinsky (the term was not defined). The President's response to lying under oath on this point rests on his definition of "sexual affair"—namely, that it requires sexual intercourse, no matter how extensive the sexual activities might otherwise be. According to the President, a man could regularly engage in oral sex and fondling of breasts and genitals with a woman and yet not have a "sexual affair" with her.

Second, in his civil deposition, the President also denied a "sexual relationship" with Ms. Lewinsky (the term was not defined). The President's response to lying under oath on this point similarly rests on his definition of "sexual relationship"—namely, that it requires sexual intercourse. Once again, under the President's theory, a man could regularly engage in oral sex and fondling of breasts and genitals with a woman, yet not have a "sexual relationship" with her.

The President's claim as to his interpretation of "sexual relationship" is belied by the fact that the President's own lawyer—earlier at that same deposition—equated the term "sexual relationship" with "sex of any kind in any manner, shape or form." The President's lawyer offered that interpretation when requesting Judge Wright to limit the questioning to prevent further inquiries with respect to Monica Lewinsky. As the videotape of the deposition reveals, the President was present and apparently looking in the direction of his attorney when his attorney offered that statement. The President gave no indication that he disagreed with his attorney's straightforward interpretation that the term "sexual relationship" means "sex of any kind in any manner, shape, or form." Nor did the President thereafter take any steps to correct the attorney's statement.

Third, in an answer to an interrogatory submitted before his deposition, the President denied having "sexual relations" with Ms. Lewinsky (the term was not defined). Yet again, the President's apparent rejoinder to lying under oath on this point rests on his definition of "sexual relations"—that it, too, requires sexual intercourse. According to President Clinton, oral sex does not constitute sexual relations.

Fourth, in his civil deposition, the President denied committing any acts that fell within the specific definition of "sexual relations" that was in effect for purposes of that deposition. Under that specific definition, sexual relations occurs "when the person knowingly engages in or causes contact with the genitalia, anus, groin, breast, inner thigh, or buttocks of any person with an intent to arouse or gratify the sexual desire of any person." Thus, the President denied engaging in or causing contact with the genitalia, breasts, or anus of "any person" with an intent to arouse or gratify the sexual desire of "any person."

Concerning oral sex, the President's sole answer to the charge that he lied under oath at the deposition focused on his interpretation of "any person" in the definition. Ms. Lewinsky testified that she performed oral sex on the President on nine occasions. The President said that by *receiving* oral sex, he would not "engage in" or "cause" contact with the genitalia, anus, groin, breast, inner thigh, or buttocks of "any person" because "any person" really means

> "I have never had sexual relations with Monica Lewinsky. I've never had an affair with her ..."

"any *other* person." The President further testified before the grand jury: "[I]f the deponent is the person who has oral sex performed on him, then the contact is with—*not with anything on that list, but with the lips of another person.*"

The President's linguistic parsing is unreasonable. Under the President's interpretation (which he says he followed at his deposition), in an oral sex encounter, one person *is* engaged in sexual relations, but the other person *is not* engaged in sexual relations.

Even assuming that the definitional language can be manipulated to exclude the deponent's receipt of oral sex, the President is still left with the difficulty that reasonable persons would not have understood it that way. And in context, the President's semantics become even weaker: The *Jones* suit rested on the allegation that the President sought to have Ms. Jones perform oral sex on him. Yet the President now claims that the expansive definition devised for deposition questioning should be interpreted to exclude that very act.

Fifth, by denying at his civil deposition that he had engaged in any acts falling within the specific definition of "sexual relations," the President denied engaging in or causing contact with the breasts or genitalia of Ms. Lewinsky with an intent to arouse or gratify one's sexual desire. In contrast to his explanations of the four preceding false statements under oath, the President's defense to lying under oath in this instance is purely *factual*. . . .

By contrast, the President's testimony strains credulity. His apparent "hands-off" scenario—in which he would have received oral sex on *nine* occasions from Ms. Lewinsky but never made direct contact with Ms. Lewinsky's breasts or genitalia—is not credible. The President's claim seems to be that he maintained a hands-off policy in ongoing sexual encounters with Ms. Lewinsky, which coincidentally happened to permit him to truthfully deny "sexual relations" with her at a deposition occurring a few years in the future. As Ms. Lewinsky noted, it suggests some kind of "service contract—that all I did was perform oral sex on him and that that's all this relationship was."

The President also had strong personal, political, and legal motives to lie in the *Jones* deposition: He did not want to admit that he had committed extramarital sex acts with a young intern in the Oval Office area of the White House. Such an admission could support Ms. Jones's theory of liability and would embarrass him. Indeed, the President admitted that during the relationship he did what he could to keep the relationship secret, including "misleading" members of his family and Cabinet. The President testified, moreover, that he "hoped that this relationship would never become public." . . .

At the time of his civil deposition, the President also could have presumed that he could lie under oath without risk because—as he knew—Ms. Lewinsky had already filed a false affidavit denying a sexual relationship with the President. Indeed, they had an understanding that each would lie under oath (explained more fully in Ground VI below). So the President might have expected that he could lie without consequence on the belief that no one could ever successfully challenge his denial of a sexual relationship with her.

In sum, based on all of the evidence and considering the President's various responses, there is substantial and credible information that the President lied under oath in his civil deposition and his interrogatory answer in denying a sexual relationship, a sexual affair, or sexual relations with Ms. Lewinsky.

Document 6.4: Statement to the Nation by President Bill Clinton

- *Date:* August 18, 1998
- *Where:* The White House, Washington, DC
- *Significance:* Faced with media reports and the then-impending formal submission of The Starr Report, President Clinton made a live televised address to the nation, admitting that he had been involved with Monica Lewinsky and that he had tried to cover it up, but denying criminal wrongdoing. The address was an unsuccessful last-minute attempt to head off impeachment—and an unprecedented moment in the history of the relationship between the American people and their leader.

Good evening. This afternoon in this room, from this chair, I testified before the Office of Independent Counsel and the grand jury.

I answered their questions truthfully, including questions about my private life, questions no American citizen would ever want to answer.

Still, I must take complete responsibility for all my actions, both public and private. And that is why I am speaking to you tonight.

As you know, in a deposition in January, I was asked questions about my relationship with Monica Lewinsky. While my answers were legally accurate, I did not volunteer information.

Indeed, I did have a relationship with Miss Lewinsky that was not appropriate. In fact, it was wrong. It constituted a critical lapse in judgment and a personal failure on my part for which I am solely and completely responsible.

But I told the grand jury today and I say to you now that at no time did I ask anyone to lie, to hide or destroy evidence or to take any other unlawful action.

Comparative View: "Vive Le Difference": The Private Lives of French Politicians

During the impeachment of Bill Clinton, an American comedian joked, "In France, they'd impeach the president if they found out he *didn't* have a mistress!" And indeed, things are different in France when it comes to the private life of public figures.

François Mitterrand was one of the dominant figures of French politics in the late twentieth century, serving two terms as president of the republic from 1981 to 1995. A socialist, he was also an openly avowed atheist—a religious sensibility that would have made it impossible for him to be elected president in the United States and many other countries. Mitterrand was rumored to have had many extramarital affairs, one of which produced a daughter named Mazarine Pingeot. Pingeot's identity was kept secret until near the end of his presidency, by which time she was an adult. In a memorable scene in 1996, Pingeot and her mother, Anne, were photographed grieving at the former president's coffin—standing alongside Mitterrand's wife, Danielle, and their sons.

The French presidential election of 2007 brought with it even thornier issues of marital relations. The Socialist Party candidate, Ségolène Royal, had four children with a partner, François Hollande, who was also the head of the French Socialist Party. Despite 30 years of involvement, the two had never married, and they separated shortly after Royal's defeat in the election. Royal accused Hollande of having a new love interest and vowed to wrest control of the party from him, then became the romantic partner of another high-ranking official in the Socialist Party.

The winner of the 2007 election, the conservative Nicolas Sarkozy, also had a notably tumultuous relationship with his wife, Cecilia, who in the late 1980s left her first husband to live with Sarkozy—even though at the time he was separated but not divorced from his own first wife. In 2005, Cecilia left her husband to live with another man in a well-publicized affair, during which time Sarkozy is said to have conducted a public affair of his own. The two appeared to reconcile in 2006, but Cecilia was absent during most of the key events of the presidential campaign, and public records revealed that she had not voted in the election.

In mid-2007, the couple abruptly divorced, provoking little more than a jaded Gallic shrug. Later that year Sarkozy began dating Carla Bruni, an Italian singer-songwriter and former supermodel. This liaison did leave many French grumbling, but less about a sex scandal than that Sarkozy's high profile cavorting was distracting him from his day job. Less than six months after their divorce, both Sarkozys were married again, Nicolas to Bruni and Cecilia to the man with whom she had had the 2005 affair.

In June 2008 French president Nicolas Sarkozy, right, and his wife, Carla Bruni-Sarkozy, arrive at an official dinner at the residence of Shimon Peres, president of Israel, in Jerusalem. (AP Photo/Menahem Kahana, Pool)

I know that my public comments and my silence about this matter gave a false impression. I misled people, including even my wife. I deeply regret that.

> "Indeed, I did have a relationship with Miss Lewinsky that was not appropriate. In fact, it was wrong."

I can only tell you I was motivated by many factors. First, by a desire to protect myself from the embarrassment of my own conduct. I was also very concerned about protecting my family. The fact that these questions were being asked in a politically inspired lawsuit, which has since been dismissed, was a consideration, too.

In addition, I had real and serious concerns about an independent counsel investigation that began with private business dealings 20 years ago, dealings, I might add, about which an independent federal agency found no evidence of any wrongdoing by me or my wife over two years ago.

The independent counsel investigation moved on to my staff and friends, then into my private life. And now the investigation itself is under investigation.

This has gone on too long, cost too much and hurt too many innocent people.

Now, this matter is between me, the two people I love most—my wife and our daughter—and our God. I must put it right, and I am prepared to do whatever it takes to do so. Nothing is more important to me personally. But it is private, and I intend to reclaim my family life for my family. It's nobody's business but ours. Even presidents have private lives.

It is time to stop the pursuit of personal destruction and the prying into private lives and get on with our national life.

Our country has been distracted by this matter for too long, and I take my responsibility for my part in all of this. That is all I can do. Now it is time—in fact, it is past time—to move on.

We have important work to do—real opportunities to seize, real problems to solve, real security matters to face.

And so tonight, I ask you to turn away from the spectacle of the past seven months, to repair the fabric of our national discourse, and to return our attention to all the challenges and all the promise of the next American century.

Thank you for watching. And good night.

Document 6.5: The Articles of Impeachment

- *Date:* December 15, 1998
- *Where:* U.S. House of Representatives, Washington, DC
- *Significance:* With this document, for only the second time in American history, the House of Representatives impeached a president. The two articles of impeachment were then sent to the Senate, where neither received the necessary two-thirds majority to remove the president. Critics of Clinton argued that he had brought the impeachment upon himself; supporters contended that the punishment vastly outweighed the alleged crime.

Resolved, That William Jefferson Clinton, President of the United States, is impeached for high crimes and misdemeanors, and that the following articles of impeachment be exhibited . . . (Reported in House)

HRES 611 RH
House Calendar No. 281

105th CONGRESS 2d Session

H. RES. 611[Report No. 105-830]

Impeaching William Jefferson Clinton, President of the United States, for high crimes and misdemeanors.

IN THE HOUSE OF REPRESENTATIVES

December 15, 1998

Mr. HYDE submitted the following resolution; which was referred to the House Calendar and ordered to be printed

---

RESOLUTION

Impeaching William Jefferson Clinton, President of the United States, for high crimes and misdemeanors.

Resolved, That William Jefferson Clinton, President of the United States, is impeached for high crimes and misdemeanors, and that the following articles of impeachment be exhibited to the United States Senate:

Articles of impeachment exhibited by the House of Representatives of the United States of America in the name of itself and of the people of the United States of America, against William Jefferson Clinton, President of the United States of America, in maintenance and support of its impeachment against him for high crimes and misdemeanors.

Article I

In his conduct while President of the United States, William Jefferson Clinton, in violation of his constitutional oath faithfully to execute the office of President of the United States and, to the best of his ability, preserve, protect, and defend the Constitution of the United States, and in violation of his constitutional duty to take care that the laws be faithfully executed, has willfully corrupted and manipulated the judicial process of the United States for his personal gain and exoneration, impeding the administration of justice, in that:

On August 17, 1998, William Jefferson Clinton swore to tell the truth, the whole truth, and nothing but the truth before a Federal grand jury of the United States. Contrary to that oath, William Jefferson Clinton willfully provided perjurious, false and misleading testimony to the grand jury concerning one or more of the following: (1) the nature and details of his relationship with a subordinate Government employee; (2) prior perjurious, false and misleading testimony he gave in a Federal civil rights action brought against him; (3) prior false and misleading statements he allowed his attorney to make to a Federal judge in that civil rights action; and (4) his corrupt efforts to influence the testimony of witnesses and to impede the discovery of evidence in that civil rights action.

In doing this, William Jefferson Clinton has undermined the integrity of his office, has brought disrepute on the Presidency, has betrayed his trust as President, and has acted in a manner subversive of the rule of law and justice, to the manifest injury of the people of the United States.

Wherefore, William Jefferson Clinton, by such conduct, warrants impeachment and trial, and removal from office and disqualification to hold and enjoy any office of honor, trust, or profit under the United States.

Article III

In his conduct while President of the United States, William Jefferson Clinton, in violation of his constitutional oath faithfully to execute the office of President of the United States and, to the best of his ability, preserve, protect, and defend the Constitution of the United States, and in violation of his constitutional duty to take care that the laws be faithfully executed, has prevented, obstructed, and impeded the administration of justice, and has to that end engaged personally, and through his subordinates and agents, in a course of conduct or scheme designed to delay, impede, cover up, and conceal the existence of evidence and testimony related to a Federal civil rights action brought against him in a duly instituted judicial proceeding.

The means used to implement this course of conduct or scheme included one or more of the following acts:

(1) On or about December 17, 1997, William Jefferson Clinton corruptly encouraged a witness in a Federal civil rights action brought against him to execute a sworn affidavit in that proceeding that he knew to be perjurious, false and misleading.

(2) On or about December 17, 1997, William Jefferson Clinton corruptly encouraged a witness in a Federal civil rights action brought against him to give perjurious, false and misleading testimony if and when called to testify personally in that proceeding.

(3) On or about December 28, 1997, William Jefferson Clinton corruptly engaged in, encouraged, or supported a scheme to conceal evidence that had been subpoenaed in a Federal civil rights action brought against him.

(4) Beginning on or about December 7, 1997, and continuing through and including January 14, 1998, William Jefferson Clinton intensified and succeeded in an effort to secure job assistance to a witness in a Federal civil rights action brought against him in order to corruptly prevent the truthful testimony of that witness in that proceeding at a time when the truthful testimony of that witness would have been harmful to him.

(5) On January 17, 1998, at his deposition in a Federal civil rights action brought against him, William Jefferson Clinton corruptly allowed his attorney to make false and misleading statements to a Federal judge characterizing an affidavit, in order to prevent questioning deemed relevant by the judge. Such false and misleading statements were subsequently acknowledged by his attorney in a communication to that judge.

(6) On or about January 18 and January 20–21, 1998, William Jefferson Clinton related a false and misleading account of events relevant to a Federal civil rights action brought against him to a potential witness in that proceeding, in order to corruptly influence the testimony of that witness.

(7) On or about January 21, 23 and 26, 1998, William Jefferson Clinton made false and misleading statements to potential witnesses in a Federal grand jury proceeding in order to corruptly influence the testimony of those witnesses. The false and misleading statements made by William Jefferson Clinton were repeated by the witnesses to the grand jury, causing the grand jury to receive false and misleading information.

In all of this, William Jefferson Clinton has undermined the integrity of his office, has brought disrepute on the Presidency, has betrayed his trust as President, and has acted in a manner subversive of the rule of law and justice, to the manifest injury of the people of the United States.

Wherefore, William Jefferson Clinton, by such conduct, warrants impeachment and trial, and removal from office and disqualification to hold and enjoy any office of honor, trust, or profit under the United States.

"Wherefore, William Jefferson Clinton, by such conduct, warrants impeachment and trial, and removal from office and disqualification to hold and enjoy any office of honor, trust, or profit under the United States."

Document 6.6: Speech by Senator Joseph Lieberman

- *Document:* Comments by Senator Joseph Lieberman (D-Connecticut) about Bill Clinton and the Lewinsky scandal
- *Date:* September 3, 1998
- *Where:* Floor of the U.S. Senate, Washington, DC
- *Significance:* Senator Lieberman's comments reflected the views of many in the United States that Clinton's behavior was shameful but that impeachment was not warranted. His status as a Democrat and a supporter of "traditional values" provided him with good standing to advance his argument; it also helped to win him the Democratic vice-presidential nomination in 2000.

I was disappointed because the president of the United States had just confessed to engaging in an extramarital affair with a young woman in his employ and to willfully deceiving the nation about his conduct. I was personally angry because President Clinton had, by his disgraceful behavior, jeopardized his administration's historic record of accomplishment, much of which grew out of the principles and programs that he and I and many others had worked on together in the new Democratic movement....

The president is not just the elected leader of our country. He is as presidential scholar Clinton Rossiter observed, and I quote, "the one man distillation of the American people." And as President Taft said at another time, "the personal embodiment and representative of their dignity and majesty."

So, when his personal conduct is embarrassing, it is sadly so not just for him and his family, it is embarrassing for all of us as Americans.

The president is a role model. And because of his prominence in the moral authority that emanates from his office, sets standards of behavior for the people he serves ...

In this case, the president apparently had extramarital relations with an employee half his age and did so in the workplace in the vicinity of the Oval Office. Such behavior is not just inappropriate. It is immoral. And it is harmful, for it sends a message of what is acceptable behavior to the larger American family—particularly to our children—which is as influential as the negative messages communicated by the entertainment culture.

If you doubt that, just ask America's parents about the intimate and frequently unseemly sexual questions their young children have been asking them and discussing since the president's relationship with Ms. Lewinsky became public seven months ago. I have had many of those conversations with parents, particularly in Connecticut, and from them I conclude that parents across our country feel much as I do that something very sad and sordid has happened in American life when I cannot watch the news on television with my 10-year-old daughter anymore . . .

The president's relationship with Ms. Lewinsky not only contradicted the values he has publicly embraced over the last six years, it has, I fear, compromised his moral authority at a time when Americans of every political persuasion agree that the decline of the family is one of the most pressing problems we are facing.

Nevertheless, I believe the president could have lessened the harm his relationship with Ms. Lewinsky has caused if he had acknowledged his mistake and spoken with candor about it to the American people shortly after it became public in January.

But, as we now know, he chose not to do this. This deception is particularly troubling because it was not just a reflexive, and many ways, understandable human act of concealment to protect himself and his family from what he called the embarrassment of his own conduct when he was confronted with it in the deposition in the Jones case. But rather, it was the intentional and pre-meditated decision to do so. . . .

The last three weeks have been dominated by a cacophony of media and political voices calling for impeachment or resignation or censure, while a lesser chorus implores us to move on and get this matter behind us.

Appealing as that latter option may be to many people who are understandably weary of this crisis, the transgressions the president has admitted to are too consequential for us to walk away and leave the impression for our children today and for our posterity tomorrow that what he acknowledges he did within the White House is acceptable behavior for our nation's leader. On the contrary, as I have said, it is wrong and unacceptable and should be followed by some measure of public rebuke and accountability.

We in Congress, selected representatives of all the American people, are surely capable institutionally of expressing such disapproval through a resolution of reprimand or censure of the president for his misconduct. But it is premature to do so, as my colleagues of both parties seem to agree, until we have received the report of the independent counsel and the White House's response to it.

In the same way, it seems to me that talk of impeachment and resignation at this time is unjust and unwise. It is unjust because we do not know enough in fact, and will not until the independent counsel reports and the White House responds to conclude whether we have crossed the high threshold our constitution rightly sets for overturning the results of a popular

> "When his personal conduct is embarrassing, it is sadly so not just for him and his family, it is embarrassing for all of us as Americans."

election in our democracy and bringing on the national trauma of removing an incumbent president from office . . .

"I am a gay American"

The Resignation of New Jersey Governor James McGreevey

One of the more startling moments in recent American political history was the sudden resignation of New Jersey Governor Jim McGreevey. Although his administration had been beset with some minor scandals, nothing could have prepared the listening audience for the governor's live televised announcement in August 2004 (Document 6.7). McGreevey, a married man with an infant child, revealed that he was a "gay American" and had had an affair with another man. His wife at his side, he asked for forgiveness while also announcing that in the interest of all involved he would be resigning.

In the days that followed, it was learned that the man with whom McGreevey had been involved was an Israeli citizen named Golan Cipel, whom McGreevey had appointed as the state's homeland security advisor despite having only marginal experience in the field. Cipel quickly returned to his native Israel, denying that the affair had been consensual and calling McGreevey a sexual predator. Some speculated that Cipel might have been threatening to blackmail McGreevey, leading the governor to preemptively resign before the story could hit the media.

Once the shock of the event wore off, it remained less than clear why McGreevey had resigned. Was it simply because he was gay? Other politicians had survived that disclosure. Was it because he had married a woman shortly before running for the governorship, prompting charges that he had been insensitive and opportunistic? Was it because he had had an extramarital affair with a man? Was it because that man was a state appointee with dubious credentials? Was there more to the story—other looming scandals?

McGreevey stayed in office until after the next election (a move timed to ensure that the next governor would be a Democrat under New Jersey's law of succession). He later wrote a tell-all book, *The Confession*, and settled into a relationship with a male partner, all while engaging in a bitter and high-profile divorce settlement with his wife, Dina Matos McGreevey.

Document 6.7: Press Conference Transcript

- **Document:** Transcript of a press conference given by New Jersey Governor Jim McGreevey
- **Date:** August 12, 2004
- **Where:** The Governor's Mansion, Trenton, New Jersey
- **Significance:** Without warning, New Jersey Governor Jim McGreevey called a press conference to announce first that he was a closeted gay man, second that he had carried on an affair with another man, and third that he was resigning. The announcement was the most dramatic of its kind in American history, and the first among such a high-ranking executive.

Throughout my life, I have grappled with my own identity, who I am. As a young child, I often felt ambivalent about myself, in fact, confused.

By virtue of my traditions, and my community, I worked hard to ensure that I was accepted as part of the traditional family of America. I married my first wife, Kari, out of respect and love. And together, we have a wonderful, extraordinary daughter. Kari then chose to return to British Columbia.

I then had the blessing of marrying Dina, whose love and joy for life has been an incredible source of strength for me. And together, we have the most beautiful daughter.

Yet, from my early days in school, until the present day, I acknowledged some feelings, a certain sense that separated me from others. But because of my resolve, and also thinking that I was doing the right thing, I forced what I thought was an acceptable reality onto myself, a reality which is layered and layered with all the, quote, "good things," and all the, quote, "right things" of typical adolescent and adult behavior.

Yet, at my most reflective, maybe even spiritual level, there were points in my life when I began to question what an acceptable reality really meant for me. Were there realities from which I was running? Which master was I trying to serve?

I do not believe that God tortures any person simply for its own sake. I believe that God enables all things to work for the greater good. And this, the 47th year of my life, is arguably too late to have this discussion. But it is here, and it is now.

At a point in every person's life, one has to look deeply into the mirror of one's soul and decide one's unique truth in the world, not as we may want to see it or hope to see it, but as it is.

And so my truth is that I am a gay American. And I am blessed to live in the greatest nation with the tradition of civil liberties, the greatest tradition of civil liberties in the world, in a country which provides so much to its people.

Yet because of the pain and suffering and anguish that I have caused to my beloved family, my parents, my wife, my friends, I would almost rather have this moment pass.

For this is an intensely personal decision, and not one typically for the public domain. Yet, it cannot and should not pass.

I am also here today because, shamefully, I engaged in adult consensual affair with another man, which violates my bonds of matrimony. It was wrong. It was foolish. It was inexcusable.

And for this, I ask the forgiveness and the grace of my wife.

She has been extraordinary throughout this ordeal, and I am blessed by virtue of her love and strength.

I realize the fact of this affair and my own sexuality if kept secret leaves me, and most importantly the governor's office, vulnerable to rumors, false allegations and threats of disclosure.

So I am removing these threats by telling you directly about my sexuality.

Let me be clear, I accept total and full responsibility for my actions. However, I'm required to do now, to do what is right to correct the consequences of my actions and to be truthful to my loved ones, to my friends and my family and also to myself.

It makes little difference that as governor I am gay. In fact, having the ability to truthfully set forth my identity might have enabled me to be more forthright in fulfilling and discharging my constitutional obligations.

Given the circumstances surrounding the affair and its likely impact upon my family and my ability to govern, I have decided the right course of action is to resign.

To facilitate a responsible transition, my resignation will be effective on November 15 of this year.

I'm very proud of the things we have accomplished during my administration. And I want to thank humbly the citizens of the state of New Jersey for the privilege to govern.

> "I am here today because, shamefully, I engaged in adult consensual affair with another man, which violates my bonds of matrimony. It was wrong. It was foolish. It was inexcusable."

"I am not gay and have never been gay."

The Arrest of U.S. Senator Larry Craig of Idaho

Few sexual scandals have been quite as distasteful as the arrest of U.S. Senator Larry Craig of Idaho in 2007, charged with lewd conduct for soliciting sex with an undercover police officer in a men's room of the Minneapolis–St. Paul International Airport. A three-term senator, Craig was a known as a rock-solid, "family values" conservative who consistently opposed gay-rights legislation. Still, rumors had quietly circulated in both Washington and Idaho that Craig might be gay, or more precisely, that he had sex with other men without necessarily acknowledging or accepting what this implied about his sexual orientation.

On June 11, 2007, Craig was arrested and interrogated by the undercover police officer; excerpts from the transcript are provided below in Document 6.8. The officer stated that Craig had peered into the stall in which he was working undercover, and then given several "signals" such as toe tapping and hand gestures reputed to indicate desire for a quick sexual contact. Craig presented the officer with his card as a U.S. senator, perhaps hoping that his status might spare him arrest. Trying to keep the entire matter quiet, Craig later pled guilty to the lesser, nonsexually related charge of disorderly conduct and paid a $575 fine.

When news of the scandal broke in August 2007, Craig claimed that his actions had been misconstrued and that he had pled guilty only to avoid further publicity. At a press conference, he said "I am not gay. I never have been gay. . . . In June, I overreacted and made a poor decision. I chose to plead guilty to a lesser charge in hopes of making it go away. . . . Please let me apologize to my family, friends and staff and fellow Idahoans for the cloud placed over Idaho. I did nothing wrong at the Minneapolis airport."

Reactions were swift, with many of Craig's ideological and partisan allies quickly condemning him and calling for his immediate resignation. In the spirit of politics making for strange bedfellows, a number of civil libertarians and gay groups came to Craig's defense. They condemned the arrest as a form of entrapment and reflective of a long-standing tendency of law enforcement to disproportionately target public sex between men, and noted that no actual sexual contact had occurred. Others pointed out that the ambiguity of the evidence meant that Craig might well have been acquitted had the case come to trial, and that his guilty plea had been a voluntary attempt to hide the incident.

The case took a strange turn when Craig first announced his intention to resign, then changed his mind and said simply that he would not run for reelection in 2008. Craig also tried to fight the charges as well, unsuccessfully submitting a motion to withdraw his earlier guilty plea, which he claimed had been coerced. The Senator became the subject of endless jokes by late night comedians and received a letter of admonition from the Senate Ethics Committee, but continued to consistently and vehemently deny both that he had done anything wrong in Minneapolis or that he was, in fact, a gay.

Document 6.8: Transcript of the Police Interview

- **Document**: Transcript of the Police Interview by Sergeant Dave Karsinia and Detective Noel Nelson with U.S. Senator Larry Craig of Idaho
- **Date:** June 11, 2007
- **Where**: Minneapolis, Minnesota
- **Significance:** Senator Craig was accused of soliciting sex with an undercover police officer in a men's room, and subsequently was arrested and pled guilty to a lesser charge of disorderly conduct.

Investigative Sergeant Dave Karsnia #4211 (DK) and Detective Noel Nelson #62 (NN)
INTERVIEW WITH Larry Craig (LC)
Case 07002008

DK: Okay. Um, I just wanna start off with your side of the story, okay. So, a . . .

LC: So I go into the bathroom here as I normally do. I'm a commuter too here.

DK: Okay.

LC: I sit down, um, to go to the bathroom and ah, you said our feet bumped. I believe they did, ah, because I reached down and scooted over and um, the next thing I knew, under the bathroom divider comes a card that says Police. Now, um, (sigh) that's about as far as I can take it. I don't know of anything else. Ah, your foot came toward mine, mine came towards yours, was that natural? I don't know. Did we bump? Yes. I think we did. You said so. I don't disagree with that.

DK: Okay. I don't want to get into a pissing match here.

LC: We're not going to.

DK: Good. Um.

LC: I don't, ah, I am not gay. I don't do these kinds of things and . . .

DK: It doesn't matter. I don't care about sexual preference or anything like that. Here's your stuff back sir. Um, I don't care about sexual preference.

LC: I know you don't. You're out to enforce the law.

DK: Right.

LC: But you shouldn't be out to entrap people either.

DK: This isn't entrapment.

LC: All right . . .

DK: All right, so let's start from the beginning. You went in the bathroom.

LC: I went in the bathroom.

DK: And what did you do when you . . .

LC: I stood beside the wall, waiting for a stall to open. I got in the stall, sat down, and I started to go to the bathroom. Ah, did our feet come together, apparently they did bump. Well, I won't dispute that.

DK: Okay. When I got out of the stall, I noticed other other stalls were open.

LC: They were at the time. At that time I entered, I, I, at the time entered. I stood and waited.

DK: Okay.

LC: They were all busy, you know?

DK: Were you (inaudible) out here while you were waiting? I could see your eyes. I saw you playing with your fingers and then look up. Play with your fingers and then look up.

LC: Did I glance at your stall? I was glancing at a stall right beside yours waiting for a fella to empty it. I saw him stand up and therefore I thought it was going to empty.

DK: How long do you think you stood outside the stalls?

LC: Oh a minute or two at the most.

DK: Okay. And when you went in the stalls, then what?

LC: Sat down.

DK: Okay. Did you do anything with your feet?

LC: Positioned them, I don't know. I don't know at the time. I'm a fairly wide guy.

DK: I understand.

LC: I had to spread my legs.

DK: Okay.

LC: When I lower my pants so they won't slide.

DK: Okay.

LC: Did I slide them to close to yours? Did I, I looked down once, your foot was close to mine.

DK: Yes.

LC: Did we bump? Ah, you said so, I don't recall that, but apparently we were close.

DK: Yeah, well your foot did touch mine, on my side of the stall.

> "I don't, ah, I am not gay . . . I'm a respectable person and I don't do these kinds of . . ."

LC: All right.

DK: Okay. And then with the hand. Um, how many times did you put your hand under the stall?

LC: I don't recall. I remember reaching down once. There was a piece of toilet paper back behind me and picking it up . . .

DK: Okay. You, you travel through here frequently correct?

LC: I do.

DK: Um.

LC: Almost weekly.

DK: Have you been successful in these bathrooms here before?

LC: I go to that bathroom regularly.

DK: I mean for any type of other activities.

LC: No. Absolutely not. I don't seek activity in bathrooms.

DK: It's embarrassing.

LC: Well it's embarrassing for both. I'm not gonna fight you.

DK: I know you're not going to fight me. But that's not the point. I would respect you and I still respect you. I don't disrespect you but I'm disrespected right now and I'm not trying to act like I have all kinds of power or anything, but you're sitting here lying to a police officer.

LC: I, I, I . . .

DK: I just. I just. I guess, I guess I'm gonna say that I'm just disappointed in you sir, I'm just really am. I expect this from the guy that we get out of the hood. I mean, people vote for you.

LC: Yes, they do. (inaudible)

DK: Unbelievable, unbelievable.

LC: I'm a respectable person and I don't do these kinds of . . .

DK: And (inaudible) respect right now though

LC: But I didn't use my left hand.

DK: I thought that you . . .

LC: I reached down with my right hand like this to pick a piece of paper.

DK: Was your gold ring on your right hand at anytime today.

LC: Of course not, try to get it off, look at it.

DK: Okay. Then it was your left hand. I saw it with my own eyes.

LC: All right, you saw something that didn't happen.

DK: Embarrassing, embarrassing. No wonder why we're going down the tubes. Anything to add?

LC: Uh, no.

DK: Embarrassing. Date is 6/11/07 at 1236 interview is done.

LC: Okay.

"Client 9" and "Kristen": The FBI Investigation of New York Governor Eliot Spitzer

Four years after the sudden and unexpected resignation of James McGreevey as the governor of New Jersey, the neighboring state of New York was rocked by a sex scandal of its own when it was revealed that Governor Eliot Spitzer had been a client of a high-priced prostitution ring. Faced with evidence from a federal investigation that he had spent tens of thousands of dollars hiring prostitutes, Spitzer quickly apologized and resigned his office, abruptly ending a meteoric rise that many had once speculated would end in the White House.

Barely a year earlier, Spitzer had come to office amid tremendous popularity and with the largest electoral landslide of any governor in New York State history. During a stunningly successful eight-year tenure as New York State Attorney General, Spitzer had brought high-profile prosecutions, including against several "escort services," which he harshly and publicly condemned. Because Spitzer had come to office as an outspoken ethics reformer and a strong law-and-order proponent, it was all the more shocking when news broke on March 10, 2008, that he had been captured by a federal wiretap soliciting the services of a prostitute named "Kristen."

On the wiretap, Spitzer—who used a false name—was identified as "Client 9" of Emperor's Club VIP, a Web-based prostitution ring that charged $4,000 or more per night for their services. On February 13, 2008, Spitzer paid for "Kristen" to travel from New York to his hotel room in Washington, DC. The wiretap indicated that he was considered a "difficult" client who wanted to do things that might not be "safe," a statement interpreted by many to mean that he did not want to use a condom during intercourse. Key portions of the FBI's affidavit in the case are presented in Document 6.9.

Independently wealthy, it did not appear that Spitzer had misused public funds. But his attempts to hide that he was moving and transferring large sums triggered first a bank alert, then an IRS investigation, and—finally—the FBI wiretap that led to the scandal and potentially to legal charges. The FBI was initially concerned that the funds might be related to public corruption, such as that the governor had been paying off opponents or was being blackmailed. So when news broke that the money had been used to pay for prostitutes, it was all the more ironic that someone who had always claimed the moral highroad was brought low by such a sordid scandal. Further, as a prosecutor, Spitzer should have known that his actions could easily be traced and used against him, revealing an astonishing degree of personal recklessness.

The scandal peaked quickly, and mostly passed within a week, without Spitzer addressing the substance of the scandal but simply apologizing to his wife, to his three teenaged daughters, and to the people of the state. In a brief initial statement, Spitzer said, "I have acted in a way that violates my obligations to my family and violates my, or any, sense of right and wrong." Two days later, the one-time potential presidential contender had resigned, "From those to whom much is given, much is expected. I have been given much—the love of my family, the faith and trust of the people of New York, and the chance to lead this state. I am deeply sorry I did not live up to what was expected of me ... Over the course of my public life, I have insisted—I believe correctly—that people, regardless of their position or power, take responsibility for their conduct. I can and will ask no less of myself." A week after the news first broke, Spitzer's lieutenant governor, David Paterson was sworn in as his successor. Paterson's first act as governor? To call a press conference to corroborate—and thus to try to move past—rumors that both he and his wife had been unfaithful during a rocky patch of their marriage several years earlier.

Document 6.9: Affidavit Regarding a Federal Wiretap

- *Document:* Affidavit filed by FBI Special Agent Kenneth Hosey regarding a wiretap implicating New York Governor Eliot Spitzer
- *Date:* March 5, 2008
- *Where:* United States District Court, Southern District of New York, New York City
- *Significance:* Known as a law-and-order advocate, New York State Governor Eliot Spitzer was implicated by a federal wiretap as the anonymous "Client 9" of a high-priced prostitution Web site. The scandal led to his abrupt resignation, barely a year after winning a landslide victory.

On February 11, 2008, at approximately 10:53 p.m., TEMEKA RACHELLE LEWIS, a/k/a "Rachelle," the defendant, using the 6587 Number, sent a text message to CECIL SUWAL, a/k/a "Katie," a/k/a "Kate," the defendant, at the 3390 Number. In the text message, LEWIS: "Pls let me know if [Client-9's] 'package' (believed to be a reference to a deposit of money sent by mail) arrives 2mrw. Appt wd b on Wed."

SUWAL sent a text message back to LEWIS, stating: "K."

On February 12, 2008, at approximately 2:37 p.m., TEMEKA RACHELLE LEWIS, a/k/a "Rachelle," the defendant, using the 6587 Number, called a prostitute who the Emperors Club marketed using the name "Kristen." During the call, LEWIS left a message for "Kristen" that the "deposit" had not arrived today, but that they should be able to do the trip if the deposit arrived tomorrow.

At approximately 4:03 p.m., LEWIS received a call from "Kristen." During the call, "Kristen" said that she had heard the message, and that was fine. LEWIS and "Kristen" then discussed the time that "Kristen" would take the train from New York to Washington, D.C. LEWIS told

"Kristen" that there was a 5:39 p.m. train that arrived at 9:00 p.m., and that "Kristen" would be taking the train out of Penn Station.

LEWIS confirmed that Client-9 would be paying for everything—train tickets, cab fare from the hotel and back, mini bar or room service, travel time, and hotel. LEWIS said that they would probably not know until 3 p.m. if the deposit arrived because Client-9 would not do traditional wire transferring.

At approximately 8:12 p.m., TEMEKA RACHELLE LEWIS, a/k/a "Rachelle," the defendant, using the 6587 Number, received a call from Client-9. During the call, LEWIS told Client-9 that the "package" did not arrive today. LEWIS asked Client-9 if there was a return address on the envelope, and Client-9 said no.

LEWIS asked: "You had QAT . . . ," and Client-9 said: "Yup, same as in the past, no question about it." LEWIS asked Client-9 what time he was interested in having the appointment tomorrow. Client-9 told her 9:00 p.m. or 10:00 p.m. LEWIS told Client-9 to call her back in five minutes.

At approximately 8:14 p.m., TEMEKA RACHELLE LEWIS, a/k/a "Rachelle," the defendant, using the 6587 Number, called MARK BRENER, a/k/a "Michael," the defendant, at the 0937 Number. During the call, LEWIS told BRENER that Client-9 had just called about an appointment for tomorrow, and that he had around $400 or $500 credit. SUWAL said that she did not feel comfortable saying that Client-9 had a $400 credit when she did not know that for a fact.

In March 2008 New York governor Eliot Spitzer announced his resignation from office following the revelation that he was under investigation in connection with a prostitution ring. (AP Photo/Stephen Chernin)

SUWAL and BRENER talked in the background about whether Client-9 could proceed with the appointment without his deposit having arrived. At approximately 8:23 p.m., LEWIS called Client-9, and told him that the "office" said he could not proceed with the appointment with his available credit. After discussing ways to resolve the situation, LEWIS and Client-9 agreed to speak the following day.

On February 12, 2008, at approximately 9:22 p.m., TEMEKA RACHELLE LEWIS, a/k/a "Rachelle," the defendant, using the 6587 Number, sent a text message to "Kristen." In the text message, LEWIS wrote: "If D.C. appt. happens u will need 2 leave NYC@ 4:45pm. Is that possible?" "Kristen" wrote back: "Yes."

At approximately 3:20 p.m., TEMEKA RACHELLE LEWIS, a/k/a "Rachelle," the defendant, using the 6587 Number, received a call from Client-9. During the call, LEWIS told Client-9 that they were still trying to determine if his deposit had arrived.

Client-9 told LEWIS that he had made a reservation at the hotel, and had paid for it in his name. Client-9 said that there would be a key waiting for her, and told LEWIS that what he had on account with her covered the "transportation" (believed to be a reference to the cost of the trainfare for "Kristen" from New York to Washington, D.C.). LEWIS said that she would try to make it work.

At approximately 3:24 p.m., LEWIS, using the 6587 Number, called CECIL SUWAL, a/k/a "Katie," a/k/a "Kate," the defendant, at the 3390 Number. LEWIS explained to SUWAL what Client-9 had proposed. SUWAL told LEWIS she would call her back.

At approximately 3:53 p.m., MARK BRENER, a/k/a "Michael," the defendant, using the 0937 Number, called LEWIS at the 6587 Number. BRENER and LEWIS discussed the problem about Client-9's deposit. At approximately 4:18 p.m., SUWAL, using the 3390 Number, sent a text message to LEWIS at the 6587 Number, stating: "[P]ackage arrived. Pls be sure he rsvp hotel."

At approximately 4:21 p.m., TEMEKA RACHELLE LEWIS, a/k/a "Rachelle," the defendant, using the 6587 Number, called "Kristen." During the call, LEWIS told "Kristen" that the package had arrived, and that "they" (believed to be a reference to MARK BRENER, a/k/a "Michael," and CECIL SUWAL, a/k/a "Katie," a/k/a "Kate," the defendants) just got the mail. LEWIS told "Kristen" to get to Penn Station and call her when she picked up her tickets.

At approximately 4:58 p.m., TEMEKA RACHELLE LEWIS, a/k/a "Rachelle," the defendant, using the 6587 Number, received an incoming call from Client-9. During the call, LEWIS told Client-9 that his package arrived today, and Client-9 said good. LEWIS asked Client-9 what time he was expecting to have the appointment. Client-9 told LEWIS maybe 10:00 p.m. or so, and asked who it was. LEWIS said it was "Kristen," and Client-9 said "great, okay, wonderful." LEWIS told Client-9 that she would give him a final price later, and asked Client-9 whether he could give "Kristen" "extra funds" at this appointment in order to avoid payment issues in the future. Client-9 said maybe, and that he would see if he could do that. LEWIS explained that the agency did not want a model accepting funds for a future appointment, but that she was going to make an exception that way a deposit could be made so that he would have a credit, and they would not have to "go through this" next time. Client-9 said perfect, and that he would call her regarding the room number.

At approximately 7:51 p.m., TEMEKA RACHELLE LEWIS, a/k/a "Rachelle," the defendant, using the 6587 Number, received a call from Client-9. During the call, LEWIS told Client-9 that the balance was around "26" (believed to be a reference to $2,600), but she would give him an exact number later. LEWIS asked if when "Kristen" went to pick up the key she would have to give a name or would she be able to say that she was one of Client-9's guests for whom he left an envelope.

LEWIS and Client-9 discussed how to arrange for "Kristen" to get the key to her hotel room. LEWIS said that she would prefer if "Kristen" did not have to give a name. Client-9 said that he was trying to "think this through." Client-9 repeated that his balance was "2600," and stated that maybe he would give "her," a reference to "Kristen," "3600" and have a thousand on balance. LEWIS suggested making it "1500" more. Client-9 said that would make it "4100," and said that he would look for a bank and see about it.

Client-9 told LEWIS to let him go down and take care of this, and suggested that maybe he could put it [the hotel key] in an envelope with the concierge.

At approximately 8:47 p.m., TEMEKA RACHELLE LEWIS, a/k/a "Rachelle," the defendant, using the 6587 Number, received a call from Client-9. During the call, Client-9 told LEWIS to tell "Kristen" to go to the hotel and go to room 871. Client-9 told LEWIS that the door would be open. Client-9 told LEWIS that there would be a key in the room, but the door would be ajar.

> "Client 9 might 'ask you to do things that, like, you might not think were safe—you know . . .'"

LEWIS asked if the hotel staff might pass by the door and close it, and Client-9 said no it was okay. Client-9 explained that the door would not be visibly open, but if someone pushed it, the door would open. LEWIS told Client-9 that his balance was $2,721.41, and that if he wanted to do an additional "1500" or even "2000" it would be better. Client-9 said that he did not know if he could get to a machine to do that, but he would see.

LEWIS said that "Kristen" would go directly to room 871. Client-9 asked LEWIS to remind him what "Kristen" looked like, and LEWIS said that she was an American, petite, very pretty brunette, 5 feet 5 inches, and 105 pounds. Client-9 said that she should go straight to 871, and if for any reason it did not work out, she should call LEWIS.

At approximately 9:32 p.m., TEMEKA RACHELLE LEWIS, a/k/a "Rachelle," the defendant, using the 6587 Number, received a call from "Kristen." During the call, "Kristen" said that she was in the room. LEWIS told "Kristen" that she would call her back when she knew when Client-9 would be there.

At approximately 9:36 p.m., TEMEKA RACHELLE LEWIS, a/k/a "Rachelle," the defendant, using the 6587 Number, received a call from "Kristen." During the call, LEWIS told "Kristen" that "he," a reference to Client-9, was at the hotel. "Kristen" told LEWIS that she just talked to him. "Kristen" said that Client-9 was coming to her. LEWIS told "Kristen" that Client-9 should be giving her "extra," and that the extra should be deposited into (REDACTED). LEWIS told "Kristen" to text her when he arrived and LEWIS would start the four hours then, and also to let her know if he left early.

On February 14, 2008, at approximately 12:02 a.m., TEMEKA RACHELLE LEWIS, a/k/a "Rachelle," the defendant, received a call from "Kristen." During the call, "Kristen" told LEWIS, that "he," a reference to Client-9, had left. LEWIS asked "Kristen" what time he got there, and "Kristen" said "15 after . . . maybe 10." LEWIS asked "Kristen" how she thought the appointment went, and "Kristen" said that she thought it went very well. LEWIS asked "Kristen" how much she collected, and "Kristen" said $4,300. "Kristen" said that she liked him, and that she did not think he was difficult. "Kristen" stated: "I don't think he's difficult. I mean it's just kind of like . . . whatever . . . I'm here for a purpose. I know what my purpose is. I am not a . . . moron, you know what I mean. So maybe that's why girls maybe think they're difficult. . . ." "Kristen" continued: "That's what it is, because you're here for a [purpose]. Let's not get it twisted—I know what I do, you know." LEWIS responded: "You look at it very uniquely, because . . . no one ever says it that way."

LEWIS continued that from what she had been told "he" (believed to be a reference to Client-9) "would ask you to do things that, like, you might not think were safe—you know—I mean that . . . very basic things. . . . "Kristen" responded: "I have a way of dealing with that . . . I'd be like listen dude, you really want the sex? . . . You know what I mean." Near the end of the call, LEWIS and "Kristen" discussed "Kristen's" departure via Amtrak, the room that Client-9 had provided for "Kristen," and "Kristen's" share of the cash that Client-9 had provided to her.

BIBLIOGRAPHY

Amann, Joseph M. *The Brotherhood of the Disappearing Pants: A Field Guide to Conservative Sex Scandals*. New York: Nation Books, 2007.

Foskett, Ken. *Judging Thomas: The Life and Times of Clarence Thomas*. New York: Harper, 2005.

Gamson, Joshua. "Normal Sins: Sex Scandal Narratives as Institutional Morality Tales." *Social Problems* 48.2 (May 2001): 185–205.

Garofoli, Joe. "Why Do Wives Stand by Their Men?: The Spitzer Scandal Raises Doubts about Political Tradition." *San Francisco Chronicle*, March 12, 2008, A.1.

Hakim, Danny, and William K. Rashbaum. "Spitzer Is Linked to Prostitution Ring." *New York Times*, March 10, 2008.

Hill, Anita. *Speaking Truth to Power*. New York: Anchor, 1998.

Hilton, Stanley G., and Anne-Renee Testa. *Glass Houses: Shocking Profiles of Congressional Sex Scandals*. New York: St. Martin's Press, 1998.

Hulse, Carl, Duff Wilson, and David M. Herazenhorn. "Rising Pressure from G.O.P. Led Senator to Quit." *New York Times*, September 2, 2007, 1.1.

Kaplan, Leonard V., and Beverly I. Moran. *Aftermath: The Clinton Impeachment and the Presidency in the Age of Political Spectacle*. New York: New York University Press, 2001.

Masters, Brooke A. *Spoiling for a Fight: The Rise of Eliot Spitzer*. New York: Owl, 2007.

McArdle, John. "Craig Arrested, Pleads Guilty in Airport Restroom." *Roll Call*, August 27, 2007.

McGreevey, James E. *The Confession*. Los Angeles: HarperCollins, 2006.

Merida, Kevin, and Michael Fletcher. *Supreme Discomfort: The Divided Soul of Clarence Thomas*. New York: Doubleday, 2007.

Rich, Frank. "The Gay Old Party Comes Out." *New York Times*, October 15, 2006, 4.13.

Roberts, Robert North. *Ethics in U.S. Government: An Encyclopedia of Investigations, Scandals, Reforms, and Legislation*. Westport, CT: Greenwood, 2001.

Saletan, William. "Hypocritical?: Don't Ask." *The Washington Post*, September 2, 2007. B-2.

Senate Ethics Counsel. *The Packwood Report*. New York: Three Rivers, 1995.

Waisbord, Silvio. "Political Scandal: Power and Visibility in the Media Age." *Contemporary Sociology* 31.4 (July 2002): 439–441.

Williams, James A., and Paul Apostolidis. *Public Affairs: Politics in the Age of Sex Scandals*. Durham, NC: Duke University Press, 2004.

SELECTED RESOURCES[1]

---

[1]Notes in quotations indicate material is being directly cited from the organization's mission statement.

WOMEN'S EQUALITY AND REPRODUCTIVE RIGHTS

International Organizations

Equality Now
www.equalitynow.org
Founded in 1992, Equality Now is an international human rights organization whose main drive is to dispense information about human rights abuses, protest harmful policies worldwide, and generally promote gender equality on a global scale.

From links that allow users to "Take Action" to those connecting users to databases, references, and current events articles, Equality Now's Web site contains a wide array of gender-parity related material.

Madre
www.madre.org
Partnering with women worldwide and communities in many continents, MADRE seeks to address human rights (especially gender) abuses around the globe.

Mainly action oriented, this site contains informative links to essays and bulletins relating to gender abuses in the key countries in which MADRE works. Links to a variety of press releases, articles, and blogs are present.

The Sisterhood Is Global Institute (SIGI)
www.sigi.org
An international nonprofit non-governmental organization (NGO), SIGI is dedicated to raising global awareness of women's rights. Co-founded by the late Simone de Beauvoir, the institute works to ensure sustained ongoing support for indigenous women's needs and grassroots empowerment for women globally.

International Women's Rights Action Watch (IWRAW)
http://www1.umn.edu/humanrts/iwraw/index.html
Founded in 1985, IWRAW is an international group advancing equal treatment of women at the regional, national, and international levels, as well as promotes advocacy and understanding for all international treaties affecting human dignity.

The Network of East-West Women (NEWW)
http://www.neww.org
Since 1991, the NGO NEWW holds a special consultative position with the Economic and Social Council (ECOSOC) for the United Nations and has registered members in over 30 countries who promote equality between the sexes and the establishment of human rights.

United Nations Commission on the Status of Women (CSW)
http://un.org/womenwatch/daw/csw/index.html
CSW works with UN's ECOSOC, a commission established to carry out investigations into the policy implementation of international treaties of human rights, especially equality for women, running statistics regarding representation, violence and other topics affecting women globally.

United Nations Inter-Agency Network on Women and Gender Equality (IANWGE)
http://www.un.org/womenwatch/

With access to a number of online resources, the IANWGE offers a wide array of information concerning the global community of women, monitoring violence, sexual abuse, and enfranchisement.

United Nations Division for the Advancement of Women (DAW)
http://un.org/womenwatch/daw
Monitoring the implementation of the Convention for the Elimination of All Forms of Discrimination Against Women, DAW is a division of the United Nations offering access to a number of resources, to newsletters and current events, and to useful statistics.

United Nations Development Fund for Women (UNIFEM)
http://www.unifem.org/
Committed to eliminating violence against women, the subjugation of women among patriarchic societies, and funding the empowerment of indigenous women, UNIFEM is a leader among the international gender equality movement, providing users with a wide assortment of data.

U.S. Agencies[2]

U.S. Agency for International Development (USAID), Women in Development
http://www.usaid.gov/our_work/cross-cutting_programs/wid/
"Provides technical assistance to USAID missions and develops approaches to new and emerging issues; sponsors projects on education, economic growth, trafficking, and violence against women that promote women's development."

U.S. Commission on Civil Rights
http://www.usccr.gov
"Studies and collects information relating to discrimination or a denial of equal protection of the laws under the Constitution because of race, color, religion, sex, age, disability, or national origin, or in the administration of justice."

U.S. Department of Health and Human Services, Including:
The Office of Women's Health (OWH), U.S. Food and Drug Administration
http://www.fda.gov/womens/
"Serves as a champion for women's health both within and outside the agency. Works to correct gender disparities in drug, device, and biologics testing and regulation policy; monitors progress of priority women's health initiatives; and partners with government and consumer groups, health advocates, professional organizations, and industry to promote women's health."

Office of Research on Women's Health, National Institutes of Health (NIH)
http://orwh.od.nih.gov
"Serves as a focal point for women's health research at the NIH; promotes, stimulates, and supports efforts to improve women's health through biomedical and behavioral research on the roles of sex and gender in health and disease, in addition to numerous other critical capacities in the name of women's issues."

The Office on Women's Health, Office of Public Health and Science, Office of the Secretary
http://www.womenshealth.gov/owh

---

[2]It should be noted that the Hyde Amendment prohibits federal funding under Medicaid for the abortion procedures and limited explicit federal support exists for abortion procedures.

"Provides leadership to promote health equity for women and girls through sex/gender-specific approaches. The strategy OWH uses to achieve its mission and vision is through the development of innovative programs, by educating health professionals, and motivating behavior change in consumers through the dissemination of health information."

U.S. Department of Justice, Including:
Office on Violence Against Women
http://www.usdoj.gov/ovw/
"Provides federal leadership to reduce violence against women, and to administer justice for and strengthen services to all victims of domestic violence, dating violence, sexual assault, and stalking. This is accomplished by developing and supporting the capacity of state, local, tribal, and non-profit entities involved in responding to violence against women."

U.S. Department of Labor, Women's Bureau
http://www.dol.gov/wb/
"Serves as a public policy advocate for working women to improve their status, improve their working conditions, increase their efficiency, and advance their opportunities for profitable employment."

U.S. Department of State, Including:
Office of International Women's Issues
http://www.state.gov/s/gwi/
"Serves as the Department's coordinating body for all foreign policy issues related to the political, economic, and social advancement of women in democracy worldwide."

Bureau of International Organization Affairs
http://www.state.gov/p/io/
"Coordinates U.S. participation in U.N. bodies that deal with human rights, humanitarian relief and refugees, women's issues, trafficking in persons, and disability issues."

Non-Profit Organizations

Abortion Access Project
http://www.abortionaccess.org/
"The Abortion Access Project is committed to access to safe abortion for all women in the U.S. We believe that by being clearly focused on abortion within the context of our broader values we will make a significant contribution to women's health and autonomy."

The Guttmacher Institute
http://www.guttmacher.org/
"A nonprofit organization focused on sexual and reproductive health research, policy analysis and public education."

The National Abortion and Reproductive Rights Action League (NARAL)
http://www.naral.org/
"National organization advocating for and providing comprehensive information on reproductive rights in the US Numerous local affiliates."

Planned Parenthood Federation of America
www.plannedparenthood.com

A backbone in the advancement of family planning policies in the United States, Planned Parenthood pioneered contraception and abortion in the struggles before and after *Roe v. Wade*.

Concerned Women for America (CWA)
www.cwfa.org
Bringing Biblical principles to grassroots mobilization efforts, CWA is the conservative voice of women in the United States, disavowing same-sex marriage, abortion, and fiscal liberalism.

The Family Research Council
http://www.frc.org/issues
"Family Research Council (FRC) champions marriage and family as the foundation of civilization, the seedbed of virtue, and the wellspring of society. FRC shapes public debate and formulates public policy that values human life and upholds the institutions of marriage and the family. Believing that God is the author of life, liberty, and the family, FRC promotes the Judeo-Christian worldview as the basis for a just, free, and stable society."

National Council of Women's Organizations (NCWO)
www.womensorganizations.org/
Representing over 11 million women in the United States, the NCWO seeks to work with policy makers and interest groups in the hopes of advancing gender parity in areas of politics, education, science, and technology as well as reproductive rights of abortion and contraception.

National Organization for Women (NOW)
www.now.org
One of the oldest organizations for the advancement of equal gender rights, NOW promotes equal pay, equal access to politics and employment, and social parity for women.

Blogs/Online

Abortion Clinics Online (ACOL)
http://www.gynpages.com/
"ACOL is a directory service comprised of websites of over 400 providers of abortion services and other reproductive healthcare. They may be private physician's offices, state licensed abortion clinics, private abortion clinics, or hospital abortion services."

Genders
www.genders.org
Publishing essays concerning gender in socioeconomic, political, and artistic contexts, Genders showcases artistic expression beyond socially defined gender borders.

Women's Voices for Change
www.womensvoicesforchange.com
A site for news and commentary, with an emphasis on the more seasoned womanly opinion, Women's Voices for Change focuses on many dynamic issues facing women in the United States.

Appetite for Equal Rights
www.appetiteforequalrights.blogspot.com
A blog encompassing equal rights in gender and LGBT spheres, Appetite for Equal Rights has sections on abortion, birth control, and other diverse issues.

Blogher
www.blogher.com
An online community of women bloggers, Blogher showcases the everyday to politically controversial, the maternal to the monetary, in a predominantly female perspective.

Feminist Review
www.feministreview.com
First describing itself as a socialist and feminist journal, the Feminist Review is an online repository for interdisciplinary approaches of the study of women's issues.

Documentaries

Not for Ourselves Alone: The Story of Elizabeth Cody Stanton and Susan B. Anthony
Ken Burns and Paul Barnes
PBS
1999
Track key events of the suffrage movement, delve into historic documents and essays, and take a look at where women are today.

From Danger to Dignity: The Fight for Safe Abortion
Dorothy Fadiman, Beth Seltzer, and Daniel Meyers
Concentric Media
1995
Contains two parallel stories: the evolution of underground networks that helped women find safe abortions outside the law, and the intensive efforts by activists and legislators to decriminalize abortion through legislative and judicial channels.

SEXUAL EXPRESSION AND SEX EDUCATION

International Organizations

AVERTing HIV and AIDS (AVERT)
www.avert.org
Primarily involved with the control of HIV/AIDS proliferation worldwide, AVERT also endorses and supports meaningful additions to comprehensive sexual education as a part of its global efforts to curb sexually transmitted infections of all kinds.

Family Health Organization (FHI)
www.fhi.org
Primarily a public health organization, FHI provides information to that end as well as establishes public health programs, including the adoption of comprehensive sexual education internationally.

Marie Stopes Organization
http://www.mariestopes.org.uk/Home.aspx
A registered charity, Marie Stopes International also works around the world in 42 countries. Funds from the U.K. clinics, help support vital sexual and reproductive health care programs in some of the world's poorest regions.

U.S. Agencies[3]

U.S. Department of Health and Human Services (HHS), Including:
HHS Index
http://www.hhs.gov/children/index.html
Listing information pertaining to health among families and women, HHS's Web site provides useful resources, fact sheets, and links to medical organizations.

Administration for Children and Families (ACF)
http://www.acf.hhs.gov/
Providing family-related services and resources relating to the government's initiatives on the status of family planning, ACF provides up-to-date information and useful links to related data.

U.S. Department of State, U.S. President's Emergency Plan for AIDS Relief
http://www.pepfar.gov/index.htm
Provides guidance and outlines U.S. policy concerning "healthy" sexual practices overseas to stem the spread of HIV/AIDS overseas, especially the ABC approach to sexual health.

Non-Profit Organizations

Advocates for Youth
http://www.advocatesforyouth.org/
"Established in 1980 as the Center for Population Options, Advocates for Youth champions efforts that help young people make informed and responsible decisions about their reproductive and sexual health. Advocates believes it can best serve the field by boldly advocating for a more positive and realistic approach to adolescent sexual health."

American Civil Liberties Union (ACLU)
www.aclu.org
A committed and leading non-profit organization for the protection of Constitutional rights and absolute protection from government censorship, the ACLU has long been a champion of both expressive liberties and access to abortion unburdened by the political process.

The Family Research Council
http://www.frc.org/issues
"Family Research Council (FRC) champions marriage and family as the foundation of civilization, the seedbed of virtue, and the wellspring of society. FRC shapes public debate and formulates public policy that values human life and upholds the institutions of marriage and the family. Believing that God is the author of life, liberty, and the family, FRC promotes the Judeo-Christian worldview as the basis for a just, free, and stable society."

Sexuality Information and Education Council of the United States (SIECUS)
www.siecus.org
"Today, despite the government's continued promotion of abstinence-only-until-marriage policy and an agenda that favors ideology over science and common sense, SIECUS continues its fight for comprehensive sexuality education and sexual health promotion. SIECUS gives

---

[3]U.S. agencies have adopted a pro-abstinence sexual education policy.

families, educators, and policymakers access to fact-based sexuality information through publications, websites, trainings, and myriad other resources."

The Coalition for Positive Sexuality
www.positive.org
An organization whose mission aims at youth, the Coalition's Web site contains information on a variety of aspects related to sex education and links to various resources.

The Heritage Foundation
www.heritage.org
For the formulation and promotion of conservative public policy, Heritage is one of the right-wing public policy research institutions in the United States. A part of its mission is the ongoing study and dissemination of information concerning sexual education in American public schools.

Blogs/Online

Campaign for Our Children
www.cfoc.org
Includes programming ideas and fact sheets, as well as information on various aspects of sexual health, FAQs, and links to other online resources.

Families Are Talking
www.familiesaretalking.org
Includes information for parents and for youth regarding all aspects of sex education, free publications, and links to other online resources.

Documentaries

The Education of Shelby Knox
Marion Lipschutz and Rose Rosenblatt
Incite
2005
Covering the spectrum of sexual education and sexual expression in America's public schools, *Education* looks through the eyes of a young secondary education student in Lubbock, Texas.

It's Still Elementary: Talking about Gay Issues in School
Debra Chasnoff, Director/Producer
Groundspark
2007
It's Still Elementary tells the history of why and how the 1996 film, *It's Elementary*, was made, the response it provoked from the conservative right, and the questions it raises about the national safe schools movement today.

SEXUAL IDENTITY AND ORIENTATION

International Organizations

International Lesbian and Gay Association (ILGA)
www.ilga.org
Global LGBT alliance formed to promote equal rights for those in the LGBT community, with national and regional partners. This site contains links to a variety of resources, from a list of countries and their respective LGBT policies to a "library" of categories containing articles that cover community-oriented information.

International Gay and Lesbian Human Rights Commission (IGLHRC)
www.iglhrc.org
A leading international organization for the protection of rights among the LGBT community on a global scale, IGLHRC is a U.S. non-profit with international scope. Contains a number of links to articles of current events and scholarly inquiry.

Gay/Lesbian International News Network (GLINN)
http://www.glinn.com/news/index.htm
Online association with access to numerous articles of current events pertaining to the LGBT community. This site contains useful links to a variety of timely and archival articles covering economic and political issues relating to the LGBT community. A link to historical databases for LGBT research is also present.

U.S. Agencies[4]

A number of state-based, non-profit organizations currently exist to promote equal rights for the LGBT community. Since sexual identity and orientation are still hotly contested political issues in U.S. legislatures, interest groups have been the manifestations in which organization and mobilization has primarily taken form. A short list of such organizations follows:

Basic Rights Oregon
www.basicrights.org
"Founded in 1996, Basic Rights Oregon (BRO) is the state's chief advocacy, education and political organization dedicated to ending discrimination based on sexual orientation and gender identity. Basic Rights Oregon has twelve full time staff plus a contract lobbyist, three offices around the state, more than 10,000 active contributors and 5,000 active volunteers."

Equality North Carolina
www.equalitync.org
"Equality NC works by effectively lobbying the North Carolina General Assembly, executive branch, and local governments on issues like inclusive anti-bullying policies, employment discrimination, hate violence, privacy rights, sexuality education, adoption, domestic partnership, HIV/AIDS, and more. We also work to engage North Carolinians with educational programming and outreach efforts."

---

[4]Currently, efforts are being undertaken to include sexual orientation and gender identity among listed protections in U.S. federal agencies. Although a number of U.S. agencies have adopted pro-sexual orientation policies, there are no nondiscrimination statutory controls inclusive of sexual orientation and identity.

Equality Utah

www.equalityutah.org

"Equality Utah works to secure equal rights and protections for lesbian, gay, bisexual and transgender (LGBT) Utahns and their families. Toward this mission, Equality Utah drafts legislation and coordinates efforts to ensure its passage; lobbies legislators and other elected officials; builds coalitions, educates, empowers and energizes individuals and organizations to actively participate in the political process."

New York Association for Gender Rights Advocacy (NYAGRA)

www.nyagra.com

NYAGRA was founded as a non-profit for the freedom of gender identity and expression in the state of New York and all of the United States. Its policy efforts include transgender protections in employment and work toward the inclusion of gender identity in state equal protection laws.

Non-Profit Organizations

American Family Association

www.afa.net

AFA is one of America's largest conservative advocacy forces in the United States. Founded on Christian beliefs, the AFA lobbies Congress and mobilizes public opinion to halt what is known among their constituents as the "homosexual agenda" and liberal promulgations of sexual identity.

Parents, Families & Friends of Lesbians & Gays (PFLAG)

www.pflag.org

PFLAG is a leading non-profit for LGBT equality as well as advocates for acceptance among American families, offering access to press releases, opinionated articles, and current events related to the LGBT community.

Gay and Lesbian Advocates and Defenders (GLAD)

www.glad.org

Striving for equal justice, GLAD is an LGBT organization advocating the legal pursuits of its community for political equality. Its mission is to eliminate discrimination on the basis of sexual orientation, HIV status, and gender identity in America.

Human Rights Campaign (HRC)

www.hrc.org

Standing as the largest, and certainly one of the most influential non-profit organizations for the advancement of LGBT civil rights, HRC strives for political equality among sexual minorities.

Lambda Legal Defense and Education Fund

www.lambdalegal.org

"Lambda Legal is a national organization committed to achieving full recognition of the civil rights of lesbians, gay men, bisexuals, transgender people and those with HIV through impact litigation, education and public policy work."

Intersex Society of North America (ISNA)

www.isna.org

Primarily focused on ending misconceptions about the transgendered community, ISNA is a non-profit that offers access to news and information concerning the intersexed community and those who wish to increase their knowledge about gender, both physical and nonphysical manifestations of it.

National Gay and Lesbian Task Force (NGLTF)
www.ngltf.org
Promoting civil rights for gays and lesbians in the United States, the NGLTF has been instrumental, along with other non-profit LGBT organizations, in the continuing struggle for same-sex marriage and employment nondiscrimination.

Family Research Council
www.frc.org
FRC is a fundamentally Christian organization that attempts to promulgate their Christian understanding of family and policy through media, lobbying and mobilizing efforts in order to limit areas of marriage, sexual expression, and liberally applied women's rights.

Christian Coalition of America
www.cc.org
"The CC is a political organization, made up of pro-family Americans who care deeply about ensuring that government serves to strengthen and preserve, rather than threaten, our families and our values. To that end, we work continuously to identify, educate and mobilize Christians for effective political action."

Blogs/Online

365 Gay
www.365gay.com
Offers stories of U.S. and international scope concerning the LGBT community.

The Gay Patriot
www.gaypatriot.com
For the gay American conservative, the Gay Patriot contains the politics of Republican LGBT members and their perspectives on all things right-of-center politics.

Right of the Rainbow
www.rightrainbow.com
The right-wing perceptions of members of the LGBT community, Right of the Rainbow blogs are one part irony and two parts controversial.

Bay Windows
www.baywindows.com
New England's largest LGBT newspaper, publishing stories of politics and community, with a central mission of promoting equal rights of the LGBT community at the regional and national levels of government.

Documentaries

Before Stonewall: The Making of a Gay and Lesbian Community
John Scagliotti, Greta Schiller, and Robert Rosenberg, Directors
First Run Features

1985

A classic of LGBT-related history, *Stonewall* traces the establishment of an identifiable gay and lesbian community in the United States from the 1920s until emerging as a visceral force of social change in the 1969 Stonewall Riots.

Overruled! The Case that Brought Down Sodomy Laws
Johnny Bergmann, Director
Studio 4, LLC
2008
Following the legal struggles of the two men who sought to overturn the sodomy laws in the state of Texas, *Overruled!* examines the cultural impact of the Supreme Court decision that followed.

SEXUAL PARTNERSHIPS

International Organizations

International Lesbian, Gay, Bisexual, Trans and Intersex Association (ILGA)
www.ilga.org
"The International Lesbian, Gay, Bisexual, Trans and Intersex Association is a world-wide network of national and local groups dedicated to achieving equal rights for lesbian, gay, bisexual and transgender and intersex (LGBTI) people everywhere."

International Gay and Lesbian Human Rights Commission
www.iglhrc.org
"The International Gay and Lesbian Human Rights Commission (IGLHRC) is a leading international organization dedicated to human rights advocacy on behalf of people who experience discrimination or abuse on the basis of their actual or perceived sexual orientation, gender identity or expression. Learn more about our work by clicking on the links below."

U.S. Agencies[5]

A number of state-based, non-profit organizations have sprung from the debate concerning marriage for same-sex couples, including organizations with the prefix "Equality" and the like; these organizations work with a comprehensive message of LGBT rights and marriage equality as a prong of their mission. A brief listing of these organizations appears here.

Equality California
www.eqca.org
"Founded in 1998, EQCA celebrates its 10th anniversary in 2008, commemorating a decade of building a state of equality in California. In the past 10 years, Equality California has strategically moved California from a state with extremely limited legal protections for lesbian, gay, bisexual and transgender (LGBT) individuals to a state with some of the most comprehensive civil rights protections in the nation."

---

[5]There are currently no organs of the U.S. government that explicitly support marriage among same-sex couples, pursuant to the stipulations of the Defense of Marriage Act of 1996. As many states, pursuant to DOMA, have adopted constitutional amendments banning same-sex marriage, state-based non-profit advocacy has proliferated in response.

Equality Maryland
www.equalitymaryland.org
"Equality Maryland works to secure and protect the rights of LGBT Marylanders by promoting legislative initiatives on the state, county and municipal levels. Our professional lobbyists and legislative team work with our allies in the General Assembly to shape and pass positive legislation in Annapolis and to beat back discriminatory legislation."

MassEquality
www.massequality.org
Massachusetts-based organization for the advancement of marriage rights for same-sex couples, MassEquality works with national organizations as well in the development of ongoing civil rights strategy for the LGBT community.

Non-Profit Organizations

Lambda Legal Defense and Education Fund
www.lambdalegal.org
"Lambda Legal is a national organization committed to achieving full recognition of the civil rights of lesbians, gay men, bisexuals, transgender people and those with HIV through impact litigation, education and public policy work."

Marriage Equality USA (MEUSA)
www.marriageequality.org
Springing from the early social and legal debates surrounding the landmark *Baehr v. Lewin* in Hawaii and the Defense of Marriage Act, MEUSA is a national organization working to mobilize efforts for a comprehensive, federal endorsement of marriage rights.

The National Gay and Lesbian Task Force (NGLTF)
www.thetaskforce.org
Promoting civil rights for gays and lesbians in the United States, the NGLTF has been instrumental, along with other non-profit LGBT organizations, in the continuing struggle for same-sex marriage and employment nondiscrimination.

Freedom to Marry
www.freedomtomarry.org
Freedom to Marry is a national organization promoting marriage rights for same-sex couples and keeping open the dialogue and case for marriage equality among policy makers nationwide.

Human Rights Campaign
www.hrc.org
"The Human Rights Campaign is America's largest civil rights organization working to achieve lesbian, gay, bisexual and transgender equality. By inspiring and engaging all Americans, HRC strives to end discrimination against LGBT citizens and realize a nation that achieves fundamental fairness and equality for all."

Family Research Council
www.frc.org
FRC is a fundamentally Christian organization that attempts to promulgate their Christian understanding of family and policy through media, lobbying and mobilizing efforts in order to limit areas of marriage, sexual expression, and liberally applied women's rights.

Christian Coalition of America
www.cc.org
The CC is a political organization, made up of pro-family Americans who care deeply about ensuring that government serves to strengthen and preserve American families and their values. Among others, the CC mobilizes political action for restricting homosexual access to marriage rights and denying same-sex couples legal recognition and partnership benefits.

Blogs/Online

Institute for Marriage and Public Policy, Marriage Debate
http://www.marriagedebate.com/mdblog.php
Provides viewpoints on both sides of the issue relating to marriage among same-sex couples, concerning both policy and social implications, and provides links to other useful resources.

Documentaries

Freedom to Marry: A Journey to Justice
Laurie York and Carmen Goodyear, Directors
Turtle Time
2005
Containing interviews with famous stars and seven inspiring same-sex couples, *Freedom to Marry* brings a personal face to the marriage equality movement at the height of its growing, global prominence.

Pursuit of Equality
Geoff Callan and Mike Shaw, Directors
Pursuit of Equality, LLC
2005
Covering the aftermath of the first issuance of marriage licenses in San Francisco in 2004, *Pursuit* is a study of communities—both gay and straight—and the reactions to comprehensive marriage in an American city.

GENERAL BIBLIOGRAPHY: BOOKS AND ARTICLES

Amann, Joseph M. *The Brotherhood of the Disappearing Pants: A Field Guide to Conservative Sex Scandals.* New York: Nation Books, 2007.

Bailyn, Lotte. "Individual Constraints: Occupational Demands and Private Life." Chapter 3 in *Breaking the Mold: Women, Men and Time in the New Corporate World,* 40–54. New York: Free Press, 1993.

Boele-Woelki, Katharina, and Angelika Fuchs, eds. *Legal Recognition of Same Sex Couples in Europe.* New York: Intersentia, 2003.

Byrd, Cathy, ed. *Potentially Harmful: The Art of American Censorship.* Atlanta: Georgia State University Press, 2006.

Caplan, Gary S. "Fourteenth Amendment: The Supreme Court Limits the Right to Privacy." *The Journal of Criminal Law and Criminology* 77.3 (Autumn 1986): 894–930.

Cook, Rebecca J., ed. *Human Rights of Women: National and International Perspectives.* Philadelphia: University of Pennsylvania Press, 1994.

Copp, David, and Susan Wendell. *Pornography and Censorship.* Buffalo, NY: Prometheus, 1983.

Cott, Nancy F. *The Grounding of Modern Feminism.* New Haven, CT: Yale University Press, 1987.

DuBois, Ellen Carol. *Woman Suffrage and Women's Rights*. New York: New York University Press, 1998.

Dupuis, Martin. *Same-Sex Marriage, Legal Mobilization and the Politics of Rights*. New York: Peter Lang, 2002.

Embser-Herbert, Melissa Sheridan. *The U.S. Military's "Don't Ask Don't Tell" Policy: A Reference Handbook*. Westport, CT: Praeger, 2007.

Eskridge, William N., Jr., "A History of Same-Sex Marriage." *Virginia Law Review* 79.7 (October 1993): 1419–1513.

Estrich, Susan. *Sex and Power*. New York: Riverhead Books, 2000.

Evans, Sara M. *Born for Liberty: A History of Women in America*. New York: Free Press, 1989.

Everett, Craig A. *Divorce and Remarriage: International Studies*. New York: Haworth, 1997.

Gallagher, John, and Chris Bull. *Perfect Enemies: The Religious Right, the Gay Movement, and the Politics of the 1990s*. New York: Crown, 1996.

Gamson, Joshua. "Normal Sins: Sex Scandal Narratives as Institutional Morality Tales." *Social Problems* 48.2 (May 2001): 185–205.

Garrow, David J. *Liberty and Sexuality: The Right to Privacy and the Making of Roe v. Wade*. New York: Macmillan, 1994.

Githens, Marianne, and Dorothy McBride Stetson, eds. *Abortion Politics: Public Policy in Cross-Cultural Perspective*. New York: Routledge, 1996.

Goldberg, Suzanne, and Lisa Keen. *Strangers to the Law: Gay People on Trial*. Ann Arbor: University of Michigan Press, 2000.

Goldin, Claudia, and Lawrence F. Katz. "The Power of the Pill: Contraceptives and Women's Career and Marriage Decisions." *Journal of Political Economy* 110 (August 2002): 731ff.

Gozemba, Patricia A. *Courting Equality: A Documentary History of America's First Legal Same-Sex Marriages*. Boston: Beacon Press, 2007.

Graff, E. J. *What Is Marriage For?: The Strange Social History of Our Most Intimate Institution*. Boston: Beacon Press, 2004.

Harvard Law Review Association. "Litigating the Defense of Marriage Act: The Next Battleground for Same-Sex Marriage." *Harvard Law Review* 117.8 (June 2004): 2684–2707.

Hertzog, Mark. *The Lavender Vote: Lesbians, Gay Men, and Bisexuals in American Electoral Politics*. New York: New York University Press, 1996.

Hilton, Stanley G., and Anne-Renee Testa. *Glass Houses: Shocking Profiles of Congressional Sex Scandals*. New York: St. Martin's Press, 1998.

Hixson, Richard F. *Pornography and the Justices: The Supreme Court and the Intractable Obscenity Problem*. Carbondale, IL: Southern Illinois University Press, 1996.

Hull, Katherine. *Same-Sex Marriage: The Cultural Politics of Love and Law*. Cambridge, U.K.: Cambridge University Press, 2006.

Hull, N. E. H., and Peter Charles Hoffer. *Roe v. Wade: The Abortion Rights Controversy in American History*. Lawrence: University of Kansas Press, 2001.

Hunt, Lynn. *The Invention of Pornography: Obscenity and the Origins of Modernity, 1500–1800*. New York: Zone, 1993.

Hunter, Ian. *On Pornography: Literature, Sexuality, and Obscenity Law*. New York: St. Martin's Press, 1993.

Irvine, Janice M. *Talk about Sex: The Battles over Sex Education in the United States*. Berkeley: University of California Press, 2004.

Jacobs, Jerry. *Gender Inequality at Work*. Thousand Oaks, CA: SAGE Publications, 1995.

Jacobs, Jerry, and Kathleen Gerson. *The Time Divide: Work, Family, and Gender Inequality*. Cambridge, MA: Harvard University Press, 2004.

Jansen, Sue Curry. *Censorship: The Knot that Binds Power and Knowledge*. New York: Oxford University Press, 1988.

Johnson, John W. *Griswold v. Connecticut: Birth Control and the Constitutional Right of Privacy*. Lawrence: University of Kansas Press, 2005.

Kaplan, Leonard V., and Beverly I. Moran. *Aftermath: The Clinton Impeachment and the Presidency in the Age of Political Spectacle*. New York: New York University Press, 2001.

Larocque, Sylvain. *Gay Marriage: The Story of a Canadian Social Revolution*. Toronto: J. Lorimer, 2006.

Levine, Judith. *Harmful to Minors: The Perils of Protecting Children from Sex*. New York: Thunder's Mouth Press, 2003.

Luker, Kristin. *Abortion and the Politics of Motherhood*. Berkeley: University of California Press, 1984.

Luker, Kristin. *When Sex Goes to School: Warring Views on Sex—and Sex Education—Since the Sixties*. New York: W. W. Norton & Co., 2006.

Massey, Douglas. *Categorically Unequal: The American Stratification System*. New York: Russell Sage Foundation, 2007.

Masters, Brooke A. *Spoiling for a Fight: The Rise of Eliot Spitzer*. New York: Owl, 2007.

Mayo, Cris. *Disputing the Subject of Sex: Sexuality and Public School Controversies*. Lanham, MD: Rowman & Littlefield, 2004.

McDonnell, Kathleen. *Not an Easy Choice: A Feminist Re-Examines Abortion*. Boston: South End Press, 1984.

Parkman, Allen M. *Good Intentions Gone Awry: No-Fault Divorce and the American Family*. Lanham, MD: Rowman & Littlefield, 2000.

Phy-Olsen, Allene. *Same-Sex Marriage*. Westport, CT: Greenwood Press, 2006.

Polikoff, Nancy D. *Beyond (Straight and Gay) Marriage: Valuing All Families Under the Law*. Boston: Beacon Press, 2008.

Ridini, Steven P. *Health and Sexuality Education in Schools: The Process of Social Change*. Westport, CT: Bergin & Garvey, 1998.

Riggle, Ellen D. B., and Barry L. Tadlock, eds. *Gays and Lesbians in the Democratic Process: Public Policy, Public Opinion, and Political Representation*. New York: Columbia University Press, 1999.

Roberts, Robert North. *Ethics in U.S. Government: An Encyclopedia of Investigations, Scandals, Reforms, and Legislation*. Westport, CT: Greenwood Press, 2001.

Rosenblatt, Roger. *Life Itself: Abortion in the American Mind*. New York: Random House, 1992.

Sherrill, Kenneth. "The Political Power of Lesbians, Gays and Bisexuals." *PS: Political Science and Politics* 29.3 (September 1996): 469–474.

Shilts, Randy. *Conduct Unbecoming: Gays and Lesbians in the U.S. Military*. New York: St. Martin's Press, 1994.

Solinger, Rickie. *Abortion Wars: A Half-Century of Struggle, 1950–2000*. Berkeley: University of California Press, 1998.

Soule, Sarah A. "Going to the Chapel? Same-Sex Marriage Bans in the United States, 1973–2000." *Social Problems* 51, no. 4 (November 2004): 453–477.

Strasser, Mark. *On Same-Sex Marriage, Civil Unions, and the Rule of Law: Constitutional Interpretation at the Crossroads*. Westport, CT: Praeger, 2002.

Valian, Virginia. *Why So Slow? The Advancement of Women*. Cambridge, MA: MIT Press, 1998.

Vianello, Mino, and Renata Siemienska. *Gender Inequality: A Comparative Study of Discrimination and Participation*. Newbury Park, CA: SAGE Publications, 1990.

Walter, Lynn, ed. *Women's Rights: A Global View*. Westport, CT: Greenwood Press, 2001.

Welch, Charles E., III, and Sharon Price-Bonham. "A Decade of No-Fault Divorce Revisited: California, Georgia, and Washington." *Journal of Marriage and the Family* 45, no. 2 (May, 1983): 411–418.

Williams, James A., and Paul Apostolidis. *Public Affairs: Politics in the Age of Sex Scandals.* Durham, NC: Duke University Press, 2004.

Wintemute, Robert, and Mads Andenaes, eds. *Legal Recognition of Same-Sex Partnerships: A Study of National, European and International Law.* Portland, OR: Hart, 2001.

Witte, John, Jr., and Eliza Ellison, eds. *Covenant Marriage in Comparative Perspective.* Grand Rapids, MI: Eerdmans, 2005.

Resource Guide Developed by Brandon Lee H. Aultman

INDEX

Page numbers in **bold** indicate excerpts or complete documents pages.